Praise for *Summer of Deliverance*

"In this wrenching memoir of his father and himself, Mr. Dickey tells us both the use of a poet and where he was coming from."
—Christopher Lehmann-Haupt, *The New York Times*

"A fascinating description of what it's like to be the real child of a man who lives primarily in his imagination."
—Susan Cheever, *The Washington Post Book World*

"This beautifully crafted story of the two men's faltering steps toward reconciliation is also the horrific story of all that went before . . . interspersed with moments of love and loyalty. . . ."
—Polly Paddock Gossett, *Chicago Tribune*

". . . an acute and affecting portrayal of a lost-and-found relationship between an extraordinary father and his bewildered son."
—Earl L. Dachslager, *Houston Chronicle*

"Wrenching, scorching, pedal-to-the-metal. . . . A splendidly recalled, splendidly related reminiscence."   —Henry Kisor, *Chicago Sun-Times*

"A not-to-be missed book that is one of the year's major publishing events."   —*New York Post*

"Scrupulously fair and absolutely riveting, *Summer of Deliverance* is as fine a literary memoir as I've seen this year."   —Dwight Garner, *Newsday*

". . . an absolutely riveting story of a family . . . that is both wonderfully and brutally strange."
—Cyril Jones Kellett, *The San Diego Union-Tribune*

"A brilliant memoir . . . a father-son odyssey and a classic tale of hubris, self-destruction and redemption."
—George Gurley, *The Kansas City Star*

"Dickey writes with a natural storyteller's gift for narrative. . . . A frank, unexaggerated account that evokes his long journey from anger to reconciliation with a soft touch and unflagging skill."
—Gordon Haber, *Milwaukee Journal Sentinel*

". . . a book written with more love and understanding than bitterness . . . pure moments of understanding, of reconciliation."
—Elizabeth Bennett, *Pittsburgh Post-Gazette*

". . . Often brave and painful admissions of loss, betrayal and love—mostly of love. In the book, the son pays tribute to the father, a tribute borne of unflinching honesty earned through the understanding of a man who was a lot of things to a lot of people."
—Christian Viveros-Faune, *Raleigh (N.C.) Spectator*

". . . by turns angry and elegiac, but always well written and affecting. It is Christopher Dickey's triumph that he is finally able to redeem himself and his difficult, complicated father."
—Michael Kelsay, *Lexington Herald-Leader*

"The kind of memoir you can read in a few sittings, 80 to 100 pages at a time. Dickey shows that the truth about a parent lies in listening, understanding and accepting what one learns."
—Repps Hudson, *St. Louis Post-Dispatch*

"It is the measure of Christopher Dickey's own imagination that he neither excuses nor condemns the Great Man, content with a remorselessly detailed, cold-eyed reminiscence that mysteriously emerges—you can't imagine how—as a deeply moving portrait and a kind of benediction."
—Peter Kurth, *Salon Magazine*

"Christopher Dickey's prose elevates this searingly honest book to a higher plane. . . . A most compelling book."
—Charles Sermon, *The State* (Columbia, S.C.)

"In the rich, heartbreaking literature that deals with the subject of fathers and sons, Christopher Dickey has produced a book that is a high-water mark in the genre. Because of this book, we now know that James Dickey produced a son worthy of his poems and novels."

—Pat Conroy

"I knew, and valued highly, Christopher Dickey's father and mother. Scalding as his account of their lives may seem, it ultimately awards them the redemption they earned—the deep comprehension and eventual gratitude of a son who is both a keen-eyed witness and a writer with the gifts for telling their story."   —Reynolds Price

"By turns droll and heartbreaking, Christopher Dickey's beautifully written narrative is not only the portrait of a great poet in the throes of self-ruination but an unflinchingly honest self-portrait as well."

—William Styron

SUMMER of

*The author with his father,
the poet James Dickey*

DELIVERANCE

A Memoir of Father and Son

Christopher Dickey

A Touchstone Book
Published by Simon & Schuster

For Carol, who took me home

TOUCHSTONE
Rockefeller Center
1230 Avenue of the Americas
New York, NY 10020

Copyright © 1998 by Christopher Dickey
All rights reserved,
including the right of reproduction
in whole or in part in any form
First Touchstone Edition 1999
TOUCHSTONE and colophon are
registered trademarks of Simon & Schuster Inc.
Designed by Edith Fowler
Manufactured in the United States of America

10   9   8   7   6   5   4   3   2

The Library of Congress has cataloged the hardcover
edition as follows:

Dickey, Christopher.
    Summer of deliverance : a memoir of father and
son / Christopher Dickey.
        p.   cm.
    Includes bibliographical references and index.
      1. Dickey, James—Family.   2. Authors,
American—20th century—Family relationships.
    3. Fathers and sons—United States.   4. Dickey,
Christopher—Family.   I. Title.
PS3554.I318Z88   1998
811'.54—dc 21
[B]   98-23452   CIP
ISBN 978-0-684-85537-0

The author gratefully acknowledges permission to reprint material from the following works:

Excerpts of poems, notes, and letters used with the permission of James L. Dickey III.

Excerpts from "If There Is No New Dickey, We Will Have to Invent Him," by Joe Cumming Jr., March 2, 1980, © 1980 by The Atlanta Journal and The Atlanta Constitution. Reprinted with permission from The Atlanta Journal and The Atlanta Constitution.

Excerpt from "Deborah Dickey Gets Two Years' Probation," by John Allard, May 1, 1991, © 1991 by The State (Columbia, South Carolina). Reprinted with permission from The State.

Excerpts from "The Great Grassy World from Both Sides," by Peter Davison, in One of the Dangerous Trades: Essays on the Work and Workings of Poetry, University of Michigan Press, 1991. Reprinted with permission from Peter Davison.

Excerpts from Self-Interviews (1970), Sorties (1971), The Zodiac (1976), and Alnilam (1987), by James Dickey, reprinted with permission of Bantam Doubleday Dell.

(permissions continue on page 288)

. . . Come, son, and find me here,
In love with the sound of my voice.

—"The Owl King: The Call"

CONTENTS

OVERTURES

I thought that I could save my father's life.

For most of twenty years I did not see him, couldn't talk to him, could not bear to be around him. I believed—I *knew*—that he had killed my mother. He belittled and betrayed her, humiliated her and forgot about her, then watched her over the course of a few years quietly, relentlessly poison herself with the whisky she had at her right hand all day long every day until she died, bloated, her liver hardening and the veins in her esophagus erupting, bleeding to death at the age of fifty.

My father was a great poet, a famous novelist, a powerful intellect, and a son of a bitch I hated, and that last fact was just a part of me. It was a cold knot of anger that I lived with, and that helped drive me to do the things I wanted and needed to do in my own life. I became a foreign correspondent—as far from him as I could be.

Anger was so much easier to deal with than love. And he made it so easy to be angry. He was drunk himself for most of those twenty years. If I didn't get him on the phone before eleven in the morning, there was no point in calling at all. He wouldn't remember, or couldn't speak coherently enough. And he never called me. So those times I got out of El Salvador or Nicaragua, Libya or Lebanon feeling lucky to survive and in love with the world, I could just barely bring myself to call him. We'd talk, but not much, and I'd say "I love you" when I said goodbye, and "Fuck you" when the phone hit its cradle. What a shame, I would think, that I still loved him at all.

But I did. And that disturbed me much more than the anger. I understood my hurt. I didn't understand him. I didn't begin to understand us.

I thought that there was a time when I was a little boy when everything was basically right. My childhood was an adventure story, not a horror show. My father and mother had adored and spoiled me. I was "the firstborn son," as he liked to say, and for seven years, until my brother, Kevin, was born, I was my parents' only child. Together, as a family, we traveled all over the United States and Europe. We made friends quickly, but said goodbye almost as easily. We felt self-contained. We lived in Texas, France, Florida, and Georgia before I was five; Italy, Oregon, California, and Virginia before I was sixteen. But by then the corrosion had set in. My mother had begun to drink heavily, steadily. You could hear that tinkling of ice cubes in the kitchen at six in the morning. When I was seventeen, I went to college; at eighteen, I was married and a father myself.

I was making my escape by instinct, and my father knew the distance between us. The morning after the wedding he gave me the galleys of his novel *Deliverance*. "On the first day of the new life, and with every love," he wrote, and signed it: "James Dickey." But none of us was ready for what happened then.

My father had been working on that first novel from the time I was ten, and his fame as a poet had been growing all along. He won the National Book Award. He became the Poetry Consultant at the Library of Congress. *Deliverance* was just one of his projects, something to talk through on our long drives across two continents. Now here it was. And as I read it that night after my marriage, in a motel on the New Jersey Turnpike, I had to admit it was very damn good. Much as I wanted to, I couldn't put it down. The book appeared in the stores the summer of 1970, and quickly became a best-seller. The next summer, it was made into a movie with Jon Voight and Burt Reynolds. And after that, nothing good was the same.

The story of four suburbanites who head down a wild North Georgia river that runs straight to redneck hell was so compelling it became part of American culture. Its success was so big, and such a surprise to us, that for a long time after I left home I blamed *Deliverance* for what happened to my father and our family. It was a line of demarcation between making it and made it, between success and stardom, the beginning of a new life. The Big Break. It was the definitive end of my childhood.

It seemed to me then and for a long time afterward that forces of self-indulgence and self-destruction, which were always there in my father but held in check, were now cut loose. And worse. Because the poet in the public eye is a particular kind of spectacle. And my father was a special kind of poet, who had known from before I could remember that he wanted to create a new kind of poetry. "I have written some fair poems, but no really good ones this summer," he wrote to my mother in 1953. "But, in each, I am nearer what I want: each one has more of the fast, athletic, imaginative, and muscular vigor that I want to identify as my particular kind of writing. I am learning how to do it."

By the time *Deliverance* happened, my father was middle-aged, and well known, and he had done that thing, and it wasn't enough to write muscular, vigorous, *virile* poetry. There was an expectation you'd live it. Be it, somehow. And people loved the show. *Playboy* magazine did a profile of my father in 1971, and the first page told the tale. "THE STUFF OF POETRY," said the headline, was "a little guitar picking, fast-water canoeing, booze, archery and weight lifting—if you happen to be James Dickey in search of deliverance."

The show eventually became a parody. Then a bore. A columnist in the *Atlanta Journal* picked up on the theme, mincing his words for the sake of libel laws and a tone of gentility. Dickey had been "everybody's darling—the moonshot poet who gave us the inspired new perspective on ourselves with 'the blue planet'; he toured with Russian poets; visited Picasso in Spain. Then his fame turned infamous. Stories floated about of unseemly and unsober behavior, even as his popularity grew as a guitar-pickin' reader of poetry on the college circuit. The little wine and cheese faculty affairs became a legacy of Dickey trying to convert them to larger affairs with faculty wives. He became the South's favorite gossip topic. We had need of such—a naughty native son to be scandalized by. You see, at this time all our old snorting demagogues who used to shock and delight us had mutated into being bland, boring or president."

The pickin' and singin', drinkin' and whorin' regional poet. The naughty native son.

And he was so much better than that. So much better.

And his own two sons were pulling away, extracting themselves from him.

And his wife was dying.

And there didn't seem any way to make contact with him. He had always been interested, he liked to say, in "the creative possibilities of the lie." He believed the poet "is not trying to tell the truth, but to make it." But the lying wasn't limited to the poem. And, in truth, he lied the most about the people who loved him most, until we came to feel he didn't so much know us as imagine us. Which is not to say that he couldn't see us for what we were. He could, sometimes. And his disappointment was impossible to endure.

He would always make things worse. Two months after my mother died, he married a girl who'd been in one of his classes. I read about it in *People* magazine: "FOR NEWLY WIDOWED POET JAMES DICKEY, DELIVERANCE IS A BRIDE NAMED DEBBIE." She was younger than me; less than half his age. They posed with mock formality for the invited paparazzo. "The day began," the caption coyly informs, "with a champagne brunch." And what I thought was: "Somebody needs to take care of you, Dad, and better her than me." Then the stories started coming about the violence. There was something about her stabbing him with a broadhead arrow. There were press reports about his drinking. There was a scandal, but I wasn't sure what, about a trip they took to Mexico as cultural envoys for the Carter administration. A decade later, in 1986, he had surgery on his brain to relieve the pressure of bleeding beneath the skull. He denied then that Debbie had hit him, but no one believed him.

By then they had had a little girl. I did not know, and dared not think, how she was being raised. There was nothing I could do, I told my father's friends. He had decided on this woman, this life, this late-in-life child. I couldn't do anything about the decisions he'd made. I took refuge in my helplessness and I kept my distance. My first marriage fell apart and I made another, better one, and left the United States. In Central America, the Middle East, Europe—in guerrilla wars and Gulf conflicts—I thought I was getting on with my life.

But blood doesn't let go of you.

By the early 1990s, I was as much my own man as it was possible for me to be, and nothing that I wrote or did was identified with my father in anyone's mind—except my own. Despite all the years and all the distance, the knot of anger inside me had become a void I didn't know how to fill.

I would start to write a novel about prisons and see it veer toward a tale of surrogate parents. A piece I did for *Vanity Fair* about an old explorer of Arabia's Empty Quarter became an allegory of the search for fathers. I labored over a profile of Jacques Cousteau, and found myself fixated on the alienation of his sons. I started another novel, about terrorism, and it turned itself into a story of broken families and angry loneliness. But I couldn't talk to him, couldn't see him. We would meet for an afternoon in New York every couple of years, as if by accident. Once we saw each other during layovers in the Delta Terminal at La Guardia. My father had finished a couple of whisky miniatures before I got there, and downed another before I'd left.

Finally, in the summer of '94, at my wife's insistence, I went back to South Carolina, back to my mother's grave among live oaks in a little churchyard and to our house near the coast, steeling myself in middle age against all the madness I knew still lingered there. And I discovered that I was right about the horrors. There were more than I could have imagined. But I was wrong to have stayed away so long.

One of the first things I found was that Deborah, my father's wife, was a convicted drug addict, and her condition was much worse than anything the local papers knew or dared to print. My family— my father and the baby sister I barely knew—had been introduced to a world of thieves and murderers. In 1991, Deborah was caught in an abandoned building injecting cocaine with the help of a man she said was a stranger. My father forgave her, always. When she pleaded guilty to one count of possession, he told the court he would "stand beside her until death and mourning."

No one had told me anything. And I had been glad not to know. But now that I was back on the scene, Deborah wanted to talk, and talk, and talk about it all, as if telling some of the worst incidents over and over again would mean all of the past could be forgiven, forgotten. And repeated. As long as my father was sleeping or drunk twenty out of the twenty-four hours in the day, she'd always been able to count on that. It was a system she'd learned to play. She was good at it. She'd be taken care of, provided for, protected. And so there was no real need to get better.

But death and mourning were closer than we knew. In October 1994, my father was hospitalized with alcoholic hepatitis. Deborah, by turns protective and abusive, slid deeper into madness and addiction. But I couldn't walk away this time. Because of Bronwen, my sister, it was no longer possible to say there was nothing to be done. For thirteen years she had learned how to survive, and even to excel, in the dense atmosphere of madness and love, drunkenness and genius that surrounded my father. She was intelligent, pretty, perceptive, funny. But things were just too crazy now. Something had to be done for her. And through her, I believed, something could be done for all of us. Over Christmas, we two grown sons and this young sister entered into a kind of conspiracy to break the cycle of destruction, to save Bronwen and assure her future, to rescue our father, maybe even to salvage Deborah, and finally to save our exiled souls.

Jim Dickey had survived an attack of liver disease so fierce that 80 percent of patients in a similar condition die. His body cavity was filled with fluids like a water bed. His face was skeletal and shrunken. The hole where fluid was drained from beneath his skull nine years before showed a deep pit in the skin of his forehead. It was clear that he was afraid—physically terrified—of his wife. "Do you see this?" he said, touching the hole in his skull as he spoke into my tape recorder, putting his last wishes on the record that Christmas after he fell ill. "She did this. . . ." She had struck the blow that had caused the bleeding. "But don't let her get hold of that tape," he said. "It would be worth my life."

He was very weak, physically shrunken, desperately out of breath from a fibrosis of the lungs that got worse even as his liver got better. But he was sober. And he spoke now, as he had not for many years, with dazzling lucidity. Within three months, Bronwen had been accepted at the best boarding schools in America. Within a year, Deborah had moved out of the house, and was more seriously committed to treatment for her addictions than ever before. We were scattered, but drawing together.

So, every few months, I went back to the South and, sitting in the mist by the Atlantic, or driving along the Carolina flatlands from the coast, or at the house in Columbia, among his books and bows and guitars and manuscripts piled as precariously as wooden building blocks around his armchair, my father and I talked about much that went before that summer of *Deliverance* and, slowly, some of what had happened after. We were feeling our way delicately toward each other through fields of abandonment and anger. From the mildewed boxes in his garage and the depths of my own basement; from old journals and police blotters and yellowed copies of the *New York Times Book Review;* from the anecdotes of madness and despair that friends and colleagues and acquaintances of my father and the family recounted to each other like a collection of dirty jokes, we remembered—and we learned.

We both saw that we had been given this tremendous gift: the chance to set everything right. What I had done so far had worked. And by the summer of 1996, when I started on this book about him, and me, and *Deliverance*, I thought that if I could save my father's life I could fill the void forever.

I thought I could.

FATHERS

I touched my wife. I saw my son, unborn,
Left living after me, and my Self,
There, freed of myself,
In a stricken shade dancing together. . . .

—"Dover: Believing in Kings"

THE LANDINGS

The house at Litchfield had been neglected for a long time.

When my father bought it, in the early 1970s, I remember it felt so *modern*. It soared upward, a cedar-sided tower rising three tall stories toward a top floor with skylights and long windows looking through twisted branches. It was set close among other, lower vacation houses in a small development built on an old South Carolina indigo plantation. There was in fact a big white house at the end of a long allée of live oaks and Spanish moss, with tall columns and porches that looked out over salt marshes where deer and alligators edged up to the well-trimmed lawn. The benign ghost of the man who had built the plantation house was said to leave cold footprints on the back stairs at night. But that was not our place.

Ours was about newness. It was bought with movie money and it had smelled like clean air conditioning and fresh affluence. My mother decorated it with white rugs and pastel furniture and abstract art, her own special memories and her own sense of order. Later, my father liked to say he bought the house as a tribute to her. He liked to show that James Dickey, the intellectual and poet that he was, and the whisky-slugging *Deliverance* novelist-screenwriter celebrity that he'd become, could buy her by far the best house in this elegant country-club community. Certainly it had become her refuge. In the end, not least, from him. After she died in 1976, nobody came here much.

Now, twenty years later, the grounds were maintained just enough for appearances, but only if you didn't look too close. The wood near the front door was covered with black lichens. The oval metal plaque with the name that my father gave the house, "Root-

Light," hung loose on a single nail. In the living room, the picture window was replaced after a hurricane blew through it, but the white wall-to-wall carpet was left with the rot and water-marks of the storm. The curtains were never put up again. Small creatures from the marshes found their way into the house and died and dried in the sun. Wasps by the hundreds lay on the sills or embedded in the rug. Two little chameleons were mummified on top of the television. There was no vacuum cleaner that worked, and, that afternoon when we arrived in July of 1996, no will to clean up.

It had been a long drive down from Columbia. Just before we got to Litchfield, we had gone past my mother's grave, a few hundred yards up the road, but we hadn't stopped. We would come back there, we said. We had tried to settle into the house. My wife, my fifteen-year-old half-sister, and my father's secretary had gone to sleep. My father and I had watched the last recap of the first day of the Atlanta Olympics. Now it was after midnight, and the ceiling lights in the living room didn't work, and the few lamps left in the house had been broken, bent, smashed. All the lampshades had disappeared. I wasn't sure why. The bare-bulbed glare in the living room was oppressive.

"Let's roll," said my father, bracing himself for the climb to the bedroom on the third floor, beneath the skylights.

"You could sleep down here," I said. All he had to do was stretch his long, fragile body on the sofa where he was sitting. I'd bring a blanket and make a bed for him. Then there would be no need to move the oxygen-generating machine; no need to get out the backup bottles of air; no reason to strain the lungs, hardening with fibrosis, that worked so hard to take in so little. No chance of a fall. The machine sat safely in the corner of the room whispering shhhhh, pausing, shhhhh, with its own reliably calibrated breath, feeding pure blood-reddening oxygen to him at 3.5 liters a minute through a thirty-foot plastic tube coiled near his feet. "It would be easier."

"No," he said, adjusting the plastic loop draped over his ears and beneath his nose that sifted the air to him. "I want to be in my room."

"I know," I said.

We had strategized the ascent to the bedroom like Alpinists, from base camp to summit. First, we had to get to the staircase. I shoved aside the battered coffee table, clearing a path. Focused and determined, decrepit when he moved, but still oddly athletic when he thought about moving, my father made his way twenty feet to a little camp stool at the bottom of the stairs and sat down, exhausted.

We waited. "It'll get easier," I said.

"Sure," he said. "Sure it will."

"Ready?"

He stood with concentrated effort and an upward push of his body—and lost his balance. I caught him, held him up, then, slowly, steadied him. One step. Two. I touched his arm as lightly as I could and watched the fear on his face give way again to determination. Three, four—eight steps to the first landing, where a chair was waiting. He eased himself down into it, completely winded.

"I'll take the machine up," I said.

He held up his hand, ordering me to be quiet. A minute passed slowly. "Okay," he said, shaking his head to clear it.

"It'll just take a second to get it up there," I said. He'd keep the little plastic hose with him, but for a couple of minutes no air would come.

He waved his hand; said nothing.

The machine was about as big as a hotel minibar and probably as heavy. I held it next to me as I climbed, afraid that I'd lose my balance. I'd always tensed up around my father, always been clumsy. I was forty-four years old and that hadn't changed.

One flight, the landing, one flight, the second floor, another flight and another landing, and finally the last flight, to the top floor. I set the machine down delicately, then stood up and stretched with some slight sense of accomplishment as I felt the muscles in my back and shoulders pump up a little from the strain. I found a plug, hit the switch. The machine sighed to life. The little ball floating in a tube on the front climbed to the 3.5-liter line and steadied.

"Five!" he shouted from below, and I wondered where he got the breath. "Five! Got to have it!"

I adjusted the knob, watched the ball rise. "You got it," I shouted down. I couldn't see him from where I was. I shook out the long plastic tube to make sure it wasn't kinked and he had some slack. It went taut. And jerked.

Then jerked again.

And again.

Damn!

"Chrissy?" His voice sounded as okay as it could.

"Chrissy? What's that?" He jerked on the tube again, like a fish striking a line.

He was playing. Ah, God. He was calling up memories of summer vacations forty years ago on a long pier in Florida; memories of a father teaching a son the secrets he'd held on to from his own childhood, that code you build up over a lifetime: how to hold a marble and aim it and shoot it; or how to make a predator-call from a blade of grass between the thumbs; or how to know when a fish was striking a hand-line, or a crab was just sawing at it. I jerked gently on the tube to set the hook, just like he taught me, and went back downstairs smiling.

When my father had been drunk, he would tell the same stories again and again, like he was playing tape-recorded loops. It was all one-way communication. You could hear it, but if you responded the machine didn't pick up. Sometimes the anecdotes were about places we had been and things we'd done. Or he'd just re-enact scenes from the movie *Deliverance*. For no reason, except that he was bored and wanted to stop the conversation, he'd launch into the speech Burt Reynolds makes when the suburbanites are deciding what to do with the body of a redneck they've killed. "You believe in *democracy*, don't you?" Strangers enjoyed the show. And if he played the same loops for people who lived with him and loved him, and they didn't enjoy them, well, fuck them.

Now that my father drank Ensure instead of malt liquor in the mornings, even when he told some of those same old stories they were the beginning of a dialogue, not a way to break it off. He was trying to remember. He was trying to help me remember. And I thought that, if I could just remember enough, understand him enough, I would have what I needed to keep him going.

"We'll stay here a while, here on the landing," he said, when he could get any words out at all. I sat on a step waiting, looking out the big window at a few leaves that were lit by the spotlights outside, and a lot of darkness that was not. Finally he said, "What do you think of the movie?," and he shook his head.

There was a new script to work on that week. My father's third novel, *To the White Sea*, the one about the murderous American loner let loose in wartime Japan, had been bought by Hollywood, and the producer was enthusiastic, as producers tend to be. But the project was out of my father's hands. Others had written the screenplay this time, and the old man had been mulling what had been done to his work, and looking to make it better.

"The string," I said.

"Yeah."

He'd fixed on the vignette where Muldrow, the killer and the hero, has been discovered by two little children on a moonlit night near a Japanese farmhouse. Muldrow might murder them, but instead he weaves a little string figure, a sort of cat's cradle, with his fingers.

The screenplay made this a brief, odd encounter. But my father wanted to draw it out, as it was in the novel, for all the tension it could hold. He wanted Muldrow to weave a string ladder with his fingers and hold it up against the moon for the children to see, and move it so the moon climbed the diamond-shaped rungs. Then he wanted Muldrow to take this circle of string and hang it around the neck of one of the little children, so that, as you saw the knot at the throat, you couldn't be sure if Muldrow would strangle the little boy or not.

As my father talked, I saw the string as he had woven it for me one afternoon on the steps of his mother's house in Atlanta in the 1950s. Maybe I was three or four. Anyway, I was still small enough for him to coax a thrilled little-boy laugh out of me by tossing me in the air on a long, warm afternoon after a Sunday dinner with the family. But he'd gotten tired of that game and wanted to show me another, and he had brought out a circle of string from someplace. "I'm going to cut off my head," he said, wrapping the thread around his neck, then lacing it through his fingers. And I knew it was just a trick. But my heart still picked up speed. And then he clapped his hands and, as if by magic, the string passed through his neck. But his head was still there. And I was amazed.

Another trick with the string was one he called "the seesaw." He put one loop in his mouth and another on each hand, then I took a fourth, and as he pulled his hands apart, he pulled my loop of string closer to him. Back and forth, and back and forth. It was the kind of game you never want to end when you're three or four. But he was still building to the climax of his repertoire: Jacob's ladder. His powerful fingers, made for holding a football or pulling a bow, now wove the string as delicately as the legs of a garden spider knitting its web. And then, with a turn of his wrists, there appeared, stretched between his hands, the ladder. "Climb it with your fingers," he told me, and when I reached the top rung, he drew the strings together to catch me there.

"I'll show you something else," he said. "Jacob's coffin." He shifted the loops on his fingers and drew them tight, and the wide rungs of the ladder closed into a tight little knot suspended in an X of string. "You see Jacob there in the middle?" he said, as his black nurse Corinne must have said to him when she taught him these things. "You see Jacob there in his coffin?" That question was part of the ritual of the trick somehow. But I didn't see it, really. I wasn't sure then what a coffin was. And how could that little twisted knot be Jacob?

"Teach me to do it," I pleaded, the way little children do. "Teach me. Teach me." And my father said he would, but the secrets of this magic had to be kept just between us. And there, on those steps at the front of the Atlanta house that were slick with green moss and smelling of pine needles and damp cement, I entered into his conspiracy, and he put the string on my tiny fingers and showed me how to work it.

What I did not learn or did not register until a long time later, when I was reading back through a collection of my father's poems and read the one called, simply, "The String," was that his brother, the one who died before he was born, the one whose death, in my father's mind, was the reason for his birth, had lain in his sickbed making string figures hour after hour.

> Except when he enters my son,
> The same age as he at his death,
> I cannot bring my brother to myself.
> I do not have his memory in my life,
> Yet he is in my mind and on my hands.
> I weave the trivial string upon a light
> Dead before I was born. . . .

The image haunted and reassured me. It seemed such a perfect expression of family, of loss and regeneration, this story of "a skeletal, blood-sharing child."

> A man, I make the same forms
> For my son, that my brother made,
> Who learnt them going to Heaven. . . .

Right there at the old house in Atlanta, where the air smelled of green moss and pine straw.

And then, this evening, on the first landing at Litchfield, I asked him about his brother and the string.

"I made that up," he said.

"Yeah?"

One of the great lessons he'd learned in poetry, he said, was from Monroe Spears, who taught him at Vanderbilt in the 1940s, and was just telling him what he needed to do to improve a particular poem—"What should happen here is . . ."—when my father had said, or so he said he said, "It didn't happen that way." And Spears had told him, "No artist is bound by the truth." A great lesson, my father thought. "And later," my father said, "I saw it was Nietzsche: 'No true artist will tolerate for one minute the world as it is.' "

We sat there on the landing for a while longer, not talking, waiting for breath from the machine.

"But you're a journalist," my father said. "So the truth is important."

"In journalism it is."

He considered that proposition for a time, as if waiting for more or better air.

"Remember this," he said, "as if these were my last words. No matter what anybody says."

"I'm listening."

"Remember what I was—to you."

THE COLLECTOR

My father liked to collect the things he cared about. Books. Guitars. Bows, arrows, knives. Typewriters. And he liked backups. Redundancies. He liked the things themselves, and he liked the idea of the things. He would wear two watches on his wrist. Altogether he must have had a dozen guitars—six-strings, twelve-strings—and maybe twice that many bows—recurves, compounds, longbows. He built walls of books in every place we ever lived. He bought himself multiple cameras, Dictaphones, televisions. Many of these things broke, or their batteries just died and moldered, but they were never repaired, and never thrown away. At the house in Columbia he kept a typewriter in almost every room, although most of them stopped working many years ago, jammed with dust or run out of ribbon.

At the Litchfield house, in the top-floor master bedroom, he had backups of all the icons he would not be without. Here were a couple of little hunting bows with elegantly curved limbs; there were two guitars in their cases; an electric typewriter sat on a leather-topped campaign desk. I recognized them all from the early 1970s. At least one of the bows was a gift from the Bear Archery Company, which supplied the hunting equipment for the filming of *Deliverance* in 1971.

Near the floor-to-ceiling bookcase was an aluminum-framed reclining lawn chair that rocked upright or supine, depending on how you shifted your weight. We'd probably had five or six like it over the years. For as long as I could remember, in fact. There was even an old Soloflex exercise machine. Instead of weights, a Soloflex used the resistance of big elastic bands to give you a workout. My father had one just like it in his bedroom in the house in Columbia, and it had become a kind of silent valet draped with clothes. This Soloflex was just draped with the spent, stretched-out rubber bands that used to give it strength.

What I could not find in the top-floor bedroom was sheets. The king-size mattress centered beneath the skylights was covered with decades of embedded stains. Spilled drinks. Bodily fluids. It looked like there had been a lot of blood at one time or another. I tried not to look too close. But there were no sheets at all up here to cover it. Finally I found a few in the laundry room downstairs. I made the bed.

My father was waiting on the last landing. "We're ready for you," I said. He was in pain as he stood, struggling and teetering as he mounted the last eight stairs, but when he made it to the top he kept moving until he was seated on the bed that we'd been trying to reach for most of an hour. He was steady now. The oxygen machine a few feet away whispered reliably. He checked to see if I'd brought up his big glass of chocolate Ensure, and the books he'd been reading, especially a copy of Stephen Crane's *The Red Badge of Courage*, for which he was writing an introduction.

I lay down on the chaise, which rocked back with my weight. "I'll sleep here," I said.

"No," said my father. "You go along. I'll be okay." That night, in that house, in that room, my father wanted to be alone.

I checked on him again. My sister and his secretary were asleep on the floor just below. He had the phone by his side, and the light, and his books. He urinated into a bottle and I emptied it. He settled into his sheets, his bed, and I kissed him good night.

I'd be lying if I said I wasn't relieved to close the door of the Litchfield place behind me that night. The South Carolina summer air was heavy, but this late in the evening there was a hint of cool dew, and it was sweet and easy to breathe. I wheeled my rented car through the plantation toward the big house, now a fashionable bed-and-breakfast, where my wife waited in a clean, well-ordered room. Near a stand of pines, the headlights swept across a small herd of deer. Their eyes were moon-silver as they looked up. "The ghost of a deer, but a deer just the same," my father wrote somewhere in *Deliverance*. I wished that he were out here with me to see them. Even when I fled him, I missed him.

Now that I was back, he wanted to talk to me about the truth. But the deeper I got into this dialogue, the harder it was to know what answers I was looking for—or even which voice was asking the questions. Was

I the grown man talking to his aged father, or the little boy talking to his dad? I would wake up in the middle of the night and start to write in my journal about the life we led when I was seven or eight, and I became that child again, and then, when I looked in the mirror at the terribly tired, forty-something face that was there, I would be surprised. How grimly fascinating to be so old and unlike my father's son, and like my father.

I wanted to know what made him *him*. I wanted some hold on his childhood experience in the North Georgia woods at the side of his own father, that dilettante lawyer and devoted gambler who took his son with him to cockfights, or to watch raccoons chained to floating logs fighting off packs of hounds, or to just about anything else where blood and death had money riding on them. I wanted to know about his mother, the woman he thought was very nearly saintly, who ran the family from her sickbed, suffering in silence in her darkened room every afternoon from the angina that was supposed to have very nearly killed her before he was ever born. That was the risk she had run—for him, he thought—although she lived to the age of ninety, and died, in the end, of cancer. And what about his military career? I hadn't learned until I was about thirty that he was not, as he told the world, and told me all my life, a pilot in a night-fighter squadron in the Pacific. He was a radar operator, an "intercept officer." The second guy in the plane. Brave enough, with his thirty-eight combat missions and five bronze stars. But that was not enough for him. At least not for a long time.

There was no way to get at him without filtering his experiences through my own: my memories of his parents, my adolescence, my wars, my middle age. And when I would read the letters and the notebooks and the poems written by James Dickey at the height of his powers, I found a man who was just my age—no older, no younger —an accessible genius and a shadow father-brother whom I could know, I thought, I hoped, like no one else. It was as if, in all those poems, in all that he wanted for me and made of me and wrote about fathers, brothers, sons, he was waiting for this. The more I sifted through his life and mine, the more I tried to bring my father to myself, the more I realized that what I was looking for lay somewhere between truth and imagination. Long before *Deliverance*, my father had begun to make himself up. And me. He would not tolerate for a minute the world as it was.

ROOT-LIGHT

It was well after dawn, but the morning still had a little cool left in it when I got back to my father's house at Litchfield. I let myself in and made my way up the stairs, none too quietly, looking forward to waking him and to talking.

He lay on the bed utterly rigid, his hands crossed over his chest in sepulchral repose, like the figures on the tombs in Westminster Abbey. I said nothing. Surreptitiously he opened one eye to see if I was watching, then saw that I was. "Just practicing," he said.

"Dad, you are so full of shit." I let out a long sigh. "Are you ready to go down, or do you want to stay up here a little longer?" There was no TV in the bedroom. Litchfield had fallen out of use before he started collecting the huge back-projection televisions he had in Columbia, so, if he wanted to watch the Olympics, and he did, we'd have to go back to the living room and see them on the set down there, the one with the chameleon mummies on top.

We'd take it in stages, he said. It was a few more minutes before he swung his legs over the side of the bed to sit upright, waiting to start the morning ordeal of descent, which was almost as difficult as the trip up to the bedroom at night. He was looking absently at the black iron structure of the Soloflex that loomed near his desk. I browsed the bookcases, just to see what was there, and came across a first edition of Pat Conroy's powerful, excruciating novel of fathers and sons, *The Great Santini*. Conroy had been a student of my father's; had idolized him, as so many of his students did, but seemed to have pulled out of my father's life these last few years, as so many people had. The book was autographed to my brother, Kevin, in 1976, the year it came out. I guessed no one had ever told Kevin it was here.

"Chrissy? Can you do something for me?" Dad was still pondering the Soloflex. "Can you take those rubber bands and throw them away?" Sure, I said. All of them were limp, lifeless, useless. "Sure. Why?"

"They remind me of my dick," he said.

"Don't you worry about that," I said. "You're going to come back strong on all fronts."

Dad shook his head a little and smiled a little. "We'll see about that."

"You're going to be around for a long time," I said, not thinking too much about what I was saying. "Carol says the Dickeys don't die, they just kill everybody around them."

He looked at me and let that idea settle for a minute.

"I'm not afraid of dying," he said matter-of-factly. "No, really I'm not. I know just how it is." When he was in the hospital in 1994, jaundiced and bloated, he'd barely been able to move. "All I could do was curl up under the blanket. And I heard this voice, I guess it was the doctor, this voice said, 'We've lost him.' And I thought, Is this it?"

"How was it?"

"It was just like going to sleep." He shrugged.

"So you know the great secret already," I said.

"Yeah, I guess I do."

For as long as I could remember my father talking to me about poetry and poets, which was just about as long as I could remember, he'd loved to tell a story of Shelley and Byron, about how they had been swimming together when Shelley suddenly sank to the bottom —and stayed there. Byron waited for him to surface again. But he didn't. And finally Byron dived down and dragged Shelley back to the air. "Why did you do that?" Shelley wondered. "In a few moments I should have known the great secret."

That had been a hard thing for a five-year-old boy to think about, that image of the poet willfully waiting to drown while his friend panicked. Wasn't Dad a poet? And my father had always followed that story with the tale of how Shelley really had drowned at sea, and his body, washed up on the Italian shore, had been burned. But the heart would not burn. And Byron had reached into the coals and taken it out.* If Dad was a poet, he must be Byron, I thought then. But now I think I was wrong.

---

* Never mind that it was Trelawny who dived into the Arno to save Shelley, or Leigh Hunt who reached into the flames on the beach near Viareggio. "I always find the bottom of the well, and they say Truth lies there," Shelley had told Trelawny. "In another minute I should have found it, and you would have found an empty shell. It is an easy way of getting rid of the body."

"Shelley. Yeah," said my father, "I like him because I like anybody who is super-inhumanly idealistic."

There was a part of my father, a central part, that always believed he could become super-inhuman—could become, in some sort of way, a god. "Intelligence should be imperishable," Shelley said. And if you could just be intelligent enough, you would be imperishable, too. About the time *Deliverance* was being made into a movie, my father published a journal called *Sorties*. "It seems to me that I am the bearer of some kind of immortal message to humankind," he wrote on page 34, and when I read that, as a teenager, it was just the kind of bombastic bullshit I would have expected of him. But there must have been times when, drunk or dreaming, or writing or giving readings or fucking, he felt that he was getting close. You see that in the poems, if you read them all together. And I hadn't understood that. Just as it wasn't until much later that I understood—a related fact—how really afraid he was, and had been, all of his life. And of so many things.

Little Jimmy Dickey was born on February 2, 1923, at Atlanta's Crawford Long Hospital and spent the first few years of his life in his grandmother's house in Atlanta, his mother's mother's place at Pershing Point. "Grossmutter," as she liked to be called, had been born in Germany. And little Jimmy learned in the nursery some German that stayed with him for the rest of his life. Grossmutter's favorite word was *tüchtig*, do it right. She often quoted lines from a German poet— "*Es muss sein, es muss sein*," it must be, it must be—that haunted him always. If there was an air of Mozart playing on the gramophone, she would demand the house be quiet. "Silence," she would say. "There is music." And her loving severity could be fearsome. One of the first books she read to Jimmy was *Struwwelpeter*, a collection of sadistic German stories meant to frighten little children into behaving as they should. "The scissors man always comes / To little boys who suck their thumbs" was one couplet. "Ah, that was a horrible book," he'd say, remembering. "Scariest damn thing you've ever seen."

But the horror that he remembered with almost unutterable intensity was his grandmother's diabetes. She had grown very fat, this imposing and loving woman, and she had gone blind. And she had gotten gangrene in her foot, and lost her leg.

No memories he had or shared of the other branches of his family were so deep, or so disturbing. They were just the subjects of Atlanta anecdotes, the kind of thing women might talk about over iced tea, or men over a whisky. There was a woman on his mother's father's side of the family, for instance—one of the Swifts—who was said to have raised the Confederate flag in Atlanta after the Yankee general William Tecumseh Sherman took the city. She was spared hanging because she was a woman, but it was a close thing. Or so it was said. About Jimmy's father's folks, the Dickey forebears, there wasn't much talk at all. His father's brother, James Lafayette Dickey, for whom he was named, made a lot of money in real estate as Atlanta started to grow. He supposedly owned the property where the governor's mansion now stands. But if you started tracing the bloodlines back to the time of the War Between the States, well, that wasn't something you really wanted to talk about. The Dickeys lived in the mountains of North Georgia, around Mineral Bluff, and many supported the Union. A great-uncle who is still remembered in those parts was named, significantly, William Tecumseh Dickey.

Jim had a whole collection of well-honed stories about the characters found under his grandmother's roof. "Both sides in my family are specialists in ne'er-do-wells and black sheep," he liked to say. There was Mr. Huntley, Grossmutter's second husband, who used to get drunk and walk down the stairs in the main house buck naked—and playing a zither. And there was an Aunt Katie—or was it Aunt Jeanette?—"who fired a maid for breathing on her." Cousin Eugenia, according to family lore, used to go to bed every night of the year wearing a Kotex, for fear a man would rape her in her sleep and she might not otherwise know of it.

But the stories he loved to tell the most were of Uncle Tom Swift, the youngest of Grossmutter's five children, and the only boy, who grew up to be, like so many of the men in the family, a drunk. "Another alcoholic," Jim remembered, "of the most extreme and lovable kind.

"He was a heavyset fella who rather resembled Thomas Wolfe. Not that tall, but with a sort of heavy face, and a deep dimple in his chin. As a little boy, two and three and four, I became a great favorite of his, a great favorite. One day I was up in the upstairs hall, just rattling around the house, like children will do. And I passed by his door and it was open. He said, 'Come on in, Jimmy.' He was always joking or teasing. And I got about halfway across the room and I was looking at his face, and a look of the most horrible fear—or some emotion—came over him. I had never seen anything like it on a human face. I thought it was one of his jokes, but I just didn't understand what was going on. He says, 'Jimmy! Those cats. Those cats! Get those cats out!'

"I thought, What on earth? 'Uncle Tom, there is nothing, I don't see any cats. There aren't any cats over there.'

" 'The cats, Jim. Get those cats out!' He got up"—and the grown

Jim, telling the story, made as if to rise, then settled back into his chair. "He scared the shit out of me. He was having the DTs." Jim remembered Tom as "a wastrel and a bum," and loved him, and loved the sound of the phrase, too.

Little Jimmy and his parents moved to their own place on West Wesley Road, off Peachtree Street, and Grossmutter eventually got fed up with Tom's hell-raising around the house and built him his own apartment over the garage. It was heated by a big potbellied stove. "He took right to it," Jim would remember. "I heard later he'd have these huge carousers with all these reprobate friends—especially women—all these low women would come out. My poor grandmother would die to see that, I was told. And they would get drunk and—"

Jim never could keep from laughing when he got to this part, even when he was short of breath and the laughing cost him.

"—and Uncle Tom would rise and piss on the stove."

"Hell, Dad, you thought that was funny then and you think it's funny now."

"Don't you? Sssssssssshhhh. The steam!"

The house on West Wesley was very different. "My mother's life was far too secretive and withdrawn for that to happen out there. That was practically a hermitage." The image of his mother that hardened in James Dickey's poetry and his head was of the woman in his poem "Angina" whose children tiptoe into her room "overawed by their own existence, / For courtly doctors long dead / Have told her that to bear children / Was to die."

I spent a lot of time in that house on West Wesley myself when I was a little boy. It was there that my father taught me the string tricks, that the concrete steps smelled of pine needles and green moss, and it was there that my grandmother took care of me whenever my mother needed a break. I do not remember that Grandmama was very sick. Or sick at all. She was kind and sweet, as my father remembered. But she was also funny, very cutting about other adults, and gloriously, playfully indulgent with children.

Every corner of the house was open to us, whether we were in the kitchen making peanut-butter sandwiches, up in the attic raiding our father's toy chests, or in the bathroom pillaging the cosmetics and bromides in the medicine cabinet to concoct secret "ingredients." A chair lift installed to help my grandmother up and down the stairs became a Dickey family amusement ride.

All along one side of the house was a wide screen porch elevated, because of the way the property sloped, to the level of the tree branches. At one end of it was a swinging bed suspended from the ceiling by chains. It was our pirate-ship–spacecraft–stagecoach and, in the summer, a magical, frightening place to sleep. Moths fluttered against the screen seeking the faint lights inside the house, and a screech owl haunted the hidden limbs of the trees.

The yard itself was more than an acre, and every corner had its secrets. The garage was a separate building at the back of the property, and in a little corner of lawn to one side of it you could find wild strawberries in the spring. When I was very little, my grandmother used to sing me a lullaby that, like all the lullabies I grew up with, and my father grew up with, was about death. Two little children wander away from home and die in the woods: "Then one day some robins so red / brought strawberry leaves and over them spread / and sang them a song the whole day long." And I thought that Grandmama meant those woods near the screen porch, those robins that hopped along the edge of the yard, those strawberry leaves back behind the garage.

There in the back, too, my grandfather kept a chicken coop where he'd stash fighting cocks when he felt the need to bring them down from the country, where a man named Wha-cha-know Joe took care of them on a ramshackle little farm with junked cars in the yard. The chickens were mean as hell, and we stayed away from them. My father would claim later that he had to shoot a couple that got loose. More often, if they hadn't proved their mettle or been killed in the pit, they'd go to old George, the yard man, to be executed. He'd take off their heads with a hatchet, and we'd watch, fascinated, as they cartwheeled around the yard in fountains of blood.

Out front was a towering fir tree with branches that hung so low and wide we could hide beneath them as if in a cavern. Along one edge of the yard was a stand of bamboo that seemed to regenerate itself endlessly even as we grandchildren assailed it with coping saws and hatchets to harvest spears and telescopes. But those woods along the side of the house, below the screen porch, were not a place we went to much, at least not when we were little.

There were servants to watch us, certainly. Old George always seemed to be working somewhere in the yard, or waiting for a meal on the back step, near the kitchen. (He was allowed into the house only on family holidays, and then just to play the harmonica and drink one beer.) And there was Julia, the nearly toothless Hungarian cook, fat and heavy-breasted, wild-eyed and sweaty, who lived next to the furnace in the basement. But it was Grandmama who took care of the grandchildren when we were over at the West Wesley house, and we were there a lot.

She did take a nap every afternoon. But I thought even then that the point of her nap was to keep the men in the family, especially her husband, from bothering her. "Pop," as everyone called him, liked to hang out with people like Wha-cha-know Joe, people my grand-mother didn't care to know. "Why, they're just *Bettelsacks,*" she'd say. Junk people. It's the only German word I ever remember her using. But when my grandfather wasn't in the house, which was often, Grand-mama would take me to play in his room. There, where the bedcovers and the leather club chair smelled like pipe tobacco and the corners were piled high with *Grit and Steel* magazine, she'd let me twirl the dials on his big vacuum-tube shortwave and, most fun of all, play the 45s on his record player, so I could bounce and dance on his bed until I was exhausted. Her own nap, if she took it at all, didn't seem to last very long.

Other times, when she took me into her own room, my grand-mother would lie with the drapes closed against the afternoon light, and the doors closed against the rest of the house. She smelled of rosewater from the cold cream she spread over the cultivated white-ness of her face and hands. The air conditioner hummed loudly in the window. It was the only one in the house in those days. Sometimes she would listen to gospel music on the radio in the dark and tell me to hush now, to try to take a little nap. More often she turned on a light and read about the old gentleman rabbit Uncle Wiggly and the skillery-scallery alligator, who was tricked into swallowing a statue instead of gobbling up the old rabbit himself. My father grew up with Uncle Wiggly, too, and it was read to him in the same voice.

I suppose there were photographs of other members of the family in Grandmama's room, but the only one I remember was on a wall diagonally across from the bed, just where I could see it when I was snuggled against her side. It was a picture of a little boy in a sailor suit, Gene, the brother who was dead before my father was born.

The idea about his own father that hardened in Jim Dickey's mind was of the old man's indifference and apathy. "He just drifted. And because he was like he was, it filled me with, as they used to say, a burning desire for consequence. Value. To attach significance to things. Be-cause there was not anything to him that had any significance. Any." It was his father who introduced him to verse, and he never forgot the powerful rhythms of "Horatius at the Bridge" or "The Shooting of Dan McGrew." But one of the reasons James Dickey wrote poetry, he said when he was old, was to "obliterate" his father.

Little Jimmy's idols were everything his dapper, sedentary pop was not. Some were just the heroes of his time, or of any boy's life. He was fascinated by body builders. Among bits of memorabilia his mother saved for him there was a 1935 brochure from the York Bar Bell Co., "The Road to Super Strength." "You will be like the soldier buckling on his sword. Equipped for life—capable to meet every physical emergency," it promised. "The world wants strong men today more than ever. Men of action, endurance, pep, punch and power. The type of man your heart aches to see you be." Later, Jim became a fan of Charles Atlas, whose "dynamic-tension" exercises, supposedly learned from watching panthers tensing against the bars at the zoo, could turn a ninety-eight-pound weakling into Mr. America.

In a little clearing in the woods below the screen porch, twelve-year-old Jimmy Dickey hung a thick rope from a tree branch. He spent hours climbing hand over hand, or chopping stumps and logs with a heavy ax. He drove himself hard. As he wrote later, he prayed that "the chicken-chested form" he belabored

> Might swell with the breast of a statue
> From out of the worm-shattered bole,
> While I talked all the time through my teeth
> To another, unlike me, beside me:
> To a brother or king-sized shadow
> Who looked at me, burned, and believed me:
> Who believed I would rise like Apollo
>
> With armor-cast shoulders upon me. . . .

The miracle didn't come. But slowly the rope and the ax and the barbells, high-school football and high-school track and the hormones his "rack-ribbed body" had waited for, started working to make him more of what he wanted to be. There is a photograph of Jimmy Dickey taken in the back yard of the West Wesley house when he must have been about fifteen. He'd built a little sawdust pit and a high-jump bar, and the shutter caught him with his shirtless body arching forward and his arms outstretched just as he hit the apogee of his leap. He was already tall then; his chest and arms were just beginning to fill out. He was—beautiful.

His fantasy life was growing, too. Lying there in the swinging bed on the porch in Atlanta, Jimmy would read one pulp novel after another. Edgar Rice Burroughs, creator of Tarzan, was one of his favorite authors. But his Tarzan was not the Tarzan of the movies, his was Lord Greystoke, raised by the Great Apes after his parents are killed in the jungle—a man who could defeat the most powerful bull ape with nothing but a knife, but also a man who could teach himself to read from the primers left in his parents' abandoned cabin. He loved this idea that one man, alone, could educate and improve and transform himself.

But Tarzan was not the only Burroughs hero that Jimmy Dickey seized on. There was also John Carter of Mars, Carson of Venus, and David Innis at the earth's core. There are not so many of the Innis books, and Innis himself, a mining engineer turned warlord, was not so interesting, but the earth's core—which Burroughs called Pellucidar —was Jim Dickey's favorite Burroughs world. There, at the hollow center of the planet, the horizons curved upward like the edges of an enormous bowl, until they disappeared into the distance, and the sun was a molten orb suspended permanently in the center of the sky. Time almost stood still. Huge beasts and powerful, primitive men roamed jungles and plains in a world that was vast but finite, accessible, self-contained. To my father as a boy—and even as an adult telling me about it—this land of enormous animals and upward horizons seemed a world that ought to be plausible, even reachable. Pellucidar ought, somehow, to be.

But the greatest pulp hero of Jim's childhood was not a Burroughs creation. He was Kenneth Robeson's Doc Savage, the Man of Bronze, a man-as-superman who made himself superior to everyone around him through the sheer power of his discipline, the stubbornness of his will. This was a hero that little Jimmy wanted to know all about. My father would tell me how Doc Savage managed to exercise every muscle in his body even as he was performing equations or practicing new languages in his head, and it was clear to me that Dad thought, "Yeah, you could do that." That *he* could. And that *I* could.

But I don't really think it was my father wanting to be like Doc, or Tarzan, or to better himself with barbells, or even to obliterate his father, that pushed him to push himself so hard. All of that was mixed into the head of that blond boy with the so-serious expression in the family photo album. But it wasn't the driving force. It wouldn't have been enough.

Looking back from that top floor at Litchfield, I started to see, in my father's work, in his life, his lies, his obsessions, a terrifying sense of original sin. But it wasn't a religious thing. It was about family. Whether he was told it once, or often, or only overheard it, little Jimmy Dickey truly did believe that his mother had risked her life to bear him.

There was part of my father, I thought, that felt responsible for the death of that little boy in the sailor suit, as if he could have done something; as if, somehow, he should have been there. As if, reversing the order of the world by not being born, he could have brought that child back to life. Or maybe, from that top floor of Litchfield, as I listened to the oxygen machine and waited for my father to call me to help him from the bathroom, it was only I who felt that way.

What my father did know, certainly, was that his guilt could be used. "Theme of mine: The search for the (ideal) brother," he wrote in a 1950s notebook, "and the turning inward to the self in search of him, finally. Narcissus; solipsism."

FLIGHT SCHOOL

B y the time we went down to Litchfield, I knew that parts of the stories my father had told me about being a college football star and a pilot in World War II were not true. But I didn't know much else. And I'd begun to care less. It was painful, excruciating, to go over this stuff. But I wanted, selfishly perhaps, to see him as he must have been when he was a kid, when he was Jimmy, or Jim, and had no idea, for better or worse, that he'd be James Dickey, or my father. And I wanted, all at once, to break through the barrier of being a son, to find a way to tell him how much I admired him, how much I believed whatever the fuck he wanted to tell me. To tell him I loved him.

He tried.

I could see him working to get back into the head of that kid in shoulder pads, that boy in a flight jacket. But there were fifty years, all the fog, and all the guilt to get through. And all the anecdotes: so many stories repeated so often, and often so well, that they were like a wall against the past, and a wall between us.

But, still, he tried. Seventy-three and dying, he went back over all of it with me. And, yes, changed the subject, and dodged and evaded. And bore my old anger. Heroically, I'd say. And from letters locked away in a closet in Columbia, and a few of his notes here and there, I discovered at last quite a lot about how he shaped himself when he did think, every day, that he was going to die. When he was young.

If Jimmy Dickey didn't go to Clemson Agricultural College in the fall of 1942 mainly to avoid the draft, that certainly was one of the reasons. The other, the one he always talked about, was sports. Football and track had been a big part of his life at North Fulton High School. To hear him tell it, he'd been known as the Crab Apple Cannonball. "And I was," he'd always say. Then there had been a year at the Darlington School, a military prep in Rome, Georgia. And finally Clemson, up in the hills of South Carolina. To the extent that the students wore uniforms and occasionally hit the drill field, it, too, was considered a military institution. The South, where young men were taught they had a vocation to command, was full of these places. But Clemson's main fame, then as now, was football. The team, the Tigers, was coached by a rough old bastard who had his own memorable way with words. "Listen, you boys, if you feel something warm and hairy coming up your throat, don't you worry. It's just your asshole. Har, har, har." It was the way that men talked to each other, and then some.

Jimmy's father wanted him to be an engineer. His mother wanted to keep him out of the army. So Clemson made sense, even if Jimmy hated it almost from the minute he arrived. "There are a lot of country hicks around here," he wrote to his folks after his first couple of days at school. "I went out for football yesterday and did pretty well considering it was my first day. I am one of the littlest ones on the team." He played in the backfield, and figured he was better at kicking and passing than anyone else, and probably faster. "There is a fellow named 'Hoochie' Morgan who is pretty fast too. Most all the football players here have nicknames. They call me 'Peachtree.' (Because I'm from Atlanta, I guess.)"

He strained to make his letters home sound upbeat, but fell back easily into a mama's-boy whine. He wished he were in Atlanta, wished he were going to Georgia Tech "and drinking liquor and belonging to a fraternity and having dates all the time in the old home town. When I have thoughts like these, it is really a strain on the old will power not to pull out of this hell hole in South Carolina. Its all for the best, though, and when all of the Atlanta gigoloes are 'A-1 in the army' little Jimmy will be thumbing his nose and having the last, and longest, laugh. (I hope.)"

He was nineteen years old and writing to his "Dearest, dearest Mom," with pure cornball sentimentality. "I wish you would do me a favor. Give Pop a big hug and kiss for me. I was just listening to the radio, and Pete Cassel sang 'That Silver-Haired Daddy of Mine' and tears came into my eyes." He was pulling praise from her any way he could. "Mom, I know that you would be the last person in the world to say such a thing, but I feel that I have been such a disappointment to everyone. I wish sometimes I could just pass out of the picture, but then I think of my wonderful family, and that gives me strength to go on."

All his life, whenever Jim Dickey felt he was under pressure from someone who loved him, he'd play that same game. "I'm a bum," he'd say. "I'm no good." Especially when he was drinking really heavily, and you were pleading with him to stop, he'd start in with that. "I'm just a bum," he'd say, sure that you'd tell him how wonderful he really was. And from his mother he always got just the response he hoped. On the envelope of that despairing letter from Clemson she wrote in her rounded script, in the light-blue ink of the fountain pen she always kept on her desk in the West Wesley house, "Could any son write a sweeter tribute to his mother. Bless you, my darling, for loving me like this and telling me so."

In all, Jimmy played just one freshman season of college football, and a couple of games of basketball. By November 1942, regardless of what his mother wanted, he wanted out of Clemson. The war was heating up, and he could be as romantic a patriot as any kid who was far from the battlefield. At the Darlington School he'd even written, in an essay that won a medal from the Society of Colonial Daughters, "If we are to defeat the Powers of Evil who threaten us, every man, woman and child must do his part, however small." That first month at Clemson, Jimmy went to see *Desperate Journey*, starring Errol Flynn and Ronald Reagan, a tale of American fliers stranded in Germany and struggling to get across the border. "Don't miss it," he told his mother. "It's one of the best thrillers I've ever seen."

By Christmas, Jimmy "Peachtree" Dickey was no more. He'd enlisted in the Army Air Corps, and by February 1943 he'd shipped out to Miami Beach, Florida, for basic training. It had been more than a year already since the United States entered the war, and no one was sure how or when it would end. But he told his parents that he'd be in training for so long—at least fifteen months—that he'd probably never see action. He was going to be a pilot for sure, he said.

The new recruits were lined up for their first day of basic training, and an old sergeant was walking down the wavering, smirking line watching smiles dissolve and spines stiffen. But Jim Dickey, this lanky kid from Atlanta, just couldn't wipe that grin off his face until the sergeant was right there and his rough voice was blasting in Jim's eyeballs. "Now, you listen up," said the sergeant, speaking for all to hear. "You boys are gonna learn one thing in this man's army. We can't make you do nothin', but we can make you wish you had."

Jimmy spent a lot of time on KP his first few weeks in the army, and a lot of time getting sick. He wanted to be an officer, he wanted to be a pilot, and he wanted it all so bad, it scared the hell out of him. "I took the Physical today, and had 150 blood pressure. Caused from nervousness I guess. . . . If I don't measure up they'll throw me out of the Cadets. . . . Nothing ever happens the way I want it to, anyway. I knew almost from the beginning I was no good, and that something would happen to thwart my plans. It's always been that way, and it always will. I'll never even see an airplane."

He and the other cadets were sent up to High Point College, in North Carolina. Most of what he was doing there was classwork. He sent his parents letters saying just how much he liked to command as a cadet lieutenant, how he felt he was made for it. And right up to the point where he actually had to fly the plane, his military career, he reported, was "right on the beam."

It was the flying itself, with his hands on the controls, that he just could not do. He barely passed his "final check" in a little sixty-five-horsepower Piper at High Point: seventy points was a failing grade and he got seventy-two. The only part of the test in which his scores were even average was taxiing on the ground, taking off, and holding in a traffic pattern. He must have known by then, in June '43, it was going to be tough to make it as a pilot. But he didn't want to tell that to anybody back home.

By October, he was in Camden, South Carolina. If he was going to be a pilot, it would be here, in these little two-seater biplanes taking off and landing on dusty runways, that he'd make it; or it was here that he'd break. And he was beginning to think it could be where he'd die. Some of the boys had crashed. One of them was burned beyond recognition. The fear wasn't going away, it was getting worse.

"I was flying with my instructor Saturday," Jim wrote to his younger brother, Tom, "and we came in and landed and taxied up to where you parked the planes and my instructor got out and I started to [get out], but he said, 'Oh no you don't, you ??-?-@@!!. You have been trying to kill me for three weeks now, and so you can take it up yourself and bust your own ass.' "

So Jim took off again. "I was shaking so bad the plane was vibrating like Pop's '34 on the road to Wha-cha-know Joe's. I was afraid the engine would fall out, so I cut the motor and came in. . . . One of the wings was dragging in the dirt. The plane went 'round and 'round and finally stopped, but not before I banged my thumb up against the instrument panel. When I got out I expected St. Peter to greet me at the Pearly Gates, but it was only the mechanics with a hose to clean the *shit* out of the cockpit."

He was writing to Tom in the voice of a Southern schoolboy raconteur, trying not to care. But it may be, too, that he was *not* caring so much by then. Why did he wash out? "Attitude," he said one morning in South Carolina when I asked him point-blank. "This officer business, it was not for me. I didn't want to command anybody. I, first of all, didn't want to be commanded. The standards were just not right for me. I didn't like it."

And what was important to Jim Dickey by then, before he ever saw combat, was that he was writing.

Maybe it was when he was back at Darlington composing patriotic essays, or maybe it was long before, while he was lying on that swinging bed in Atlanta, that Jim Dickey got it in his head that writing was what he really wanted to do, and a writer was what he wanted to be.

He was about fourteen before he read his first serious novel, which was Somerset Maugham's *Of Human Bondage*, as he recalled. His sister, Maibelle, who was in her twenties by then, had checked it out of the Yellow Lantern Lending Library but couldn't get through it. So he found it lying around the house. "And I was outraged, because, in all the books I had read, the hero was so virtuous. Here was this novel about this crippled guy who had all these evil, lustful fantasies. I thought, 'Jesus, this guy is too much like me. They shouldn't allow this stuff to be printed.' " But the idea grew on him fast.

After he'd been in the army for a few months, Air Cadet Jim Dickey started telling his parents—gently at first—that he wanted to be a writer. The Army Air Corps had sent him and 199 others to High Point College to take college courses in physics and other useful disciplines. There was also an English class. And suddenly, after weeks of fawning letters home to "sweetheart Mom" and no-nonsense Pop, Jim Dickey sent this one back from High Point, full of unrelated accomplishments awkwardly linked in his head as he edges up to the real subject: "I know I'll be commissioned as a pilot. For something wonderful has happened. I know I am good for something. First, I can run. The coach here clocked me in ten flat yesterday. . . . But that is secondary. I can write. Always before I have had some doubt as to my ability, but not any more. The English teacher here says my themes are the best he's ever read."

In a separate envelope he sent a "rough draft" of an essay he'd written about jazz cornetist Bix Beiderbecke. "It is not at all the type of thing I intend to do in the future," he says. But "the stuff's there, and it's mellow." Written in pencil on yellow, lined notebook paper, it was called "The Rebel Soul—1931":

"Most of us are cut from the same pattern," it begins, "and, with minor variation, have practically the same interests and aims in life. But there are some, yes, many, who by the very nature of their own being, and by their particular talents, are destined to be singled out from the many and live brilliant but somehow strangely distorted and out-of-focus lives." He cites as examples Alexander the Great, Napoleon, Beethoven, Byron, and Shelley. "It is the spark, the spark of greatness that pulls them from obscurity to the heights. . . . After they have gone, everything is not quite the same. Things have been altered. Sometimes big things, sometimes small things but everything is not as it was." He gives a rundown of Beiderbecke's career: leaving school at nineteen to play "the hottest, purest kind of jazz" only to die, a cirrhotic and largely unrecognized wreck, at the age of twenty-eight. "His music never satisfied him. He was always striving, seeking new notes, combinations of notes, chord sequences, many of which were not possible to render upon his instrument," wrote young Jim Dickey, sitting there in High Point College, waiting for war. "He was a drunkard. He whored. He led the dissipated and irregular life that jazz musicians have always led. He lived ingloriously, and died as a result of his own weakness and folly." But "the music was in him, and he had to get it out. Get it out or perish."

THE COLOR OF RUST

Boca Raton, Florida. Mouth of the rat. A strip, a few hangars, AT-9 and AT-11 trainers. The barracks were in a scattered pine grove, with duckboards between them over the hot grayish sand. And one cinderblock building; that's where the secrets were. Or the secret. The trainees were searched and marched in, glancing at the barbed wire rolling over the blocks. They went into bare classrooms and were handed notebooks and pencils. No one had any idea what was coming, what they were doing there."

I sat up in the bed at Litchfield Plantation's little inn, trying not to wake my wife. Damn, I thought as I read that scene from the first chapter of *Crux*, my father's novel about the air war in the Pacific. Damn. That's what *his* war was really about. Harbelis is nothing but Intercept Officer Jim Dickey. Harbelis had washed out of pilot training because his captain had decided he "could not fly well enough for the time he had logged, and he had joined the eliminees. It did not bother him." In *Crux*, Harbelis contents himself with the idea that he is part of a secret, mystical society, and nothing else matters. In life, my father believed he'd thrown in his lot with poets, so nothing else had to matter.

Harbelis goes to gunnery school, and finds he's pretty good at blowing targets out of the air. Then he's picked for a top-secret program. Radar had saved Britain and helped change the course of the air war in Europe. Now it was going to be used to take the fight to the Japanese—at night, over the infinite black waters of the Pacific. Harbelis/Jim had washed out of pilot school and into one of the most elite programs in the service. And now he was training in Boca Raton: "In cinderblock cubicles, on which a light sweat stood and in places ran, Harbelis and the others were hooded, and in as much dark as could be made, faced into a screen where, in perverse, unreliable, grass-like electricity, danced the secret, the green-ghostly wings that could not be believed, but must be; they were the enemy's."

There had been another novel about the war, *Alnilam*, which came out in 1987 and centered on the training in North Carolina. This was supposed to be the sequel. But it was so much cleaner, more direct. Sharper. There were notes all over the page of manuscript in front of me and I had to read slowly, fitting in the changed phrases, jumping over the deleted words. But when I did I was there in front of the radar screen with Harbelis, and with my father, "far from earth in an invisible field that only he controlled, master, in total darkness, of the ultimate hunt."

I read on to the last page of the notes, wishing, praying there were more. But there were not. Only twenty-nine pages. And then, leafing back through them, I wondered where the sextants were.

For decades James Dickey had been collecting those, too. He had them in his office, the den, the living room, and the bedroom of his house in Columbia, and maybe a dozen of them lined up on the dining-room table at Litchfield. There were also thick volumes of navigation tables and a satellite-synched global positioning system to check the calculations against. "Tell me something," my grown son once wondered as he beheld the sextant-cluttered table, "are we lost?"

James Dickey had hoped his navigational trove would show him a way through to this book he had talked about a lot, and worked on very little, over the course of fifty years. It was named after Crux Australis, the Southern Cross, the most easily identified constellation in the Southern Hemisphere. One of his functions in the plane had been to navigate, and he wanted to make of the constellations, or maybe the zodiac, some sort of mystical connection. But all the sextants, and even the correspondence course he took in navigation, didn't bring him out of the alcoholic fog in which he lived, or any closer to those months in combat when he had felt the power of the radar and the guns, and felt death close at hand, for the first time in his life.

Jim had spent the last six months of 1944 training at Hammer Field, outside Fresno, California, and those had been good times. On the way out there, aboard the Streamliner *City of San Francisco*, he'd met a tall, beautiful girl named Gwen Leege who was studying at Bryn Mawr.

"In the middle of the night I heard a tremendous commotion," Gwen told me fifty years later. "There was a whole squadron of army fliers who came on this train. I walked down the steps and halfway I crashed into your father. An absolute Apollo vision. Absolutely fabulous! And he said, 'You have a face like a rose.' Do you know, the whole night long we talked together."

Jim was as taken as she was. He'd dated girls like Peg Rooney in Atlanta, whose father was a college professor, and he'd impressed some of the younger ones with the poems he'd read and learned. But here was this girl who could match him quote for quote, and throw in references to Goethe, Schiller, Kant. He hadn't met anyone quite like her before.

"I suppose you will be surprised to hear me say something good about the army for a change," Jim wrote to his parents in June, "but I am leading the best life I ever have (away from home at least)." He'd go to a few classes during the day, fly at night, and take his leaves in San Francisco with Gwen and her family. "They have a tremendous country estate, a swimming pool, and everything that I have always thought of very rich people having." Gwen's mother was "a very nice German lady, and you'd love her, if only for that." Then he said flat out, "Gwen and I are in love, Mom." The euphoria faded as she got ready to go back to school in the fall, but this rich, educated girl with her European background had made the idea of writing seem that much more important, that much more imperative.

"I have been reading enormously lately," Jim wrote home to both his folks in August. His favorite was Thomas Wolfe, but his room was filled with "a gigantic array of ponderous books." He'd been asking his mother to buy him Hemingway, Dreiser, Conrad Aiken. "I am convinced that the only thing I will ever have any interest in as a career is authorship, or something akin to it," he told her.

When Gwen went back east, Jim found another girl, Jane, "who thinks she can get a few of my better pastoral lyrics published," and he'd already been paid the generous sum of $3 for a poem in an obscure publication that he didn't name and couldn't find. ("Mom, you better not let Pop read this, in all seriousness. He would think I am out of my mind, or something.") Jim called the poem "Rain in Darkness," and said it came from thoughts of lying on the screen porch in Atlanta during a downpour, and probably was influenced by Robert Bridges's "London Snow." He asked her not to show it to anybody, and said he was "frankly ashamed of such an amateurish effort." But he copied it out by hand and sent it anyway. ". . . Pouring always / From dim heaven. Ó rain / Take not your love from us, we who need you."

. . .

At Hammer Field, Jim teamed up with a pilot named Earl E. Bradley, and, along with a buddy named Donald Armstrong and the rest of the replacement crews who were trained at Fresno, they shipped out for the Pacific on an unescorted transport called the *General A. E. Anderson* over Christmas 1944. It took them three weeks to get to New Guinea.

If Fresno had seemed like paradise, this was a long, slow trip to the inferno. The farther south they traveled, skirting Guadalcanal and the Solomons, the more intense the heat. There was almost no escape from the dense interior of the ship, and no respite. "I was the equivalent of a warrant officer, which was called a flight officer," Jim remembered. "Anybody below first lieutenant, we all ate standing up at big tables." He read in his bunk, and whenever he could, he'd go up on deck. He was fascinated by the flying fish: "They flattened into their pattern, the sun catching everywhere on it, one spark to a fish. . . . It could be a contest of some kind: not to get somewhere first but to go farthest, stay, hold out for most time in the air? Was the same one always in front? Yes, it must be, it must be that way, Harbelis thought."

For a couple of days in New Guinea, the crews from Hammer Field were shuttled around between transit camps. Then they were called by a night-fighter squadron, the 418th, way up in a forward area of the Philippines. The Allies had just taken the island of Leyte, and Jim and his buddies were flown up to Tacloban, one of the main airstrips there.

"You never saw such carnage in your life," he remembered. "I thought, 'Man, we have been talking war for years. I have been training for it. But this is the first time I have ever seen it.' I sure didn't know in my wildest dreams it would be like this. Wreckage all over the place was the first thing you saw. American planes that had ditched in the water or crashed on the beach. Japanese aircraft. Landing ships that had had direct hits on them blown in half. There wasn't any dead people around. I guess they had been gotten off in the last few days. But there was blood all over everything. Or rust." He thought about the word as he told me this, and for a second I wondered if he was short of breath. "Rust," he repeated. "Rust."

Among the papers Jim's mother saved, there was a two-page composition called "Tacloban" he sent her in 1946, after he'd made it back to the States:

> . . . Armstrong and I climbed out of the transport and walked along the narrow beach paralleling the taxiway. Wrecked airplanes, most of them American, were every-

where. We examined a crumpled P-38 resting on the edge
of the sand. The instruments had been removed and rust
covered the battered instrument panel and seat. At least
Armstrong said it was rust. I knew better, and I think he did,
too. . . .

For a long time Armstrong and I sat in the open doorway [of the transport]. . . . He sat on an old barracks bag,
his feet propped on the door, motionless, elbows on his
knees, his long thin hand holding a cigarette. I had seen him
like that, almost, many times, all the way through flying
school and at bars in the States trying to pick up girls and
be gay with them after his wife had left him, but this time
there was a difference. He looked out toward the ships and
I watched him, thinking that he was the best friend I had,
and while we were sitting there it started to rain, softly at
first and then more fiercely until we could not see the ocean
any longer. But we sat quietly and did not speak.

I do not know that my father ever learned for certain the difference between blood and rust. I do not know that he saw many, if any,
bodies in that war. Flying long distances at night, he was left to
imagine how people he knew, and people he killed, went about their
dying. One of his best poems, "The Firebombing," is, precisely, about
that remembered guilt for the distance in space and time that separates
the narrator from the slaughter: "Twenty years in the suburbs have not
shown me / Which ones were hit and which not." Two other poems of
the war are about the death of Donald Armstrong.

Practically from the moment the replacement crews arrived in Mindoro, where the 418th was based, they went into action. Jim Dickey
was climbing down out of the back of a truck when a pilot who had
been in combat for the better part of a year asked if someone wanted
to fly with him north of Manila that night to cover MacArthur's landing at Lingayen.

"I told him I would fly with him. He asked me what my name
was. I said, 'My name is Dickey.' He says, 'It says on the manifest:
James. We call you Jim?' I said, 'No, Gene. My name is Gene.'"

When my father told me this story, I didn't know what game he'd
been playing then with the veteran pilot, or was playing now, with
me. "Why did you say that?" I asked. Did he mean Gene his father, or
Gene the brother whose death he never saw and always felt?

"My father."

"But why?"

"I don't know. I said, 'Be with me, Father. This is the first one.' I don't know why I did that," my father said.

Bradley and Dickey were assigned their own plane, and Bradley, a big, square-jawed family man, wanted to name it after his wife. Dickey wanted to name it after a line from a poem by one of his poetic favorites, the raucous Roy Campbell: "The Flaming Terrapin." But for one reason and another, the Terrapin wasn't seeing too much combat. So Dickey went up with other pilots, including Don Armstrong. Don was daring, skilled, funny, and half the time didn't seem to give a shit. He took a lot of chances, and some of the older crews were leery of him. "He was a sort of cowboy pilot. Wouldn't do anything by the rules." And maybe that was what Jim Dickey liked about him. But it was what got Armstrong and his usual intercept officer, Jim Lally, killed.

Most of the missions from Mindoro went up north, but there were also a few to the south, over Panay, an island where the Japanese were supposedly using forced labor to build a new airstrip. Armstrong and Lally took a P-61 down there on a strafing run. For a fighter, the P-61 was huge, and carried a lot of firepower to direct not only at other planes but at the ground. It could carry teardrop-shaped canisters full of napalm under its wings, and it always had "six 20 mm package guns, each of them firing the same rate as a .50 caliber machine gun, with explosive heads" for strafing. Armstrong must have come roaring in toward the field about sunset, just as the light was fading, dropping low to get a better angle, the best accuracy. Too low. The plane hit the trees and started to break up. Armstrong couldn't do anything but bring it down all the way in a crash landing.

Armstrong died of his injuries in the crash, and Lally was captured by the Japanese. Soon afterward he was beheaded.

More than ten years later, my father was still trying to find a way to write about those deaths. In his first notes on a poem called "Between Two Prisoners," he imagined Lally keeping vigil beside his friend's body, waiting for his own death. Then, in "The Performance," one of his best-known poems, he imagined that Armstrong had survived the crash, and more. He dreamed that before he was to be beheaded Armstrong had managed to surprise and dazzle his executioners, breaking away from them to turn somersaults and handsprings, as he had done when he was clowning around the base, and finally astounding his Japanese captors with the perfect handstand that he'd been trying awkwardly to master for a long time. Then, in the poem,

Armstrong knelt down with dignity beside "his hacked, glittering grave, having done / All things in this life that he could."

Armstrong should have—they *all* should have—died so well, my father thought. And now they had.

By July 1945, Jim Dickey's squadron was on Okinawa, flying missions over China and mainland Japan, dropping three-hundred-gallon tanks of napalm and gasoline that lit up towns and rice paddies with "all American fire." "Reflections of houses catch; / Fire shuttles from pond to pond, / In every direction, till hundreds flash with one death." Yet, "when those on earth / Die, there is not even sound; / One is cool and enthralled in the cockpit, / Turned blue by the power of beauty, / In a pale treasure-hole of soft light / Deep in aesthetic contemplation."

Then, on August 6, the United States bombed Hiroshima.

"That was a long, long war. None of us thought we were going to come out. Especially those in the forward area," my father remembered. "There was so much celebration—the Third Fleet was out in the harbor in Buckner Bay firing off ammunition and a lot of it was falling back onto the island and killing people, Americans. So we went and stayed in the foxholes with the helmets on for three, four days after the war was over. But it was a great time. We just went around looking at each other like people that had been reprieved from some terrible catastrophe."

Joined with that moment of victory, at least in the telling, were a few lines of poetry Jim Dickey happened across in an anthology as he looked out on Buckner Bay and across the long rows of newly marked war graves that stretched before him. "Thou art divine, thou livest,—as of old / Apollo springing naked to the light, / And all his island shivered into flowers."

Reading those lines just at that moment turned my father irrevocably to poetry. Or so he said later.* The process was longer, more gradual than that, certainly. But he wrote in one of his journals from the 1950s about "the chair above the bay at Okinawa . . . where I had my first look as a poet at the world." And I believe that. Poetry and survival, for my father, were all part of the same thing. That is the essential link that was made as Okinawa shivered into flowers.

When we were talking at Litchfield, I didn't press my father for the

---

* He would make a personal cult of the work of Trumbull Stickney, the obscure American poet of the turn of the century who died young and wrote little of note apart from those lines.

truth about every wartime tale he'd told me when I was growing up. What combat veteran doesn't exaggerate, especially to his son? And what veteran doesn't deserve to?

Was he ever shot down near Borneo? Did he bail out into the Pacific, only to be rescued by a submarine? Was there another time when he was flying in from a long mission and a Japanese fighter appeared on his tail just after sunrise? Did they really outrun the Jap using "water injection" to boost the P-61's power and get safely back to base? Were these scenes from his life, or from a movie he was imagining for himself and his son? Did he have a little monkey as a pet, and if it wanted to wake you from a nap would it pull on your eyelashes with its delicate little inhuman fingers?

My father told, and retold, these stories to me when I was a child, and he told them to many other people when I was an adult. But he never mentioned them in the letters he sent home from the war. The adventures recorded there are a search in the night for a lost B-24; a dangerous return to base when the landing gear wouldn't go down; a crash landing in a C-47 on the way back from leave in Manila.

He did fly thirty-eight combat sorties over thousands of miles of enemy territory and empty, hostile seas. He strafed, he bombed, he acted as bomber escort and provided cover for landing forces and convoy attacks. He was commissioned a lieutenant overseas, and got five bronze stars for offensives in the Philippines, China, Borneo, and Japan. His discharge papers, which he used to carry as a miniature photostat in his wallet, are clear enough about all that. He knew the truth. And if he was a hero to me as a child for what he made up, he was a hero to me now for what he had actually done. We both knew more about dying now. We would let all that lie.

But there was one story I did want to ask him about. He had told it to me in strictest confidence when I was about eight. I can still remember where we were, under the portico at the West Wesley house on a sunny afternoon just before a big Dickey family dinner.

"You know, I was married before I was married to your mother," my father told me. I was embarrassed. It seemed such a strange thing to say. She had been an Australian he'd met in Sydney while he was on leave during the war, he said, and they'd decided to get married. But she had died soon after that. She'd cut herself, and gotten blood poisoning, and was gone.

I never forgot, and I remember asking after he went to Australia in 1968 if he had gone to see her family. "Yeah," he said. "Yeah." But he hadn't really wanted to talk about it. That was our secret.

And so, now that we were telling each other so much, or trying to, I wanted to know more about her. Her name. What she looked like. Anything. "I have to know," I said.

"I made it up," said my father.

"But—" I couldn't think what to say. "Why?"

"Just to do it."

"Yeah?"

"Just to do it. I felt it helped me as a writer—"

"Yeah?"

"—to imagine the situation."

"Yeah."

"I have never done anything in anything I have ever written. I have made it all up."

But this, too, was a lie. "Did you write a poem about her?" I asked when I was able to collect my thoughts a little.

"No, never did."

"You were just making that up for you—and for us."

"Yeah."

My wife was listening to this conversation. "Did Maxine know it was a story?" she asked.

"I never said anything about it to her, I don't think. No."

ALL SAINTS

My mother, Maxine Syerson, was a town girl in Nashville, Tennessee, when my father was at Vanderbilt University after the war. She worked as a reservations clerk for American Airlines. She was pretty, hardheaded, self-sufficient, and lonely.

Her mother, Maxine Webster, was one of those women who grew up in the 1920s and remained flappers for the rest of their lives. Maxine Webster came from the little town of Union City, Tennessee, and she was courted, so family legend has it, by an heir to the Jack Daniel's whisky fortune. But she decided to leave him one summer to go on a trip out west with some girlfriends. At a big campground in Yellowstone Park, after offering up a campfire rendition of "Pistol Packin' Momma Don't You Two-Time Me," she was approached by a middle-aged Danish immigrant named Val Syerson, who married her, then two-timed her, and left her a few weeks after my mother was born.

Abandoned and bitter, my mother's mother went to work in Nashville, where she was a secretary for various officials in the state government, including, by the time I knew her, the attorney general. She lived in a grim little efficiency apartment in a women's hotel, leaving my mother to be cared for by sisters who lived in a big house in soot-stained Birmingham. My mother went to Catholic schools, got married as soon as she got out, and divorced soon after that. Then she moved to Nashville, got her job as a ticket clerk with American Airlines, and met my father.

Jim Dickey had been lost at the end of the war. "They dropped the A-bomb and everything stopped just like that. I was really terrified, because I didn't know anything but flying and navigating—tracking aircraft." Back home in Atlanta in early 1946, it was no longer enough to imagine a life as a writer. His mother and his girlfriends might have encouraged him, might even have regarded him as some sort of local genius, but they wondered, too, when he was going to settle down. Jim's letters from those days are full of talk about marriage; mainly Jim explaining, none too patiently, why it didn't interest him. He had escaped death in the war, but now he felt sucked into the torpor of Atlanta society.

He went to Vanderbilt on the GI Bill in the fall of 1946, and as always he was pushing himself hard. "I just started as a first-term freshman at the age of twenty-three and went on through there all year round, and went some more at night to try to finish. Because I knew that if I would ever pull out of college again I would never go back." To keep himself fit, he ran the high hurdles. He wasn't as fast as his brother, and that bothered him. But in track, too, he was ferociously disciplined.

There was time for women, if they had time for him, and many did. Jim Dickey was handsome, a veteran, and just reckless enough to be really seductive. But his unrelenting focus on himself must have been hard for many of them to take. They plunged into life with him, then eased back out. Or escaped.

He'd started to see Gwen Leege, his Bryn Mawr girlfriend, again after the war. She had taken him to New York and introduced him to Frances Steloff at the Gotham Book Mart. He'd saved $3,000 of his GI pay to buy poetry, novels, anything and everything he'd thought about reading when he was in the Pacific. Here at the Gotham, where any afternoon the greatest writers in America might be found browsing the shelves, and where anything ever written could be ordered, my father was in heaven. Gwen might have been "a rich man's woman," as he liked to say in later years. But she'd given him this. She'd understood what he wanted to do, and wanted to be. And when she left him to take a teaching job with the Allied occupation forces in Germany, he came to the boat in a rage. "You are going to the enemy!" he screamed from the dock.

At Vanderbilt, Jim was dating his math teacher. She was only a little older than he was, but she decided to break up with him, she said, because dating a student might put her job at risk. "She was very regretful about it," he recalled. And she offered to hook him up with one or another of her girlfriends. As my father remembered the choice, one was supposed to be "very, very nice-looking, presentable, and a lot of fun and good company"; the other "has got a smashing figure

and is extremely pretty, too." My father remembered saying, "I'd like
to meet both of them, but let me meet the one with the figure." He
paused. "And that was your mother."

Dad's face gentled out. The lines of concentration and pain eased
as he slipped into the rhythm of this story he loved to tell.

"She lived downtown, in a little sort of residential hotel. And I
went down there and called up to the room. And she came down in
her American Airlines uniform. And I looked at her and I thought,
'What have I lucked into? Where has she been hiding?' And we went
out and gradually we fell in together."

My mother was, indeed, beautiful. There was something of the
young Elizabeth Taylor in her face, but with more innocence. She had
never been to college, never read poetry or serious fiction, never
seriously imagined a life outside the circles of Tennessee politicians
and small-town gentry in which her mother lived and worked. Jim
Dickey was like no one she had ever met before. All she knew how to
do for him was to make love to him, to make a home for him, to bear
his children, to be his wife. And at first that had seemed enough.

"You came before me, poem about to be spoken," he wrote to her
in the summer of 1948. "Half-revealed, the foam at your ankles, / The
drift of the sea-burst about you, / Behind you the sun and ceaseless
waver of water / And my knowledge of the darkness."

They were married in November, as he liked to tell the story,
over a feed store in Ringgold, Georgia, by an assistant justice of the
peace with papers that my father liked to suggest were somehow
dubious. "To this day," he would often say when telling this tale, "I'm
not sure Maxine and I are *legally* married." But the GI Bill bureaucracy
accepted the wedding as it was, and so did my mother. Her mother
sent out engraved announcements. His mother gave her the diamond
solitaire ring that had been in the family for years. They went to
Quebec for their honeymoon.

"We didn't have any money. We lived mainly on her salary from
American Airlines," my father remembered. He was on a roll now,
bringing her back to him. "She was a genius in finding places to live
and economizing. I never saw any talent like that in my life, in any
subject. She found us a place that was a renovated attic in the home
of a guy who was a minor state official—who really wanted to be an
inventor. He"—Dad laughed slyly—"he invented a glass awning. He
was trying to get it patented. Sort of like having a—a cut-glass fly
swatter." He laughed until he started to cough, then settled himself
down, and chuckled. "They were very eccentric, George and Jean."

When my father went to work on his master's degree, he and my mother moved into an apartment owned by a man who, as he recalled, had lost a leg working on the railroad. This place was bigger, but more expensive. And my mother had to work that much harder to support them. "A lot of the times, we would just meet on the stairs. She'd be going out to work and I'd be coming in from school. Or I would be going out to school and she'd be coming in. But every two weeks we had four days, and we would spend all of those together, as much as we could."

During the summer of 1950, after he'd gotten his master's and before he took up his first teaching job, my father and mother had nowhere to live, and not much money to live on. The GI Bill had quit paying his way. So they decided to accept an invitation from Val Syerson, my mother's long-estranged father, to come stay in an apartment he had in Clearwater, Florida, above his little insurance office. He "was trying, I suppose, to make up for something," my father said. But it was Florida's Gulf Coast in July, and no air conditioning. "It was like fire, boy. It was mighty hot. And we just stayed there to sleep at night. Mainly we stayed out on the beach. And I earned a little money as a lifeguard."

At the end of the summer of '50, they headed for Houston, Texas, and Rice College, where he'd gotten a post as an instructor. He loved the idea of teaching. "I had my own ideas of how I was going to go about things," Dad recalled as we thought back over five decades. "But it was such a short time before I was recalled, I didn't really get into it like I wanted to." The Korean War intervened. "And one thing after another happened. It is a long, long story. Long story."

"A long life, Dad."

"Yeah. I noticed that Yeats was seventy-four when he died. And without exception the commentators say he was also exceptionally lucky in having had a long life. Yeah. Older than me."

We were packing up to leave Litchfield. We had finished the last descent of the stairs. I had brought the oxygen machine back down. My father's secretary was loading up her car, and Bronnie, my sister, was all excited. She'd just gotten her driver's license, and the secretary was going to let her drive part of the way back to Columbia. My wife, Carol, looked around the Litchfield house to see if there was anything that could be done to leave it a little tidier. She had scoured the kitchen and tried to sanitize the bathrooms. But she hadn't been able to face the wasp holocaust or the mummified chameleons. They were left where they were.

I gathered up the oxygen bottles that gave my father his traveling supply of air, then waited for him to steel himself for the walk to the car. It was not far, but the way was slippery, and because of that it was suddenly frightening. "He has done this for me," I thought. I had hoped he would get better here, near the sea, near some different and better memories. I'd thought that a little bit of exercise might help. The doctors were constantly encouraging him to get physical therapy, to try to build up what was left of a lung capacity that was shrinking a little more every month. But he had made this trip, essentially, for me. And maybe—no, certainly—to see my mother's grave.

"So I had my first teaching job at Rice," my father said. He wanted to go on with the story. "And I taught for several months, just till Christmas. And then I was recalled. Right back to the air force and a training command."

Jim and Maxine wound up living near the base in Waco. By the middle of June 1951, my mother was seven months pregnant. "It was so hot there in central Texas in the summer that I remember Maxine leaving the refrigerator door open to try to get some cool to come into the house." My father shook his head very slowly. "We had real rough times. But she stuck in there. She was good. She could adapt to anything."

The little cemetery at All Saints Waccamaw Church is only about half a mile from the entrance to Litchfield Plantation. There's a large headstone there on my mother's grave, visible from the road, under a live oak dripping with Spanish moss. "The church wrote me and asked me if I wanted to sell our other plots," my father said as I pulled to a stop. "I told them, No, I want to use them."

Carol and I got out to put some flowers on the grave. Dad stayed in the car, where he could see it well enough. When we had come here the year before, we had stood there in front of the headstone, and he had half leaned, half lunged, telling her "I'm coming, Maxine. I'm coming." But there weren't going to be any scenes like that today.

At the top of the stone was a little carved owl. She had collected owls. The inscription read, "In loving memory of Maxine Syerson Dickey. 1926–1976. Wife of James Dickey. Mother of Christopher and Kevin." And then, below it, two lines from Henry Constable: "I do love thee as each flower / Loves the sun's life-giving power."

Carol and I closed the little cemetery gate and got back into the car, and as we pulled away my father started to reminisce about my mother's funeral. How there'd been this tall, beautiful girl there standing at the back and he'd gone up to her and said, "Aren't you in one of my classes?" And she'd said she was. And did she know Maxine?

"No, not really," he remembered her saying, but she had just thought that she would come to the funeral for no special reason. There was a tear coming out of her left eye, he remembered.

"And you know who that was," my father said as we drove on toward Route 17.

"Yeah, I know."

He meant the woman he'd married just two months after the funeral. The woman who was calling him "God" at the time. "I love you, God, mucho," she used to say. He was lying, of course, about how well he had known her, and he knew I knew it. He looked over at me with one of those mean, feral looks he sometimes got when he was waiting for a fight. But it hardly seemed worth the trouble now.

SONS

Homeowners unite.

—"The Firebombing"

THE TWO-CAR
GARAGE

University librarians, knowing that my father was sick, had begun sniffing around to see if they could get him to give away his books and papers. "Look at that garage," said one of a team lobbying Dad from the University of South Carolina, "God only knows what's in there. We could come over some weekend and clean it out for you."

Carol had heard that and, when dinner was over, said with the authoritative clarity I love her for, "We should clean the garage ourselves."

It was a bigger job than we ever imagined. It was hot that July weekend in Columbia, humid. The work was sweaty, sordid, horrifying, fascinating. A whole lifetime had been piled into the two-car garage of that low-eaved ranch house by the man-made lake, and forgotten. Mostly it was my father's life with my mother that was shunted away there. But the mess—the mutual, corrosive destruction —of his second marriage, to Deborah Dodson, was in there, too, all intermingled indiscriminately with the mildewed suitcases, the broken 78-rpm records, the rusting exercise equipment. There were hidden bourbon bottles and discarded medications. Manuscripts for poems from forty years ago were stained by melted suppositories. Photographs of the family, of poets, parts of the literary life and history of my father, were mixed in with small dunes of roach shit and the jumbled detritus of craft projects—rehabilitation projects—from quilting to Christmas ornaments, never undertaken. There were multiple copies of Debbie's *The Big Book*, the one you get each time you start the Alcoholics Anonymous program. There were all the AA diaries, which lasted no more than a couple of pages each. There were so many lists of things to do.

My father sat inside the house, in the cool, reading and talking on the phone. Every so often I would bring in something I thought would be of special interest to him. There was a letter opener from Toledo, Spain, that his crazy cousin, Eugenia, had given him in 1955, and that he'd kept on his desk at home when we lived in Atlanta. There was an old copy of the *Atlanta Journal Magazine* from July 1947 with a profile of his brother, Tom, who had managed to stay out of the war, and was looking to get into the 1948 Olympics running the four-hundred-meter dash.

I was dripping, streaked with dust and cobwebs, flecked with the wings of roaches.

"It's hot out there," said my father.

"God, yeah. But it's good in here," I said. "Are you okay?" I no longer heard the sighing of the oxygen machine. I would only hear it now if it stopped.

"I'm fine, son."

I was looking for something to say. I was angry, in fact, about all that I had been seeing, and remembering, and reliving in the garage. And I didn't want to be angry any more. "Remember—when the only air conditioning in the South was in the movie theaters? You'd go to see anything—*anything*—just to cool off."

"Amen," said my father.

Movies were something we talked about a lot, a way for both of us to remember feelings, I guess, without having to search for details. Long before I was born, and still when I was little, my father did a lot of thinking and dreaming in movie theaters.

Once, he remembered, when he and my mother were first married and staying in her father's stifling little guest apartment in Clearwater, he had gone alone over to St. Petersburg, "which is the hottest goddamn place on this earth." There was a little art theater there. He paid and went in and sat down. "Boy, it was blessedly cool." As far as he could see, there was nobody else in the theater at all. "It was a German movie about the life of Mozart," he remembered. I could see he was there again in his head. "And there came on a scene of a sort of a party, a big outdoor eighteenth-century party like something from Fragonard, or Watteau. And it's the first time Mozart is letting people hear his new opera. He and Constanza, they begin to sing." And my father, remembering, half sang, half breathed the aria from *Don Giovanni*. "And there was nobody in the theater, but behind me I heard somebody singing along with it. You know?" As if some invisible spirit had penetrated the cool of the theater. "I thought, 'This is ghostly.'"

"When I left the theater there *was* just one other guy, who had come in. He was just a big, fat, nondescript guy. Could have been a baker, or some merchant or something. But he knew that opera. And I thought, 'Thus is the power of art,' that this could happen. You know? Oh, that was such a nice experience." My old, sick, almost breathless father actually began again to whistle the air by Mozart. "It's so— effortless," he said.

That summer I was born, my father went to a lot of movies. He was in the training command, spending the Korean War in the United States shuffling from one base to another. As my birth approached, he was serving time in Alabama, then Mississippi, then Texas. My mother was with her mother again, back in Nashville. She read, trying to catch up with his mind somehow, and she carried me, and he waited for orders, and went to the movies with his buddy Joe Sokolewiscz, and wrote poetry, and tried, in his way, to imagine me into existence.

A few weeks before I was born, he wrote a poem called "The Son," full of mythic imagery about "the parricidal vision from the loin."

I can't imagine, really, what my mother thought of all this as she read it at the women's hotel in Nashville. My father believed, with equal measures of affection and condescension, that she didn't understand at all the books he'd given her. ("You had better read Rimbaud's 'Le Poete a Sept Ans' again if it makes you think the poet is 'dreamy.' ") So what was she to think of the mythic obscurity he was conjuring inside of her?

A few days later, from Biloxi, after an afternoon watching *A Place in the Sun*, starring Elizabeth Taylor and Montgomery Clift, my father wrote Polonius-like to my mother about what I should be taught, and what I should be:

> . . . I am thinking of you all the time, and of the child, and of our great and quiet joy and anticipation and of the fearful responsibility we have taken on, and of the even more fearful and great responsibility the child has to us, and to itself, in that it is a human being, half animal murderer, part saint, sometime Anti-christ, pardoner and the fruit and consummation of our love and the living knowledge of the guilt we all lie down in, that we may permit another to rise above us.
>
> I love you. I will write to you as soon as I get to Waco.
> Love, little Toodlum,
> Jim

My mother's letters to my father, as far as I know, did not survive. But we have another from my father, the one he'd promised from Waco, on August 28, 1951, three days before I was born. He's writing again about going to the movies. That paragraph ends three-quarters of the way down the yellow foolscap page, and without warning the next picks up in an inspired explosion of prose about the me that was imminent:

> . . . Child, child, where in what forest you lie alone tonight, hearing the horned voice of the hunter break through the green pools and the unharmed birds cry down the feathered wind, where your face is unseen, has never been seen, and where you smile against the furred stone, and the blade moors its fires over the raining font of birth . . . son, daughter, whose life and ruin I have wrought with not one thought of forgiveness, where the great gentleness of all who have ever been kind to me will find the soft lighted mouth of your mother, and the suns gleam and make, and the great tribes of the silken and cruel sand throw down their burdens and wander to the rich pastures laid on their unhooded skin, overture, Canaan and the great of earth, I shall come to you soon, fresh in your sacramental blood and the warmth of a great room, and watch your small lips curl and try in that inarticulate music Beethoven heard when he saw the storm break over this pure deafness, and we shall then meet, and what speech we shall have together is already in whatever richness you have been allowed to proceed, cautiously and cruelly, from, and has been in my heart from the time I was myself conceived, to lie wrecked and new and unsheltered save by love on what cast and lone shell of time the tremendous unceasing wind that blows us full of breath filled that night, and this night of all my love, and my litten and hallowed wife.
>
> Jim

I was kind of a morose little kid. "Half animal murderer, part saint, sometime Anti-christ . . ." I had no idea about all that, of course. It would be hard to say that the little boy in the family albums, in a floppy cowboy hat, with a cap-pistol six-shooter on his belt, was carrying the weight of genius—evil or benign, mine or others'—on his narrow shoulders. I was watching Roy and Dale and Hopalong Cassidy, and splashing in the wading pool and teetering on my bike with training wheels, and begging for a BB gun and pasting construction-paper Christmas trees on kindergarten greeting cards to my parents. But I spent a lot of time, too, just worrying.

I was afraid of time. From somewhere—from my father, no doubt —I got the notion, all the worse for being true, that time was irretrievable. He loved to tell me over dinner, usually after he'd had a couple of drinks and I was putting off my homework, how much Mozart had done at my age. Silly, painful stuff. But serious, too, when I was six or seven. I'd suddenly find myself upset by the idea that I would never be that age in that place with those people around me again. That this moment, and the next, and all moments would be lost. And, of course, that people would die. Like my mother. Like my father.

Any child, I suppose, has these flashes of mortality. But they came to me a lot, almost whenever I was bored, filling me with anguish that was sometimes pure melodrama, and sometimes unforgettably real. I remember a moment in one of those big old Atlanta movie theaters still decorated vaguely like a mosque from the days when Valentino movies showed there, with an orchestra pit up front. I was wandering quietly in the aisle during some part of a film that didn't interest me, and I just stood and stared into the pit, and thought about what it would be like when my parents, seated back there behind me in the theater, died. And I thought then that I could feel the hurt. But I was just a little boy.

SERPENTS

My father loved to tell me that the first movie he ever took me to see was a sword-and-sandal epic with Victor Mature called *The Egyptian*. "Daddy," he'd remember me asking, "which one was the Egychman?" And he thought this was cute, and funny—and he just liked the sound of the made-up word—for as long as he lived. Another first movie he took me to was *Gentlemen Prefer Blondes*, with Marilyn Monroe. When he asked me how I liked it, I said, "Pretty girls dancing." And he liked this trenchant observation, and remembered it always, and often repeated it to me. And maybe I did say those things. Why not? But there were so many times over the years when he remembered me saying and doing things that I never said and never did, that I have to wonder. The first film I actually do remember going to see was called *Them!*, a science-fiction thriller in which enormous nuclear mutant ants are hunted through some kind of sewer. What I remember is being terrified. What Dad remembered was that I peed in my pants.

I was only two. But many images from that time remain clear in my head. We moved around so much when I was growing up that I can associate memories with places, and from that know more or less what age I must have been. My earliest identifiable recollections are of the lawn where I played among the faculty apartment buildings at Rice, and of my father. Once there were a bunch of kids trying to make a clubhouse out of a wooden packing crate. They wanted to put a window in it, but couldn't punch through the wood. My father—I remember he was wearing track shorts and nothing else, not even shoes—came over to see what was happening, and with one swift kick opened up a window for us. Another time he was pushing me in a swing. It was a cloudy day, and when he pushed me up hard and high I, for some reason, let go. I flew out of the swing, tumbling up through the air, and when I hit the ground there was no wind left in me. My father was terrified, angry, amused, panicked, all at the same time. Or so it seemed. Or seems, in memory. My mother and he fought about me, over me, as she held me in her arms.

My third birthday was in a park in England, and I remember it, I suppose, partly because the little cake my mother bought had candle holders that looked like the guards at Buckingham Palace, and she kept those for years afterward, and every time I came across them in the kitchen drawer the memory came back to me.

It was on that same trip to Europe that I had a terrible fight with my mother, the way only three-year-olds can. "Jim, you deal with this," she'd said. And my father took me outside—we were on a terrace in the mountains—and he told me to go easy on my mother, that she loved me very much but didn't really understand me, because, I should understand this, I really was smarter than she was. At three. I remember this because it was something he told me again, in various ways at various times all the while I was growing up, and because secretly I was so proud to believe it when I was little, and, when I was grown, so ashamed that I'd been proud.

We had gone to Europe in 1954 on a Sewanee Fellowship arranged by Monroe Spears and the coterie of Southern writers, including Andrew Lytle, who often helped my father in those days.

Afterward, we would measure every event in our family's life as "before we went to Europe" and "after we went to Europe." As little as I was, I had this sense that our trip had changed everything. In the minds of my parents I believe it had.

Before Europe, Jim Dickey put in about two years teaching at Rice. He'd gone straight back there after his tour in the air force and picked up where he left off, but he soon grew weary of the academic world. ("It is part of the plan at a university that no one ever listens.") Teaching English from a rigid syllabus to bored freshmen seemed too high a price to pay when the pay he was receiving was so abysmally low. He was thirty years old and making $2,720 a year. And my mother, while trying to raise me, was also working as a receptionist at a hillbilly radio station. "I can remember calling up and hearing a sprightly voice," my father recalled, " 'KNUZ Radio Ranch. Can we help you?' "

In the summer of 1953, my parents separated for reasons they told themselves were mainly monetary. To save money, my mother took me up to Nashville for a couple of months to stay with her mother in her tiny efficiency there. And Jim went back to Atlanta, back to the swinging bed on the screen porch at 166 West Wesley, back to his mother and to a life of comfortable privilege. West Wesley was a place where he could be pampered, indulged, and done for as he always had been. Jim Dickey would talk all his life about the times when he was poor. He'd say the family had no money during the Depression. He'd talk about his meager salary as a teacher. But there was always a reserve of his mother's money to back him up, and when he started to earn more there were times—many times—when we lived extravagantly. If he worked hard for his salary and to save, it was to establish his independence—to support his decision to be a poet. But at the age of thirty, when his wages were still low, he'd find his way back to Atlanta to live easy in the family home, and leave Maxine to pay the price of his self-imposed poverty.

He sent my mother several letters a week, always reporting progress on the novel that he was supposed to be writing, and always saying he was saving. But his letters from that time aren't so much about work as they are about distractions. He jokes about lusting after Julia, the snaggle-toothed, ever-sweaty cook who lived next to the furnace. He's watching the Wednesday-night fights on television with Pop. He's reading Forster and Sartre ("the best description of vomiting I have ever come across") and starting new poems. His mother takes him to buy a new suit. He's playing tennis. He seems to be working hard on a tan, and spending a lot of time at the Venetia, a public pool and gym. He's really fit, he keeps telling my mother. And he is starting, as he would do all their married life, to see her as fat, and to tell her so. "How is the little duck-hunter?" he writes, asking after little Chris. "I sure do miss him, and his waddling mama. How is the great weight-losing project coming along. Lost *any* yet?"

It wasn't a great time for the marriage.

There was a smell of books in the Columbia house, and of disinfectant and of the unwashed but unsweated body and hair of my father. He did not want to stand in the shower, did not want to step into the tub. He was afraid of falling, although he wouldn't say that. And he did not want to be bathed by Mayrie, the woman who took care of him now as she had taken care of his baby daughter before him. It was not a disagreeable smell: must, age, paper, father. Sometimes, when we were talking, Jim would ask Mayrie for a disposable razor and shave himself without soap or water, so that his face was flame-red when he finished, and anyone who came to visit who didn't know what he'd done thought he was even worse off than he was. For most of his life he also shaved his chest to show off his build. But, of course, he didn't bother with that now.

His feet had begun to give him a lot of trouble, but there was nothing new about that. Jim Dickey had a fungus that gnarled his toenails. He had it all his adult life, and as a result they were a hideous mess: thickened, ingrown, callused in odd places. His macabre toes, especially the little ones, absolutely fascinated me when I was little, and every couple of years, even when I was a teenager, I'd ask him: "Really, Dad, how did your feet get like that?" And he'd always say his family was very poor during the Depression and his mother got him shoes that were too small for him, so his feet had been deformed. Grandmama was very upset when I asked her about this. It was pure Jim Dickey perversity. As my father got old and got sick, the ingrown nails and lack of circulation started to cause infections. Then Bronnie, my thirty-years-younger sister, would ask him the same question. He'd tell the same story.

Once I bought cream at the pharmacy and rubbed it into the dry, flaking skin of his little-used legs and his feet. He was embarrassed and even a little annoyed, I think, but I was glad to do it, hoping that I could keep him from getting new infections in his cracking skin, and also happy just to touch his skin, just to know he was there.

It's not easy to remember the first time you *remember* your father's touch, but it is possible with fathers as it is not with mothers, whose caresses one feels from before memory, from birth. My first memory of my father's touch was of his unshaven face one night in the residential hotel in Nashville. I guess he'd just arrived back from Atlanta on one of those summer nights in 1953, and I jumped up to hug him and discovered his face like an imagined porcupine, and his kiss so wet on my face that I wiped it off.

If we had not gone to Europe a year later, I'm not sure how long my mother and father would have stayed together. But the trip was, as it was meant to be, the beginning of a new life, one far from freshman English and residential hotels and the swinging bed in Atlanta. Europe then was a place for a writer—and a writer's wife—to invent themselves in their own minds. And that is what they did. "A whole world opened up," my father remembered. Here was a universe of creativity, of license, that he'd been thinking about at least since he'd read his first serious novel. It understood writers. It revered them, and excused them. In a notebook from the time, he wrote an enigmatic line that was very French-intellectual, but also very much him. "The poet is one who, because he cannot love, imagines what it would be like if he could."

We went from London to Paris, where a friend from Rice, Lester Mansfield, and his French mistress, Malou, introduced Dad to a little Left Bank bookstore, Le Pont Traversé, on Rue St. Séverin. It was owned by Marcel Béalu. "I still have a lot of books from Marcel," my father said one afternoon in Columbia. "He was awfully sweet. He was interested in any American poet. And everything in his life was devoted to poetry. There was a *whole bookstore* devoted to poetry. Boy, for me it was like throwing Brer Rabbit into the briar patch."

In late September 1954, we headed south to the Côte d'Azur, looking for a cheap villa where we could stay in the off season. There was nothing in St. Tropez, my parents' first choice, but down the coast, in Cap d'Antibes, they found a ramshackle house called Lou Galidou, just at the bottom of the stairs that lead up to the old lighthouse, and just up from the beach, the Plage de la Garoupe, where Gerald Murphy had entertained Scott Fitzgerald, and Hemingway, and Picasso. The yard was big and full of cactus and unkempt undergrowth, more a subtropical jungle than a lawn. *"Serpents?"* my father asked the woman who owned the place. *"Des serpents ici?" "Pas de serpents,"* she said.

"That was a great relief to me," he laughed, looking back. "NO snakes."

Ah, I thought, you were scared of that yard, too.

There was a game my father liked to play at Galidou, but only at night. He would pretend that a magical creature had left a little gold-web bag of chocolate wrapped like gold coins hidden in the bushes. "Let's go find it," he'd say, and take the old square French flashlight that looked like a miner's light and start down the dark, winding driveway with me to search the bushes. I get scared even today as I think about it, and I was just petrified then. "Now, you take the light," he'd say, and then fall back out of sight, so that, a moment later, when I was wondering where he was, he could jump out of the bushes and scare me into a screaming-laughing fit. After a while, the chocolate money didn't seem worth the price of being frightened so badly, and I just wouldn't play.

"Des serpents ici?" My father's ideas of nature, for all that he wrote about it, were mostly imagined from movies safely watched in air-conditioned theaters or on living-room televisions, whether a Disney documentary following a wolverine through the *White Wilderness*, or Cousteau's undersea adventures, or even the early Hollywood expedi-

tions to Africa, like the first Johnny Weissmuller *Tarzan* movie or, better yet, *Trader Horn*, shot on locations from Mombasa to the Congo in 1929. And that imagined experience of the wild became a part of the code that Dad was devising for us from before I could remember.

"How is that boy?" my father wrote to my mother in 1953. "I dreamed about him last night. It's really very funny: I dreamed I was taking him to see 'Trader Horn,' the great jungle picture [from] when I was a kid, and by God I look in the paper this morning and the picture is playing here in town."

When I was a little boy, I couldn't think that my father could be scared of anything, of course. But it wasn't until he was old and sick that he started to give me clues about the sources of his fears. And even then I had to wonder if they were real, or whether he made them up as clues to a deeper code. "The first time I ever saw death was at Pershing Point," the home of his grandmother, he said one morning in Carolina. "One of the maids was taking me for a walk, and I was just looking into the bushes, and I saw a praying mantis behead a butterfly."

My father loved zoos: places where nature was well controlled. He took his first chaperoned dates to the Atlanta zoo. When he was alone in New York he'd go to the Bronx Zoo. In Columbia, he donated money to buy a rare owl. But none of these places were more important to him, to us, than the Jardin des Plantes in Paris. We went many times, and for me as a three-year-old, there was nothing in the city that could be more exciting. We never went in the main gate, but walked down a small street, Rue Cuvier, along a blank wall full of cracks, to find an opening that was completely unexpected. "Don't tell anyone about this," Dad would say. "It's our secret entrance." And in we'd go.

The reptile house was his favorite part of the zoo, and he would peer through the glass, with me in his arms or sitting on the rail, watching for any sign of movements from the massively poisonous Gaboon viper, or looking into the eye of a green tree snake. I guess there was a little island of snakes with a moat around it in those days. Anyway, there is in the poem "Goodbye to Serpents," in which my father writes about a last trip to the Jardin des Plantes, with me in tow, to say goodbye to Europe.

I don't go back often to the zoo in Paris, but when I do I always find my way to the little-used entrance through the wall on Rue Cuvier, and always remember the touch of my father's hand holding mine. That island of serpents is no longer there, but the little Art Deco reptile house still is, and so little changed that I have to wonder if the Gaboon viper and the green tree snake might remember, somewhere in their deadly, passive brains, that child and his father from more than forty years ago. And it was only on one of my most recent visits to the Jardin des Plantes that I realized James Dickey never did talk about the other creatures kept in that building. Because there are not only snakes there, and lizards, there are insects. In window after window, there are enormous mantises.

The first few weeks we spent in Antibes were sunny and warm, and we went down to the water all the time. I was too little to swim, so my mother and I would get in a pedal-boat and follow my father, churning after him as he snorkeled out into the little bay. The water was so transparent that as he floated it seemed he was flying, slowly and effortlessly, above the blurred shapes of fish and rocks and the ripples of sand.

When the weather turned and the *mistral* began to blow, the villa on the hill below the lighthouse got very cold. I would shiver when my mother bathed me, and dried me and wrapped me up in the towel. At night, even with the chill, we slept under mosquito nets, because somehow these huge hovering insects had learned to survive the *mistral*. During the day, Dad would go down to the basement every few hours to shovel coal into the furnace, and take me sometimes to watch, or to throw pine cones into the flames. Sometimes we would go into a café called Le Glacier, or to visit the Cumberlidge family down the road, where there was a little boy named Christian. They had a big fireplace in a small living room, and just having that heat was an incentive to be sociable. We made outings along terrifying cliff roads to Èze, and up into the high mountains to a tiny resort at Valberg, where my father tried a little skiing. He didn't like it much, but kept the boots and used them to weight his feet when he was doing leg lifts.

Picasso and his mistress Françoise Gilot were still very much in evidence around Antibes in those days, and my father remembered seeing both of them several times. There was only one occasion when words were exchanged, and I remember it myself, vaguely, because I was at the center of it. We were in a museum, I'm not sure which one, and we saw a group of people there, and my father started to whisper to my mother, "Picasso!" As Dad would tell the story later, the artist was taken with me enough to make a quick sketch as we stood there, and my father reached out to receive it, thinking Picasso meant to make it a gift, a homage, as it were, to me. Or to my father's son. Picasso shook his head, and clutched it to him. So my father said.

I don't know. I remember the group of people as a group, and the older children with them, more clearly than the old man whom my father was so surprised and delighted to meet. Maybe there is a sketch of me somewhere. But the only pieces of art we ever owned that were more or less by Picasso were bits of pottery made at Vallauris. They must have cost us, by our standards then, a fortune.

Whenever my father talked about Antibes, he always told the same story about my mother.

"It was kind of funny," he'd remember. "I was trying to learn the language, to read the writers and to get conversant with the literary part of it. And she would go down and learn it on the practical side among the people in the markets. And we would come back at the end of the day and compare notes. I would say, 'How much French did you learn today?' She said, 'Well, not very much really, but down at the *marché* I learned something I think is going to be a lot of help to our family financial picture.' I said, 'What is this magical phrase?' She said, '*Trop cher.*' "

When Dad was away in Cannes watching movies, or down at the bookstore of Monsieur Aldon in the center of town, I'd play in the house or sit and watch my mother in the kitchen. She'd post me near the window that looked down on the street, so I could tell her when the man was coming to deliver ice. That was my little job. Then, when the iceman came, there was a whole ritual associated with bringing what seemed an enormous block up to the kitchen, and setting it into the tin compartment in the icebox. Perhaps because it seemed so un-American, so Old World, that ritual of the ice was one of the experiences we all remembered from that time. Ice, after all, came so easy in America.

Europe was difficult for my mother, and a difficult place to take care of her little boy. "Maxine was wonderful. She was so adaptable," my father would always say as he introduced the story about her learning the phrase "*trop cher.*" "It was just a glory to behold. She could go anywhere in any country, she would not know a word of the language, and by the afternoon she would have everything organized." And all that is true. But it is also the sum total of what my father ever remembered or said when he talked about *her* experience in Europe.

It must have been a tremendous vindication for Maxine Syerson to be there, though. Maybe more than it was for him. She had married this wild man from Atlanta who wanted to be, of all things, a poet. And here she was on the streets where Picasso walked, far from the grimy curtains of Birmingham or the claustrophobic rooms of the women's hotels in Nashville. And living on the edge of Maughamian decadence, where her mother's broken marriage, or her own teenage marriage-divorce to a small-town jeweler, didn't mean anything to anyone. And she did thrive. She was insecure, and she worried about all that my father did not worry about. But she came into her own as she never imagined—and as my father never imagined—she would. You can see it in the pictures. There is one extraordinary little one taken on board the SS *United States* as we set sail for New York. She is wearing a simple sweater, her hair is back in a scarf, and she has on dark glasses. She looks European. She is beautiful—more beautiful in that picture than in any other I have—and elegant and sophisticated. But I don't think my father ever allowed himself to see her, or her to be, that way for very long.

BRING HOME
THE COKE

The Pen Women of Gainesville, Florida, aspiring to genteel culture in a college town where only the Gators really counted, weren't ready for the poem my father pulled out of his pocket.

James Dickey, a new instructor in the English department at the University of Florida, had been asked to read to them some verses by other poets. He gave them a little Auden. A little Prokosch. And they, being polite, finally asked him to read one of his own. Of course he just happened to have brought along a work in progress. "The Father's Body," it was called. "It's about a little boy's discovery of his father's— about the difference of his father's body from his. They're taking a shower together. And it's the little boy's recognition that he has sort of the same equipment, but it's not, it's different." A provocative choice for the Pen Women. As he read, they sat silent, stunned, and finally, when they gathered their wits, angry. Within a few days, my father was out of a job.

"Pornography!" the scandalized reading club of Gainesville had said, and seemed firmly indignant in that conviction. But every time I read that poem I have to wonder, How did they know? It is deeply obscure. It is *obscurely* obscure. A little boy is watching his father in an outdoor stall at a beach cottage, then joins him and a little girl under the pelting water. There is a dream of transported souls and primal sexuality, its imagery as mythic as anything in *The Golden Bough.* "Something descends into the man of ruined, unarrestable statuary." There are a few references to the boy's loins, and to him "pierced by a sprig of holly / Between the double freshness of his legs." (It is easy, here, to imagine the Pen Women pricking up their ears.) In the dream "he parts the girl's terrible legs; he shouts / Out silence; his waist points / And holds and points, empowered / Unbearably: withheld: withheld—"

This was pretty mild stuff for a serious writer in the 1950s. But the Pen Women protested to the president of the university. The head of the department demanded an apology from my father, and my father refused. Making a bad situation bitter, my father had been given the job at Florida through Andrew Lytle, one of the Southern writers he admired who had helped him in many ways since he was at Vanderbilt. Lytle had supported his bid for the Sewanee Fellowship that took him to Europe the year before. Lytle was a man of principle, the kind of Southerner who might once have fought duels, and gave the impression he might still. Surely Lytle would back Jim Dickey now— would say this was a question of serious work at a serious university, and not the sort of thing to be trifled with by a bunch of frustrated menopausal matrons. But Lytle did not back Jim Dickey. Lytle scolded him for bad judgment, if nothing else. And Dickey, in a matter of days, was on his way to New York to start writing advertising copy for McCann-Erickson on Madison Avenue.

That option had been open, in fact, and my father had been considering it since before the poem emerged from his pocket. I can't tell you for sure if he planned all this. I think not. But he was glad it happened. For a second time, at a second university, the academic world had been too small, too restrictive, and too poorly paid for Jim Dickey's tastes. In advertising he'd be making twice as much money ($7,000 a year), and since McCann had just gotten the Coca-Cola account and was expanding its operations in Atlanta, Coke's home town, he'd be working there. Before the Pen Women, advertising was a gamble. Now it was a guaranteed escape from what he called "that genteel tomb" of academia. He took off for New York and backdated a telegram of resignation, breaking his contract and abandoning his classes.

It was up to my mother to deal with friends, faculty, and everything else he left behind in Gainesville: the uncertainties and fears, the closing down of the house, the packing, the move. My father even told her to make amends with Lytle, as best she could. "Do what you can to get him back on our side," Jim wrote when he landed in New York, "if all else fails, why then *tant pis*, I say." He was staying in a grim little room at the Winslow Hotel, at 55th and Madison, watching an April snowstorm. "I never felt completely right about teaching, anyway; it seems to me that there is something a man owes to his life more than sitting around talking about books all the time. And it makes literature itself boring, by divorcing it from life. This way is better, believe me, and is going to be better and *better*. I have a kind of feeling I was made for it. I think I can make Coca Cola into a *Big Thing*." The coming of spring would vindicate him, he said.

Lytle was embarrassed and annoyed. He wrote a weary, bitter letter to my father. "You have got to accept and respect the egos of people you deal with." It looked as if the university might sue for breach of contract. The strain on my mother must have been terrible. She was trying to make a home on $3,800 a year. If we were sued, there wouldn't be anything to give back. And yet I don't remember this as a time of great unhappiness. It just seemed like a continuation of the European adventure. We were always moving. That was the way life was. And there was the promise that in Atlanta we'd be close to Grandmama. While my father was away, I told my mother I would "be the daddy." I played outside in the yard waiting for the trip, or helped her pack by bringing her books from the shelves she and my father had made from bricks and boards.

There were already so many books, and even as we were packing, a new shipment arrived from Marcel Béalu at Le Pont Traversé, and she had to search through the boxes for a copy of *L'Eau fine* by Alain Borne that my father decided he really had to have with him in New York. Still, she managed. Her mother came down from Nashville and helped her pack and, as I think about it, probably helped charm Lytle, too. In less than three weeks, with the help of my uncle Tom Dickey, who was now in the real-estate business, Mom negotiated the purchase of a little house on the newly built suburban fringes of fashionable northwest Atlanta. It was only about five minutes away from West Wesley. She bundled me into the tiny, stuttering Hillman Minx we'd used to tour Europe. I knew my place, playing and sleeping in a kind of nest cleared in the back seat, watching the telephone poles go by, hypnotized by the swooping lines of the wires suspended between them. She sent Dad the copy of *L'Eau fine*. By the beginning of May, we were in Atlanta. She settled in to wait for my father to come back to her. To us.

The spring had arrived. "It is all over: the 'University of Florida' laid to rest, Andrew back in his original calm, and the teaching profession (thank God!) really, finally, behind us," my father wrote. He was on a roll now. With the help of cash from his mom and pop to tide him over, Jim Dickey was falling into the rhythm of Madison Avenue. He was put to work writing copy for *Coke Time*, a new television show starring the crooner Eddie Fisher ("Bring home the Coke, be-op be-dop, bring home the Coke"). "Eddie himself, whom I met and worked with on the commercials is a very nice, tired-looking, pocked Jewish boy who talks a good deal in the jive lingo of 'The Wild One,' " my father wrote home. It all seemed so easy, and even glamorous. "I feel wonderful and have the confidence of Achilles."

"I wish you well in this job, and I say this carefully because I think it is a dangerous job for a poet," Andrew Lytle wrote to him. "It may be that you are the one man who can take such a job and still write, for I'm told it is fast, competitive, and brutal."

With the move to New York, Jim Dickey was not only leaving teaching and going into advertising, he was moving out of Lytle's circle and, for the first time, onto the fringes of a literary scene the likes of which he'd never really experienced before. It was a little alien, but exciting and encouraging. At lunch he could go browse the shelves of the Gotham Book Mart, and bump into writers he had never in his life expected he would meet in person. "Wise men fish here," said the sign out front, and he felt like he might just be one of them. In the evenings, he could catch *Waiting for Godot*, or go to literary parties to read his poems. He might be making pitches to Coca-Cola bottlers' meetings by day, but at night he was listening to Oscar Williams read "The Relation of Poetry to Reality."

By June, it seemed as if he would never come back. We had moved all our furniture into the new house at 2930 Westminster Circle. The mud in the front was seeded and the grass was beginning to grow. I had made a few friends my age in this subdevelopment burgeoning with children, and I was happy to be close to Grandmama. But I couldn't understand why it was taking my daddy so long to come home. My mother, whom he'd taken to calling "Chubbin" and "Miss Chubby of 1956" in his letters, was beginning to wonder, too.

Jim Dickey might have stayed in New York for a full six months. That had been the plan. But *Coke Time* with Eddie Fisher "had the lowest Nielsen rating that had ever been recorded," my father would recall with bemused chagrin. "Nobody watched it." And that freed my father to go back to Georgia, closer to the home office, and to home.

"I was Atlanta's Young Businessman of the Year," Dad remembered. And what amused him, but what he couldn't quite accept, is how well he fit the role. Because, before Jim Dickey ever became a professional literary Southerner of the Vanderbilt school, much less the cracker bard of later years, he was an Atlantan. And Atlanta just wasn't like the other old cities of the Confederacy. Its people always felt a little apart, and more than a little above the shiftless flatlands of South Georgia, and the treacherous mountains of North Georgia. It was a town built by and of and for a parvenue bourgeoisie, where it took only a generation to become an old family, and the young men in society were always torn between the need to work hard to maintain appearances, and the desire to appear as if no work were needed at all.

Atlanta prospered because it was essentially open—the exact opposite of the introverted, incestuous lands around it. The city's affluence was founded on modern transportation and communication, first railroads, then airlines, and always a lot of public relations. No city in the South was a more suitable home for an advertising man. Slogans and jingles, with a little chicanery and a lot of chutzpah, were as natural to Atlanta as the rhetoric of fire and brimstone was to the rural parishes just beyond its horizons. The Swifts, my father's mother's family, made their fortune with a patent medicine called "S.S.S." that once billed itself as a sure cure for syphilis, before the law made the company reduce its claims and it became just another iron tonic. Coca-Cola, a product nobody ever needed, became the drink everybody wanted to have. Folks in Atlanta got the idea they could sell just about anything. The key to success lay in picking the right slogan. And never more so than in the 1950s. "Bring home the Coke," sure. But also Mayor Hartsfield's creed, in the midst of the integration wars, that Atlanta was the city "too busy to hate." Part wishful thinking, part willful blindness, this credo managed, nonetheless, to keep Atlantans feeling civilized while the attack dogs raged through Bull Connor's Birmingham, and crosses of the Klan burned in the dark night of the cotton fields.

Our little street in the Atlanta suburbs, Westminster Circle, was a dead end when we bought our house there, although later it would continue on to join up with other little subdevelopments off of Howell Mill Road. Near where the street ended there was a little creek and a lot of weeds and a few trees. In the summer you'd come across snakes down there. At least once I saw a cottonmouth moccasin, long and black and fundamentally viperous, with its curved fangs set in a death-white mouth. More than once I came across copperheads, their bodies harlequined in the colors of leaves. The dangers of nature were a little closer to our suburbs than anybody really wanted to admit. Once, one of the boys in the neighborhood managed to haul a monster snapping turtle back to his house to show to his friends. Its mouth was like some prehistoric bolt-cutter that could snap right through the bones of your fingers. He got his picture in the Atlanta paper. I had nightmares for weeks.

Across the street from us lived a salesman. My father would

remember that his wife was voluptuous and he was away a lot. But I remember only his lawn in front of his house, which was the best-mowed and most evenly green on the street, and the ferns far in the back of his yard, near the little creek. One summer he had a Fourth of July party. There was a street parade with crepe-paper streamers on our bicycles, and we ran three-legged races and ate Waldorf salad and fried chicken and watermelon. Dad, I remember, won the husbands' beautiful-legs contest.

A couple of doors farther up was a retired diplomat who'd served in occupied Vienna and whose son, Freddy, was one of my friends when I was in fourth and fifth grades. The actual circle that gave the street its name was a few hundred yards from our place, beautified with a crab-apple tree and shrubbery tended by the local "Garden Club," of which my mother became a member. Near the circle lived an affable real-estate man who was the brother of a defendant in a famous Atlanta murder case of the 1940s, as my father always remembered. Atlanta was still a small enough town so that a scandal in the family lingered a lifetime.

Farther up the street, toward Howell Mill, was a woman who'd survived a concentration camp and had a number tattooed on her arm. I couldn't not look at it when she would give me a ride in the carpool to school. She also had rows of little red-and-white pins on the visor of her car to show how many times she'd given blood to the Atlanta Red Cross, which seemed, to me then, just as strange and inexplicable as the tattoo. Next door to us on one side was a couple that had a ferocious dog and no kids. They were nice enough to look in on our house when we were on vacation, and it was they who discovered the flood when Mulciber, my pet hamster, escaped from his cage and gnawed his way through the washing-machine hose. Those neighbors were replaced eventually by a man who had a pistol range in his basement garage. On the other side of our house was a man named George Kirby who edited a magazine called *The Progressive Farmer*. His daughter, Ellen, was my best friend and playmate. She had a soft deformity above her eye, a huge lump that came down and obscured the vision and wasn't removed until some time, years later, after we moved away. People were shocked when they saw her for the first time, but I loved to be with her, and spent as much time as I could over at the Kirby house.

Behind us was a stand of pine trees and some undergrowth, and at the end of the Kirbys' yard there was a hedge just high enough to block the view. Behind it, as we all knew but rarely thought to talk about, there was a dirt street lined by shacks. Maybe a dozen black families lived there.

The schools I went to were never integrated while I lived in Atlanta, but there was always talk that they would be. During nuclear-attack drills in fourth grade, when we'd all be huddled under our desks to protect ourselves from Russia's atomic threat, some of the boys would say they'd heard tell there was gonna be niggers in our school, and their daddies was gonna take them out if that happened.

I thought about this a lot. I was such a *serious* little boy. I worried —I made it a point to worry, about big issues, and I took myself so seriously that, looking back, I laugh. Sort of. There is a picture of me at about the age of four or five, lying on a towel in the back yard with my hands behind my head, my shirt off, my jeans pulled up about to my rib cage, looking like I couldn't have a care in the world. But I know I was lying there trying, somehow, to solve the problems of humanity—war, the atom bomb—while getting a tan. The bigger the thing I had to think about, the more distance I could put between myself and whatever it was close at hand that I feared or failed to understand. So much is obvious when you're an adult and looking back through the lens of forty years. But I realize, from a line or two in the poems and the novels and my mother's letters, that my parents were really puzzled by the things I chose to fix on, and the things I failed to see at all. It was like a scene in *Deliverance*, in the back of Ed Gentry's home in Atlanta before he sets out on his canoe trip. He picks up his little boy and looks out at the trees behind their suburban house. "I kissed him and he held me close around the neck," writes the father. "He was not ordinarily an affectionate child, and his acting this way made me nervous."

LONERS

M y father would say later that he was "making my head." He
had his own version of the Socratic method, and sometimes
on a rainy weekend afternoon we'd lie on his bed in the back of our
little Atlanta house and he'd ask me what I thought, for instance, about
the distribution of wealth. He steered me toward the idea that people
should produce according to their abilities and be paid according to
their needs, but I don't think it was a concept that really meant very
much to him. Once, I remember, we started *Huckleberry Finn* together
on the bed. But the language was too rich for me, and Huck's drunk,
brutal father was not someone I wanted to hear about.

Mostly, though, my father read to me in one or another of the
two big armchairs that my mother bought soon after we moved to
Atlanta. They were covered with a gray-and-white flowered fabric and
positioned in a more or less formal living room where carpenters had
built floor-to-ceiling walls of books. And from Atlanta to Oregon
to California to Virginia, where they were re-covered in wide-wale
corduroy, to South Carolina, they stayed with us for the rest of our
lives. And so did the walls of books.

My grandmothers might indulge me with Uncle Wiggly, but I
can't recall that Dad ever read me any children's stories. Not even
Tarzan, or John Carter or Doc Savage. He liked to tell me those tales
as if he were making them up. And the education in the armchair
never included picture books either. Instead we would leaf through
my father's big, oversized volumes of art. Some were of modern paintings: the great splashes of color in Emil Nolde, or the romantic and
excruciatingly real temperas of Andrew Wyeth. That Andrew's father

was a great illustrator, not least of *Treasure Island,* was something my father never failed to talk about when we came across *Christina's World* or that painting of a windblown scarecrow in a cornfield.

There was a big coffee-table book of world mythology, and Dad would read me its versions of *Beowulf,* or the labors of Hercules, or, his favorite, Theseus and the Minotaur. He'd been leading me into the old world of the old gods at least since we were in Florence, on that first trip to Europe, when we would stand looking at Cellini's bronze of Perseus with the head of the Medusa in his lightly clenched fist. There were dinosaurs in that big chair, too. We had a huge book, too big for me to lift when I was a little boy, with full-color plates of triceratops, brontosaurus, and, of course, *Tyrannosaurus rex.* Science, there in the chair, was a kind of mythology without a narrative, a collection of wonders in the picture pages of our books.

Architecture became the same sort of adventure. By the time I was nine or ten, the art books we looked at the most were a boxed set that surveyed the works of Louis Sullivan, Le Corbusier, Oscar Niemeyer, Alvar Aalto, Gaudí, and Mies van der Rohe. But it was Frank Lloyd Wright who interested my father most. For hours, as I snuggled against his side, we would look at the sketches and photographs of the two Taliesens, and Falling Water, and the Guggenheim Museum, and the Johnson's Wax headquarters. He loved Wright's draftsmanship, which was so precise, and the art of his vision, with its historical references and surprising juxtapositions of form. And he loved the arrogance of Wright's genius. Did the roof of Wright's chapel in Florida collapse? "Everybody is entitled to one mistake," Wright had said. Or so my father told me.

The literature my father shared was usually strange and often scary. Sometimes he'd have me read a haiku to him like a page from *Dick and Jane.* But I liked—*he* liked—limericks better, especially those by Edward Lear. I would read the five-line verses to my father, puzzling out the words, not getting, quite, the crazed connections they made. I'd pore over the weird, scraggly pictures Lear drew as illustrations. Then Dad would read me the more serious nonsense about the Owl and the Pussycat, or the Jumblies, who went to sea in a sieve, or the Dong with the Luminous Nose, as lonely a figure as exists in English literature.

We didn't read the Brothers Grimm, we read John Collier: "Bird of Prey," in which a couple buy a pet parrot, and the things it says to each while the other is away feed their jealousies and lead them to murder. And "Evening Primrose," about people who live in department stores after the doors are closed. To hide during the day, they pose as mannequins. At night they have their own closed societies. Among them are children who were lost and forgotten by their parents in the store. And if any try to escape, they will be taken away by the people who live and hide in funeral parlors. And God knows what *they* eat.

When my father told me stories about himself, they were mostly about the war. All those stories about being a pilot. With his hand swooping through the air, he'd show me about barrel rolls and loops and Immelmanns. He'd guide my hands and feet to show me how to use the rudder and stick. He'd tell me how he escaped that Jap Zero, how he'd been rescued by the submarine. And he'd say he never wanted to go back to war again, and, gently, he'd say he felt like a survivor.

The only poem I remember us reading in that armchair was *The Rime of the Ancient Mariner,* and that we read over and over again from an edition with menacing illustrations by Mervyn Peake. Part of the fascination was Coleridge's macabre romanticism. "*Her* lips were red, *her* looks were free, / Her locks were yellow as gold: / Her skin was as white as leprosy, / The Nightmare LIFE-IN-DEATH was she, / Who thicks man's blood with cold." But there was something here, too, of the war, of navigation, of islands that shivered into flowers.

My father would always ask the same question about the poem, as if he'd just discovered this bit of knowledge, and was proud to pass it on. "The Sun came up upon the left, / Out of the sea came he! / And he shone bright, and on the right / Went down into the sea," my father would recite. "Now, Chrissy, which way were they going?"

"South, Daddy."

"That's good. Most people don't get that."

"Alone, alone, all, all alone, / Alone on a wide wide sea!" I would read aloud to him. "And never a saint took pity on / My soul in agony."

"Good. Good. Now the next lines." These were the ones that seemed to be the most important to him.

"The many men, so beautiful! / And they all dead did lie. . . ."

"I was a *businessman,* by God," my father marveled almost forty years later in Columbia. He was sitting in the old chair that had been with us so long. The re-covered corduroy arms were shiny from his hands' bracing on them when he tried to stand. The cushion had been worn down beneath his emaciated form. I sat on the arm beside him and showed him the pictures I'd brought in from the garage. They were eight-by-ten glossies from an advertising presentation, and he was the model in one of them, sitting at a mocked-up lunch counter waiting to be served a Coke. I'd forgotten that, when we were in Atlanta, Dad not only wrote the ads, he wasn't averse to appearing in them. At one point he made a television spot for S.S.S. that showed him wearing a business suit and trudging up a hill of loose sand. His blood was tired, too little iron. Then, after a dose of the family firm's magic elixir, he sprinted to the top of the hill with no problem. When I was about nine, he even started putting me in television commercials. The one I remember best was for Sunshine Pickled Peaches. An ideal mom comes back home with the groceries, tosses a jar of peaches to the ideal dad, who tosses them to me so I can put them up on a shelf with a perfectly radiant American suburban smile.

In *Deliverance*, the narrator, Ed Gentry, knows that he fits into his small, moderately prosperous world, and that makes him feel moderately uneasy. His friend Lewis "wanted to be immortal." But Ed is just glad his graphic-arts studio is doing well enough. "I had no wish to surpass our limitations, or to provide a home for geniuses on their way to the Whitney or to suicide." There must have been a part of my father that reacted the same way, that was lulled into acceptance of a moderately good life. But he fought it with a vengeance. And I—I, like most kids, just wanted to be like everyone else. But I couldn't. That wasn't the way my head was made.

By second grade, my teachers at Morris Brandon Elementary School, not sure what to do with me, decided I should skip third grade and go straight into fourth. And my father sat me down one night to talk about what that would mean. I was already one of the youngest children in my class. Now I would be at least a year younger than everybody else. It would be hard, he said, especially when I was a teenager. I would feel out of step with everyone around me.

"Do you think you can handle that?" Dad asked.

"Yes, I guess. I don't know, Daddy. I think so."

"I know you can," he said. "You're like me. You're a loner. I wouldn't wish that for you. But you are."

We were in my father's tiny study in the third bedroom of the Westminster Circle house when we had that talk, and it seemed strange to me to be there after supper. At night this was the place Dad worked, and it wasn't a place for little boys, he'd say. His desk, an unvarnished door laid across two filing cabinets, looked out on our quiet little street. Around his old typewriter there were stacks of paper, often a ream or more, that would be the draft of a single poem. Sometimes there would be a piece of "dad-shirt cardboard," as it used to be called, with individually typed and cut-out words carefully arranged and rearranged on it in a kind of poetic Scrabble my father played against himself to find new ways to put the words together. An old radio was tuned to one of the rare FM stations in Atlanta in those days, and eventually he crammed a small record player in there, too. He listened to classical music or Burl Ives and Bob Gibson. And sometimes he would listen for hours to comedy albums by Jonathan Winters, whose insanity appealed to him. Across the top of the doorway there was a chinning bar where Dad would do leg lifts, wearing his old ski boots for weight, bringing his feet up until they touched the lintel above him, marking it with two dark smudges from the impacts.

My father would work five days a week at the agency, then in that room for hours more at night and on the weekends: "Selling my soul to the devil during the day, buying it back at night," he liked to say. But in that tension between the workaday world of suburbia where he dwelled and the mythic universe of war and hunting and ecstatic lust that he dwelt on in his study, he began to find his real artistic voice. In the small notebook he kept on the desk that looked out on Westminster Circle, he wrote in red ink, "Poetry comes when the utmost reality and the utmost strangeness coincide."

GOD'S SCRIPT

The cold settled onto the surface of the North Georgia lake and started to cut through the little car-coat that I wore. I was only about eight, and thin, and the ice that was in the air as night came on got under my ribs and into my guts, so my teeth chattered if I wasn't careful. And even if I was. We were up in the mountains, surrounded by forest, my father and I alone. He had put up a little mountain-tent, and we were trying to build a fire, but there was no dry wood to be found. Dad went off into the forest looking, and took his bow with him. "Maybe I'll get us a fox," he said.

I had a pocket knife and tried to cut some twigs. The blade was small and dull, and I concentrated and sawed and whittled, but it seemed like an awful lot of work for one or two sticks. I picked up a stone and threw it into the lake, watching the rings spread out over the still water. I shivered and put my hands in my pockets, feeling loose kitchen matches I had ready in case we ever found anything that would burn.

Through the leaves and tree trunks I heard my father's voice, distantly. "Chrissy?" It sounded like he was shouting. "Chrissy?"

"Daddy?"

"Chrissy, where are you?"

"Here, Daddy." I hadn't wandered very far. Why was he looking for me? I was right near the tent and the station wagon. I didn't understand.

And he shouted again, and I shouted back, until, after a few minutes, he came into our little camp. And it wasn't until I was grown that he told me that he had been the one who was lost, and afraid for himself, and afraid for me without him.

As he laid the fire with the wood he'd found, I was nervous and excited, looking forward to the warmth. The campfire seemed to be our reason for being here. In my pocket I rubbed the matches together, not thinking. There was a flash at my fingertips. Searing pain shot through my hand. Smoke poured from the pocket of my coat.

For a second my father didn't realize what had happened, and by the time he got to me I was crying from the burn and embarrassment. He looked at my hand. There were no blisters. He kissed it to make it better. The tears dried in the cold. We managed, at last, to start the campfire. But it didn't burn for long, a thin drizzle began to fall, and soon after dark we started to try to sleep.

My father knew nothing about camping. We hadn't brought anything to put between our two sleeping bags and the half-frozen ground except a canvas sheet. It was like sleeping on a block of ice. As we lay there talking, we could hear the rain start to drum heavily on the roof of the tent. I turned on the flashlight, and we could see the beads of water forming slowly on the inside surface. They started to drip onto me, and onto my father, and we narrowed the space we were in, snuggling together, trying to stay dry, until he said, "Come on and get in with me." He put one sleeping bag inside the other, and I, with my smoke-smelling car-coat still on, wriggled into them beside him, as immobilized as a swaddled baby against the warmth of his body.

"Did you hear the owl?" my father whispered a few hours later when he felt me stirring in the still-dark morning. He said it had come down and sat on top of the tent. Hadn't I heard it? Really? But I had been sound asleep.

When I was middle-aged and he was old, my father would say that he had taken me into the woods of North Georgia because he wanted to give me a little something of what his father had given him. It was a strange thing to say. My father never thought that his father had given him much at all. And when Grandpapa had come up to these woods, it was for chicken fights, or coon-on-a-log, or to listen to foxhounds running through the night after their prey. It was for blood sports. When my father and I came to the forest, even though we talked about hunting and took our bows, and I thought we wanted to kill something, we never did. And it wasn't just because we were not very good shots. It was because the blood my father was looking for was in his imagination, not in the pulsing veins of the animals. He didn't want to kill them. In his head, he wanted to *be* them. "Try to get the sense of metaphor and of participation in the cosmos that an animal would have," he wrote in his green notebook at about the time we went up to camp by the lake.

In the formal stanzas of "The Heaven of Animals," he was looking for a kind of animal immortality, where the predator and the prey kill and are killed and are resurrected endlessly, and he would keep working on that idea until, in his poem "For the Last Wolverine," he found its perfection:

> *Lord, let me die   but not die*
> Out.

He could laugh at himself, sort of. "Springer Mountain" is a wonderful, ludicrous, mystical, powerful poem in which a suburbanite bow-hunter strips naked to run with the deer through the frozen woods, as my father might have thought of doing that evening by the lake. And maybe as he did—maybe that's why he was lost. But it's in "Listening to Foxhounds" that he tells the truth about those trips he took with *his* father to the woods, about the loner-child sitting by the campfire with the men and listening to the baying of the dogs, and becoming the fox.

Among the stories my father read me in the armchair in Atlanta, there were a handful about animals. "Leiningen Versus the Ants" and "The Most Dangerous Game" were classic adventure tales. Then, as if it were the same genre, my father would slip into our reading list James Agee's "A Mother's Tale," about a wounded cow that escapes from a slaughterhouse, or "The God's Script" by Jorge Luis Borges.

That was the story that really haunted me, because I didn't really understand what it was about, but it seemed so important to my father. In it an Aztec priest, Tzinacán, is imprisoned by Alvarado in a dungeon cell near the cage of a jaguar that is "measuring with secret and even paces the time and space of captivity." Once a day, at noon, the jailer drops slabs of meat through a hole, and there's enough light for the magician to see the beast nearby. "I imagined my god confiding his message to the living skin of the jaguars." And he begins to decipher it. And after years, he succeeds.

> It is a formula of fourteen random words (they appear random) and to utter it in a loud voice would suffice to make me all powerful. To say it would suffice to abolish this stone prison, to have daylight break into my night, to be young, to be immortal, to have the tiger's jaws crush Alvarado, to sink the sacred knife into the breasts of Spaniards, to reconstruct the pyramid, to reconstruct the empire. Forty syllables, fourteen words, and I Tzinacán, would rule the

lands Moctezuma ruled. But I know I shall never say those words, because I no longer remember Tzinacán.

The idea of secret writing hidden on the skin of an animal was so appealing to my little-boy's code-breaking heart that I would ask my father to read it to me again and again. But I had no idea, until much later, what it was really about—poetry—and why it interested him so much.

There were never any guns in our house when I was growing up. And there was only one afterward, when someone gave my mother a Derringer pistol toward the end of her life in Columbia, because she was alone a lot, and afraid. My father hated guns. "Because of the war," he said. But there was also something about their mechanical potency that he found unappealing. If you could look at a deer through a telescope and kill it with the pull of a trigger, then, at least as far as my father was concerned, there was no link between you and it. But if you could draw down on it with an arrow, even if you missed it, there was some sort of mystical connection. Hunting was about *instinct.* And the kind of archery my father practiced and that he taught me was called, literally, instinct shooting. You drew back the arrow, you looked at your prey or at your target, and from practice, and control, and instinct, you knew when you released the string that the arrow would go where you aimed—where you *willed* it to be. There was something here of Eugen Herrigel's *Zen in the Art of Archery.* "Fundamentally the marksman aims at himself and may even succeed in hitting himself." But in hunting, of which Herrigel says nothing, the target is the animal—is the self-as-animal—and the idea of instinct hits at two levels or more. That was Dickey in the art of archery.

I just wanted to kill things, or thought I did. And it was in the rituals of making things to kill things that my father and I spent a lot of our time together. He first got interested in archery when we lived in Florida and my mother gave him a lemon-wood longbow from a local sporting goods store. She was "very high on bows and arrows," he remembered. Maybe he'd been reading Herrigel even then, and she thought she would touch him with such a gift. Maybe she had been good at archery when she was in Catholic high school. My father said he had "no idea" why she gave him his first bow, and there's no one left now to ask. But by the time we got to Atlanta, the passion for archery was something he'd taken over completely.

Bows were not our only weapons. Somewhere my father had learned that you could make a very effective blowgun out of a six-foot aluminum pipe. The darts, cut from segments of coat hanger with paper cones taped to them, were sharpened on the pavement of the driveway. At twenty yards, driven by an explosion of my father's breath, they would penetrate almost an inch into a pine tree. When I would spy a snake down in the creek, he'd come looking for it and skewer its head from several feet away. There was no trouble aiming. The dart flew from the middle of your face straight to the target. And if you pointed the blowgun into the sky, the thin wire and cone of paper would sail high, out of sight. Once my father got in trouble with the local police for shooting old darts into the tops of the trees behind our house, unaware that, when they cut through the leaves and went onward, they landed in the yards of another suburban development. Housewives lying in their lawn chairs watched in horror as the little projectiles descended from the skies. Dad lost his enthusiasm for blowguns for a while after that.

But archery was about more than just the shooting, or even the hunting. It was about escape. A friend named Dave Sanders, who lived across the street from Dad's brother, Tom, had introduced Dad to the archery ranges in the woods outside Atlanta, and almost every weekend, if the weather permitted at all, he'd head out to the Cherokee Archery Club in Smyrna. It was not so different from a golf course, Dad would say. You walked along a trail from stake to stake, shooting at targets up to eighty yards away. He just preferred being in the woods. But this wasn't a country club, of course, this was redneck country.

After a tournament, Dad would sit around for hours with a frame-turner from a local Ford plant, drinking beer and listening to his stories about hunting wild hogs, missing shots, climbing trees; talking about how to put a good edge on the broadhead tip of a hunting arrow, and who was the best hunter in the world—Howard Hill, who taught Errol Flynn to be Robin Hood, or the dour-faced Fred Bear, who was starting to make the best mass-produced bows on the market. "I tell you," Dad's friend the frame-turner used to say, "that Fred Bear looks like he mighta been takin' ugly pills." These men and the few women they brought with them were a lot like the people you might meet up at Wha-cha-know Joe's, where Grandpapa kept his fighting chickens. They'd have been right at home watching a raccoon chained to a floating log trying to fight off a pack of hounds, or listening to the baying of the dogs running through the dark after a fox. They sure didn't know much about Zen. And Dad would say that's what he liked about them. But if Grandpapa had felt comfortable among mountain people, there was a part of Dad that could not help feeling superior to them. A long time afterward, he would say, oddly, that the frame-turner was "a flunky, an industrial flunky," as if even his claim on the woods was inferior. These were the kind of people my grandmother would call *Bettelsacks*.

Dad started to take his own friends from Atlanta with him to the range, and up into the woods.

MOONSHINE

We'd been waiting since dark for Dad to get home. He was just running a little late, Mom said. He'd be back soon. We'd see the sweep of the headlights coming around the house. Through the louvered glass in the kitchen door we'd hear him slam the door of the station wagon, and under the yellow light of the carport we'd see him, dirty and damp in his old military-surplus flight suit, dragging stuff out of the back. Bows, arrows, paddles, more wet clothes, maybe a life jacket. That's the way it would always happen. Sometimes his friend Lewis King would be behind him in another car, or Al Braselton, who worked with him at Liller, Neal, Battle and Lindsey. They'd come in for a beer or a highball, and talk about the river, or call their wives, and maybe stay for dinner. But it was getting real late now. Supper was made, and some of it eaten in the kitchen, and the rest of it grown cold.

"You go check on Kevin," Mom would say every so often. Because my little brother, Kevin, who was about two by then, was getting restless, too. The cartoons were over on television. No more Quick-draw McGraw, no more Deputy Dawg. Nothing to hold our interest. And it was bedtime, but none of us wanted to say that. Because Dad wasn't home yet.

Mom called Dave and Ann Sanders. Sometimes—a lot of times —Dad would just disappear over at their house after work, or after he'd been out at the range with Dave. And Mom would worry, and call, and when Dad came back to our house at last there would be a fight.

"Jim, why don't you come *home?*" Mom screamed, angry and desperate.

"Because when I'm there I feel *happy!*" he'd say. "Can't a man feel happy?"

"You mean drunk," she'd say. "You go over there and get drunk and—damn it, Jim, I don't know what you do."

But he kept going back there, even so. And got meaner about it. More resentful. And stayed longer.

The night my mother got a phone call telling her that her father had died, it was one of those evenings when Dad had left the office but hadn't come home. My mother had called over to Dave's and had left a message for Dad. And maybe Dad had been there, and maybe he hadn't. But he'd taken a real long time to get back to the house.

"But, Mom," I said, "don't cry."

"He was my father," she said. "My *father.*"

"We never saw him," I said. "How can you cry about somebody you never see?"

And then Dad had come back, and I thought there would be a very big fight. But there wasn't. Mom just cried. And he held her.

But now, when Dave and Ann said they didn't know where Dad was, she believed them. And she called Joan King, and Polly Braselton, and they hadn't heard from the boys either.

It probably wasn't all that late—maybe nine-thirty or ten—when the headlights finally did sweep across the back yard and into the carport. But we were scared enough. Lewis's car, with a canoe on the top, pulled into the driveway behind them. They talked, and Lewis left. We could see all that through the louvered glass in the door. But we didn't open it.

"Mom, they're back."

"I know that, honey."

Dad came through the door first, carrying some sort of bag, and Al after him. Both of them were pale and sallow, like men who'd been sick for a long time, even though they'd only been gone for a day.

They'd busted up the canoe in a stretch of rapids on the Coosawattee, a stretch of river they were no-way ready for in a deep, narrow gorge, and Al, banged up badly on the rocks, almost drowned. The canoe had wedged up against him, filling with water, crushing him with the weight of the river. With all his strength and with all my father's strength prying and pushing, he'd only just slipped free. Lewis was supposed to be meeting them, but they didn't know where he was, and they figured he didn't know where they were. Wet and bruised— they weren't sure Al hadn't broken something—they were thinking they were going to have to spend the night out there in the gorge.

And then, like from nowhere, this redneck boy out hunting with his dog had come out of the woods. Lucas Gentry, his name was. And he'd taken them to his pa, who warmed them up with a little moonshine, and took them down to the road, where Lewis was waiting.

My mother stood there in the bright light of the kitchen, just looking at them, relieved, and furious, and relieved again. "You-all are like children," she said, and I think my father was just too tired to argue. I was listening to the adventure, and wishing, sort of, that I'd been there. "You *broke* the *canoe?*"

"Banged it up real bad. Al like to got killed."

"Al," said Mom, "you want us to call somebody?"

Al thought he'd call Polly, and be going.

"What's in the bag?" I asked Dad.

"Let's have a look," he said, and reached in to pull out a couple of jars of clear liquid that looked like water, but it clung to the sides of the jar like light oil. "That old cracker gave us this," he said as he sat the jars on the Formica counter. Corn liquor. The best you could make up there in the mountains.

"Only copper tubes," said Al. "No lead." It was what you always said about moonshine, because the fear in drinking it was that lead pipes or lead solder would contaminate it, and poison your brain or blind you. So this was good stuff. But Al, that night, didn't stay for a drink. He was headed out the door.

"And this is for Chris," said Dad. It was a stalk of sugar cane. I don't know where that would have come from up there. But there it was. And, child of the suburbs that I was, I'd never chewed anything quite like it before.

"You take that outside, before you get it all over the place," Mom told me. So I sat on the step in the carport and peeled the tough fiber off the stalk with a lot of ten-year-old concentration, and not much success, while my father talked to my mother in a voice too low for me to hear.

Ever since, and in places as wild as and much more remote than the Coosawattee, when I would bite into a peeled piece of cane and suck out the sweetness, and smell the grass smell of the stalk, I'd think of my father and Al and of the river.

The rhythm of our life on Westminster Circle was changing. Dad was speeding up the pace, multiplying his interests, intensifying his energies, and spreading them out. He was the advertising man by day, the poet by night, the archer and canoer and tennis player on the weekends. He was the father in the armchair on Westminster, the half-rebellious son at Sunday dinners on West Wesley. He was lifting weights, still, in the carport, and cruising the Buckhead strip malls in the MG-A sports car his mother bought him. (One afternoon, just to show off, he pushed it all the way up the little hill to our house.) He was narrowing the gap to forty, and he wanted to try everything.

Then he started to play guitar, too. He had played a little piano in the past. There was one in Grandmama's house, and he could still hammer out a boogie-woogie melody he'd taught himself when he was a kid. And he'd tried the cornet, like Bix. But when he first picked up a guitar, in about 1958, he thought maybe—just maybe—he really could master the thing. An office boy at Liller, Neal, where he'd gone after McCann, taught him some basic chords. And Al played. So, when they got together, they'd get it on, drinking beer and strumming, and Al singing. Because Dad, God bless him, just couldn't carry a tune.

There were a lot of would-be writers and artists around Atlanta, intelligent people with a little talent and hopes that were sure to become disappointments. "The studio was full of gray affable men who had tried it in New York and come back South to live and die," Ed says in *Deliverance*. He's not sure what to make of them. But Jim Dickey, he seemed to be fearless, and he was on a roll the gray affable men could only envy.

There was so much happening for him, and so much that he was making happen. *The New Yorker* had begun to publish his poetry, and he'd signed a contract giving them first shot at anything he wrote. He was getting to know writers and philosophers whose work he'd admired since he was a half-lost flight officer in a makeshift hut on Okinawa. There were not many serious writers around Atlanta, but Flannery O'Connor lived down in Milledgeville, and a couple of times we drove down the long back roads to her place so my father could talk literature with her and I could ride her ponies and collect the feathers of the peacocks she had wandering around her yard. Other writers, meanwhile, were seeking out our little cul-de-sac, sitting in those pale flowered armchairs, to talk and to listen to my father. The poet James Merrill, the exquisite Jimmy Merrill, came to Atlanta often to visit his mother, and a lover, and James Dickey. Another visitor was Robert Bly, who later made it a point to attack Dickey's supposed politics (which were never very political), and later still made it his profession to be a manly man. My father loved to say that Bly, from Minnesota, had a voice just like Bullwinkle the Moose.

Jim Dickey was funny, and must have been a hell of a lot of fun, too. "I want it all!" he'd say, and the *IT* was absolutely, magnificently, unspecifically, and universally applicable, the way it is when you are old enough to feel all your powers—and also old enough to see how they'll start to wane.

But the little boy that I was didn't know anything about *it*. He just knew that the daddy who'd spent so much time being with him—and making his head—was not there like he used to be. "I spend more time with my family than any man I know," Dad would say. And maybe that was true. But it didn't feel that way. He was writing ads, and writing poetry, and even writing book reviews for the Atlanta newspapers. He was giving readings at local art galleries and colleges. He was starting to travel. And we were missing him when he was away. And sometimes when he was drinking we started to miss him when he was at home.

My father thought alcohol was about joy. He didn't like the taste of it very much, he'd say, he just liked the way it made him feel. And it did seem to me there were a lot of good times made better—more joyful —by the beer, by the whisky, by the gin he was knocking back. He'd have drunk in any case, but there was no reason not to in America in the 1950s. Highballs and dry martinis lubricated every gathering, starting with the three-martini lunch. Now and again, on a summer Saturday, we'd go in Dad's MG to a little drive-in restaurant where he'd get French-fried onion rings, a little filet-mignon steak wrapped in bacon on a hamburger bun, and a couple of Miller High Life beers in crystal-clear bottles. He'd devour the meat, knock back the ice-cold beer, and it was pure, pure pleasure for him. I know it was. And it didn't seem to change him much then. Drinking was just part of the excitement. The *it*.

But toward the end of the time we lived in Atlanta, the whisky on my father's breath, a smell that seemed to come from deep in the bellows of his lungs, started to frighten me. It made the familiar unfamiliar. It meant anger, it meant threatened violence, it meant danger. It was the smell of those lost Friday nights with Dave and Ann Sanders. It was the scent of return when Dad would step, boldly and unsteadily, down the stairs from an airplane. I'd run to meet him and he'd pick me up in his arms, and I'd smell the whisky and know that whatever I said to him would go past him and whatever he replied would be words spoken to the air. He was my father still, but he was somebody I didn't know. And I was just a little boy, I didn't know how to talk to him about that. And later, he wouldn't listen. Strangeness and reality had begun to coincide in our lives. And he liked it that way.

RIVALS

. . . Ah, to play in a great field of light
With your son, both men, both
Young and old! . . .

—"Messages: Butterflies"

POSITANO

The shadows of the Mediterranean sun outlined every rock on the face of the cliff above Fornillo Beach. A man was climbing there, barefoot and barehanded. He wore torn jeans and no shirt. His hair was long and dark and curly, and the skin on his back was tanned as brown as the rock. I knew, although it was too far away to see them, that on those bare feet feeling their way among the cracks in the cliff there were small target-shaped tattoos.

"Jesus, Chrissy, look at that." My father and I were in a small rowboat rented from a fisherman, lying back in the sun, taking in the hot spring day and this unexpected show. My mother and my little brother, Kevin, were on the pebble beach, camped out on the towels they'd spread, ready to eat a picnic lunch with us whenever we managed to row back in.

That spring in Italy, we were living the happiest days of our lives as a family, and if we didn't know that then, all of us would realize it later. It was that place we always tried to get back to, but never could bear to go.

It was 1962. The year before, James Dickey published his first book of poems, *Into the Stone*, and was given a Guggenheim Fellowship. He quit the advertising business, and drove down to the unemployment office every week in his aqua-blue MG to pick up his check. Then his second book, *Drowning with Others*, appeared. He traded in the old Ford station wagon for a Volkswagen bus. And in February we sailed for Europe aboard the newly commissioned SS *France*.

A steady income, my schooling—the whole predictable package of middle-class life in Atlanta was jettisoned. And my mother was as anxious to get back to Europe as any of us. She was married to a genius, she knew, and others were beginning to recognize him as a genius—but not enough others. There were too many gray affable men in Atlanta. There were too many garden clubs. He was straining to get away from this life now, and he was getting away from her. "Jim, you are tearing yourself to pieces trying to do your own writing at night and working like hell all day for those people who ought to be paying you twice as much as you are getting," she said. In Europe, she thought, we might not have a house, but we were going to have our home together again.

"We got to make a break here," my father said. "I am almost forty. This is our chance. What will we do when we get back? I believe I have enough clout to get a job teaching—and doing it the way I want to do it, instead of teaching out of a syllabus. I am ready to gamble."

"Well, so am I," said my mother. "Let's do it."

The rest of the family was surprised, even a little threatened, by the decision. Grandmama wanted her boy to do what he wanted to do. But Pop, he was against it. "He thought I had finally brought some sort of distinction on myself instead of just rattling around doing one thing or another for not much money," my father remembered. "He was very proud of me, because he was such a ne'er-do-well himself. He didn't want another son to be the same way. He was thinking it might run in the family or something."

My mother plotted the trip for months. Periodically the den in the little Atlanta house would be turned into a chart room, with maps of Europe and deck plans of the *France* spread out across the floor. My father wrote to everyone he had met on our first trip and wanted to see again, and many people he wanted to meet for the first time. But the itinerary was still loose. We thought we might drive down to the heel of Italy and take a ferry to Greece, where Jimmy Merrill would be spending the summer. But we made no hotel reservations. If we couldn't find a place to stay, well, we had a tent in the bus for emergencies.

As my father liked to remember, my mother was "good at Europe." And all the improvisation which might have made us feel rootless and unsure gave us instead an odd sense of security. We might wake up in the morning with no idea where we'd sleep that night, but we always did find some place, and often that place was an adventure. The night of our arrival at Le Havre, we set off driving for Paris, and didn't stop until we found a little inn somewhere in the Norman countryside. On the walls were the heads of foxes and weasels, and my father took that as an omen. We were all so excited we could barely sleep.

Then the first few days turned gray and grim. We stayed in the same little hotel near Place St. Michel where we had stayed before, but nobody remembered us there. We tried to pick up old routines. The mail was starting to arrive, as planned, at American Express, whose offices were our lifeline to the United States, our vital connection to the new life my father hoped somehow to build. Every day we would make our pilgrimage to the building on Rue Scribe to check the box marked "D" for our letters. But the routines were not really the same. The city was full of fear. Gendarmes carried machine guns beneath their capes on the Eiffel Tower, and every day there were reports of new bombings as the OAS waged a savage campaign to keep Algeria French, or punish those who gave it independence. Those were the days of the Jackal, it was a time of assassins, and even a little boy thought he could feel the threat of death in the streets.

We drove back to Antibes. There we found nothing but the shuttered windows of Galidou. No fire was lit at the Cumberlidges'. Nobody was home. Monsieur Aldon had closed his bookshop and moved on. The waiters at Le Glacier said they remembered us, but didn't really seem to. The wind blew cold gray waves across the bay at La Garoupe. "You cannot go back," my father said as we drove along the corniche toward Italy. And when we arrived in Florence, my mother wrote home, "I am happier to see this town than any other we have been to yet."

My father discovered and rediscovered this world of Florentine history and art with the enthusiasm of a child—no, more than that—with the enthusiasm of the man remembering the child. He invented games, he shared knowledge, he listened for whatever unexpected thing I or Kevin might say. In the little jewelry shops along the Ponte Vecchio, he searched out agate beads among the semiprecious stones so we could use them for marbles. The Straw Market became a maze, the stalls of leather vendors mere obstacles on the way to the bronze boar with a magic nose to rub and to wish on. Perseus stood, still, where we remembered him, the Medusa hideous and beautiful in his hand. Michelangelo's *Giuliano dei Medici* held my father's eyes for a long, strange moment. He loved that sculpture, more even than Michelangelo's *David*. He felt he had discovered it for himself, and that made it his, and he would make it ours.

Slipping across the wet cobblestones and bracing against the Arno wind, we'd work our way to the chilled, cavernous halls of the Uffizi. My father's excitement was something you could feel in the air around him when he'd look at some of the paintings, especially the Botticellis. At *The Birth of Venus*, he glanced over his shoulder to see if anyone was looking, but didn't really care if anyone was. "Touch it," he told me. "Touch it." And when I had, he put his own large hand gently, as gently as humanly possible, against the surface of the paint, just to know that it was there, and that he was there.

After a couple of weeks, we drove on south toward Perugia, where it was so cold the fountains froze. We'd been in Europe more than a month now, and we had the rhythm of the trip. It was like nothing could stop us. So, when the VW bus started to skid in a snow flurry on the road to Assisi, we got out and tried to walk the last couple of miles through the storm. Fortunately, Kevin, who was not all that steady on his feet at the age of three, had the sense to stop after a few hundred yards and refuse to go farther. We went to the medieval village of Gubbio, and when my father saw a new ski lift had been built to a restaurant on a nearby peak, there was no question but that he'd take us there for lunch. It was "very safe and we all loved it," my mother wrote home to her mother that night. But she was lying. We were still shaken from the experience.

Each car on the lift was shaped like an oil drum, and about the same size. It would fit one person standing, and skis or, just barely, a parent and child. The cable ran continuously, and if the cars paused at all it was for such a short time that you had to get in on the move, then pull the door shut just before it started its vertiginous ascent. Even then, an adult was in the open air from the waist up, swinging precariously over the valley before, finally, the cars jerked and glided around the concrete ramp, and you jumped off, and they started their descent again.

All through our lunch, as Kevin and I ate our spaghetti Bolognese, which is what we always ate, and our mother and father ate their meals and drank their bottle of Chianti, which is what they always drank, I begged them to let me go down the lift by myself. Finally, as they almost always did, they relented. We lined up in front of the man taking tickets. The cars swung by. My mother got in one and sailed down and away across the chasm. I got into the next, filled with excited concentration as I shut the door behind me and floated jerkily over the abyss. But there was a commotion. I turned and saw, in the next car behind me, Kevin alone in the swinging drum as it sped toward the edge of the cliff. Maybe there had been some confusion with the ticket taker and Kevin had toddled into the car by himself before anyone could stop him. Maybe my father, his reflexes slowed by the wine, had missed a beat somehow and let my brother slip away before he could make the step himself. I watched, mesmerized. The door to the car was wide open and there was nothing to keep Kevin inside. Any shift in the wind, any fright that made him lose his three-year-old's shaky sense of balance, would have launched him in a free-fall to the valley floor. I saw my father push aside the man taking tickets. Jim Dickey, the sprinter at thirty-nine, was running after my brother, and he was gaining speed as he ran toward the edge of the cliff. The car floated out over the brink. My father wasn't there yet. The gap widened with open air. He leaped and—made it.

It was a moment of real reckless magnificent bravery that Kevin and I never forgot, but it was something that our father did not talk about much. Maybe he blamed himself for letting Kevin slip away in the first place. Maybe it was just too close a thing. But there it was. In front of our eyes he had saved the life of my mother's baby, my brother, his son. And after that moment of stupid risk and ferocious bravery at Gubbio, all our luck, our travels, our time together seemed better than ever, at least for as long as that spring and summer lasted.

For two weeks in Rome we stayed in a *pensione* just across the Tiber from the Piazza del Popolo and the Borghese Gardens. It was quiet there and restful, and the family that ran it took us in as if we were their family. Each day Kevin would finish his spaghetti with us at lunch, then go up to their private apartment and eat another couple of helpings with them. In the evening the eldest son would put Kevin on the back of his motor scooter and take him to eat ice cream at a local *gelateria*.

The city was dense with reckless glamour that spring. Everyone had seen *La Dolce Vita*, and everyone visiting Rome thought he could live that way someday—if he wasn't living that way already. It was the year of *Cleopatra*, which was filming on monstrously expensive sets at Cinecittà. The romance between costars Elizabeth Taylor and Richard Burton was the scandal of the moment, and felt like the scandal of the century. Roman decadence, Hollywood glamour, all of it seemed right at hand and wonderfully accessible, and my parents were having a lot of fun. At a bar called Bricktop's, where a friend named Walter Clemons, from *Newsweek*, sometimes played the piano, they'd see Taylor and Burton slip into the shadows of a rear table. At the Rome zoo, we'd stand in line behind Martin Landau and strike up a conversation.

I was right on the edge of all this, but outside it, a dour little boy hoping somehow to be a sophisticated man. And there were times when I must have been a real drag on the family. "Isn't Chris a mess?" my mother wrote home to her mother. I was jealous of the attention my beautiful blond baby brother, Kevin, was getting—jealous of his childhood—but also starting to feel the nervous eddies of sex and longing for women with no way to satisfy—or even imagine satisfying

—the desire. Slight and nondescript in the company of this man-god-father; contentious and sullen and scared—so often scared. And even scaring myself. My favorite novel, the first I ever read, was *Dracula*.

But there was something so peaceful, so easy about Rome in the early spring that even I lightened up. Along the Viale Giulio Cesare, beside the Pensione Losanna, there were almost no cars, and among the buttonwood trees with trunks like candelabras, swallows were in constant flight. On the roof there was a terrace, and after my mother bought my father a little guitar to knock around with, he would go up there and practice his chords, trying to pick out from a book as best he could the rhythms of "La Malagueña," then try to teach it to me. In the ruins of the Coliseum or the Circus Maximus I felt like I was living through history I knew: I'd seen *Spartacus* and *Ben-Hur*. I read Shakespeare's *Julius Caesar* and memorized Mark Antony's speech. And my father made it all more vivid still. One day as we were touring the Vatican, he heard a woman guide speaking English to some other American tourists. "Now, this," she said, "is the cross that Marie-Antoinette held in her hands as she went to the guillotine." My father's face lit up. This was the kind of tourism he liked. He signed up the guide on the spot for a tour of the rest of the Vatican and, a few days later, the Forum.

"Caesar was assassinated right in here," she told him as we stood among the ruined columns.

"Right here, where I am standing?" he said.

"No, about two feet to the right."

So he moved over to be where Caesar had been on the Ides of March, and he had me stand there, too.

Our plans kept changing. We were still making up this trip as we went along, and the notion that my parents had of taking us to Greece was abandoned when they discovered the one-way ticket on the car ferry cost $200. They had the idea that Ischia, an island off of Naples where Burton and Taylor liked to take their sun, might be a good place for us. But, again, the cost of the ferry seemed prohibitive. So they decided to stay on the Italian mainland, but they weren't sure where. We headed south to Naples with no intention of staying there—"See Naples and drop dead," as my father liked to say—and we wound up spending the night in Sorrento. Years before, my mother and father had heard about a fishing village and artists' colony called Positano perched on mountainsides above the sea a few miles away. They thought they'd give it a try.

It was a cold, rainy Friday when we arrived along the winding cliff-face road. It was April 6, and we would leave, after postponing our departure several times, on June 20. So we were only there for seventy-five days in all. But even a couple of years later we would have the impression that we'd lived in Positano—really lived there—for the better part of a year.

My mother had found someone to rent us a house within the course of the afternoon, a very little house, with one room and a little kitchen and bathroom downstairs, and one big bedroom with a balcony and a view of the sea on top. Our luggage was brought in by porters, on their backs. The VW was put away in a parking lot shaded by grapevines. The electric heaters were turned on. My father's typewriter came out of its case and was put on a table by the balcony window. We were home.

Heavy weather would roll in over mountaintops a thousand feet above our heads in the morning, and the sun would show pink and brilliant off the pastel sea that same day at dusk. The buildings were faded greens and blues, and cracked whites, and stacked around and on top of each other in a vertical jumble of habitation. Bent old women in black sat in the doorways of their houses in the upper reaches of the town. Aged fishermen, fingers blown away from fishing with dynamite in the days after the war, took their boats and nets out each night and caught their fish by lantern light.

There was a road that ran through Positano, but we never used it. Everywhere we went, we went on foot, up and down the stairs and along the narrow alleys that cut in all directions through the crags and ravines on which the town was built. The air in the alleys was heavy with the scent of wisteria, and the walkways were alive with chameleons that took in the sun for long hours, silent and still except for the pulse at their throats, then rustled away among the webs of vines in a mad scramble if you surprised them.

It was the kind of place where you made friends fast as a foreigner, because so many foreigners were there looking to make friends. An American divorcée down the road was living on alimony and the money she got from the insurance company when she hurt her hand in a taxi accident. "My finger money," she'd call it as she served artichokes on her balcony. An elegant, leathery woman named Edna Lewis had founded an artists' workshop in the 1950s and made it the center of the expat artists' life there. (At an art-show opening in the early afternoon, my mother recorded, "Instead of tea and cookies, they serve martinis and whisky over here and it was much fun.") An aging Englishwoman named Mary Norton had taken up residence with her granddaughter Charlotte in a house a few twists and turns away from ours. Norton had made herself a comfortable income with a children's book, *The Borrowers*, and its several sequels about little people and their daring adventures in the commonplace cabinets and mouse holes of a commonplace house. She was looking for another woman to share her outings in exotic Positano. My mother soon became her friend and companion, and Charlotte soon became mine.

She was a little younger than I was, and I was ten. I don't want to think now that Charlotte was only seven or eight, but I guess she must have been, with long blond hair like Alice in Wonderland and every bit as much impetuousness and perverse self-assurance. She kept blaming me as an American, I remember, for the way imported American gray squirrels had taken over the homes and food and finally destroyed the lives of the nicer, weaker red squirrels of England. It didn't seem fair to me to blame all Americans for this ecological anomaly, much less me. "But it is the truth," Charlotte kept saying, and it hadn't been fair to the red squirrels, either, she insisted. I put up with this because what I really wanted to do, without being absolutely sure why, was to see her naked.

I knew about sex by then, of course, and had for a while. At least I thought I did. My father explained it to me when I was eight years old and in fourth grade. I'd spent the night with a kid named Buzzy, and we'd stayed up late playing poker and telling bathroom jokes. He'd been asked to leave the classroom earlier in the day, as it happened, because he'd given the finger to our teacher, Mrs. Watson. "What was that all about?" I asked him. He showed me the finger: "You know what that means, don't you?" He figured I didn't and, so, patiently explained how sex began, about the time of the Civil War, and how it started out with men and then they found out you could do it better with women. The next day, still pondering these revelations, I asked my mother about fucking. "Jim," she said, "this one's for you." And he'd sat me down and told me a little about anatomy, a little about love, and—this is what he wanted to impress upon me—how evil and murderous some people could be about sex, and how I had to be careful of anybody who ever wanted to give me a ride in his car, or, as it were, offer me candy.

It must have been a difficult moment for him. His explanation was so awkward and oddly threatening. But this threshold in father-son relations was one my father was happy to have crossed. After that he could tell me some of his own dirty jokes, and teach me some of the dirty songs he remembered from the army. One of his favorites, when he was a little drunk in the Atlanta house and wanted to tease my mother, was "Friggin' in the Riggin'." "There was a first mate, name of Carter, a clever little farter. . . ." And I thought these were the funniest, most amazing verses I'd ever heard. "Oh, Jim, stop that," my mother would shout from the kitchen. Then he'd launch into a rendition of "Indian Maid," and before he could get through that first verse—". . . that some buckaroo would give her a . . ."—my mother would be in the den, her eyes angry, saying, "Jim, quit it!" And he'd laugh, and she'd be furious, and I'd beg him to sing the rest of the words as soon as she left the room. And he'd sip his beer. "No," he said, "you've got to get your mother's permission."

So my idea of sex was probably not so different from many a ten-year-old's. And I wanted Charlotte to show me hers, and I spent endless hours thinking about this as we wandered the alleys of Positano. But as far as I can remember she never did.

With us from the first week we were in Positano until the last, watching over me and taking care of Kevin, was the sixteen-year-old daughter of the people who owned the house. Her name was Laura Rispoli. Her smile, her body, her smell excited me, and I would think, "Is this what it's about?" And, yes, it was. But when you're ten, you can't be sure. And I would watch my father flirt with her, and watch her laugh, and be amazed. He would lie on his back on the pebble beach and have her stand on his hands. He heard her say that Kevin could go in the water *senza pantaloni,* and he loved the sound of those words. No pants. "Laura," he would say to her, *"senza pantaloni."* Even years afterward, when he was thinking back on that time, the phrase would come to him. *"Senza pantaloni."*

My mother watched, too, of course.

The center of our family's social life was the bar-pizzeria-nightclub called the Buca di Bacco. The cave of Bacchus. It was at one end of the main beach, and the old Byzantine-style church was at the other. In between were sunbathers, soccer players, fishing boats, and if you sat on the ceramic-tile benches facing the town rather than the sea, you could watch anybody and everybody descending the main stairways. John Steinbeck, in those days before he won the Nobel Prize, had an apartment just to the left of the Buca di Bacco with a balcony that looked out over the Mediterranean. We would watch for him to emerge bearded and blear-eyed in the early afternoon as if we were waiting for an old owl to land near his nest. "There he is," my father always said, "trying to look like Hemingway." But the men who caught my attention were a pair of Americans in their twenties. One had long red hair and a red beard, and I don't remember his name. The other, the one I sometimes talked to, had a dark beard and wavy dark hair down to his shoulders. His name was Casey Deiss, and he was the son of a writer, Jay Deiss, who had done a book on the Roman ruins and art at Herculaneum. Casey looked as if he'd stepped out of a fresco. He was always barefoot or in sandals, and if it had been a few years later he would have been called a hippie. But in those days of the Twist, when Chubby Checker was still spinning on the record player at the *gelateria*, Casey and his friend were completely original. "Here come Jesus and Judas," my father always said as they descended the stairs. "But which one is which?"

Casey moved around Positano the way no one else did. If he took the road, he was on his old Harley-Davidson, and you could hear its throbbing echo up and down the town. But he also liked to climb. A woman named Vali, who styled herself an artist and a witch, lived in a cave above the town. I never went up there, and saw her only rarely, when she descended into the village, peering into our lives with those kohl-dark eyes. It was she, Casey told me, who tattooed those little targets on top of his feet like stylized stigmata. He often climbed the cliffs to her cave, and he climbed just about every other rock surface around Positano. He used no ropes or pitons. Nothing but his bare hands and feet. He was, or at least he seemed to be, absolutely fearless. And when he died, struck by lightning near a lake a few years later, it seemed so appropriate that no one ever forgot. His thunderstruck body, it was said, could only be identified from the silver ring he wore.

As my father and I lay back in the fishing boat and watched Casey climb above Fornillo Beach, Dad must have felt a twinge of jealousy. My father was fiercely and almost randomly competitive. The ferocity was worse when he got older, and worse still when he drank, but it was always there, and he passed it on to me with all the other lessons he gave. And Casey, high above us there on the rock face, a younger man scaling the cliff as my father himself would never dare to do, must have given my father pause.

We remember scenes and sensations from childhood, but not often sequence. Each event floats in isolation from the others, a recollection of emotion, not of cause and effect. Only the adult, looking back, can begin to give it context. Was this the same day that my father dropped the anchor of the little boat about a hundred yards offshore? I think it was.

"Let's swim in," he said, and dived beneath the surface of the cold water, and started to stroke away. But swimming was the one thing that he most wanted me to do and that was most impossible for me. I could play around in shallow water with a mask and flippers. I loved to do that. But when my father tried to teach me to do a crawl across the surface, to stroke and breathe and stroke and breathe, I could not do it without choking. So I tried to swim without breathing at all, and in swimming pools that was enough for a single length. But here in the sea, this far from shore, I was lost. If I tried to dog-paddle, my father would tell me to crawl, and if I did that I would choke. Tentatively I jumped in and tried to swim away from the boat, but panicked and turned back to the anchor rope and clung to it. And hugged it. And called out to my father to come back and get me. And cried with fear, and for having disappointed him. And he did come back, and, still a very little boy, I clung to his neck and rode him to shore.

On Good Friday, my mother and Mary Norton rose at four in the morning. A procession bearing a full-size cross made its way to the mountaintop churches of Positano, and these two women followed every step of the way. No other foreigners bothered, and neither my mother nor Mary was very religious. But it was a time when everyone was having adventures, and this was theirs. "We've been treated like queens ever since," my mother wrote home.

My father was building his body every day. He was always trying new techniques, and he'd discovered something called isometrics, which meant, he said, working out against immovable objects. He'd stand in doorways and press against the sides of the frame, or against the lintel above his head, until his muscles bulged—or the carpentry started to crack. He trained himself to run up the hundreds of stairs from Fornillo Beach to our little house at 13 Via Boscariello. And he swam. God, did he swim. The main beach of Positano and the Buca di Bacco were around a point from our beach, and to get from one to another there was a path about a hundred feet up the side of the cliff. Sometimes my father would just swim the distance and I'd walk above, afraid for him, and proud of him, watching his shoulders flex and his arms churning through the open water—my powerful, amazing dad alone in that wide, wide sea.

On the meandering stairways that led up to our house, there was a little promontory where a couple of trees grew just beyond the wall that normally held you back from the brink. Sometimes when my father was alone with Kevin, he took him over the wall to sit beneath the trees and look down on the beach, the sea, and the little islands in the distance. It was a magical place for his younger son, for whom magic was more real, in those days, than it was for me. And my father wanted to share it.

Every so often my father would extract the VW from its shaded

repose and we would brave the cliff-face road to leave Positano, ven-
turing out to the ancient ruins in the shadow of Vesuvius. In Pompeii,
a lubricious guide winked at my father and escorted him alone to the
inner precincts of the Lupanar, the ancient whorehouse with its crude,
pre-Christian frescoes. ("I could be in prison, or dead, / Cast down for
my sins in a cell / Still filled with a terrible motion . . ." my father had
written after our first trip to Europe.) We waited for him in the museum, looking at the contorted images of men and women preserved
at the moment of death. There was even a terrified dog still writhing
on its short tether. All had been covered by the volcano's ash that
settled like a blizzard over the town, then hardened into rock. Their
bodies had decayed, but the hollow forms had remained to be filled,
eventually, with the plaster poured in by archeologists. I studied them
all with morbid fascination, and my father, when he came back, told
me that lovers in the brothel had been frozen that way, too. To
imagine the actual entwining of lovers was a hard thing at ten. To
imagine them frozen by hot ash was something I pondered all the
way home, and I prayed that Positano was beyond the range of the
smoldering mountain.

Everything was working out for us. A letter from Reed College
had arrived at last, after missing us in Florence, and it offered my
father a teaching job for a year. With the money he'd be making there,
and from The New Yorker, he'd have almost as much as the salary he'd
left behind in advertising. Jim Dickey in Positano had the energy of a
man who might die tomorrow, or never, and he was writing with a
sense of absolute certainty.

More than thirty years later, I wanted, in the house in Columbia
where the oxygen machine gave him his breath and the air smelled of
disinfectant, to give some of that energy, some of that magic back to
him; and maybe to get some of it back from him.

"What poems did you write in Positano?" I asked him.

"Oh God, I don't know, I'll have to look them up in the book."
He took a copy of his last and most complete collection, The Whole
Motion, off one of the high-piled stacks within reach of his withered
arm. "They would be the poems in Helmets. I wrote 'The Dusk of
Horses.' I wrote 'Fence Wire.' I wrote 'At Darien Bridge'—in Rome. I
remember sending it in from the post office down there right at the
Spanish Steps. I wrote 'Chenille.' I wrote 'On the Coosawattee.' I
wrote 'Winter Trout.' I wrote 'Springer Mountain.' "

"You wrote 'Springer Mountain' in Positano?"

"That's right."

"All right. All right! Now we're getting into it." We were going to talk about the writing of the novel and the making of the movie *Deliverance*, and "Springer Mountain" was key. A young agent in New York, Theron Raines, saw the poem in *The Virginia Quarterly Review* and wrote my father a letter wondering if he would consider writing a novel based on this idea of the suburbanite as hunter and hunted.

"Yeah." My father smiled and shook his head. "I wrote 'The Scarred Girl' in Positano. I wrote 'Kudzu' in Positano. I wrote 'The Beholders' and 'The Poisoned Man' and 'Marble Quarry' and 'A Folk Singer of the Thirties,' all in Positano."

"Damn."

"All in *The New Yorker*. I wrote 'The Being' in Positano. I wrote 'Breath,' which is a good father-son poem. I wrote 'The Ice Skin'— which is about you."

It was a poem I did not remember.

"I wrote 'Bums, on Waking,' " my father went on. "You remember those two town bums in Positano that they used to find sleeping in the church? I wrote that about them. 'Goodbye to Serpents' "—that poem about the Jardin des Plantes—"I wrote there. I wrote 'In the Child's Night' there. I wrote 'Approaching Prayer' there. I wrote 'The Driver' before I left Atlanta, and the money from *The New Yorker* on that one poem sustained us over the last of my period of being on relief. 'The Driver.' I wrote 'Horses and Prisoners.' 'Drinking from a Helmet' I started there and finished at Reed. So most of *Helmets* was written there. And the book was ready to go after that. And the whole of *Deliverance* got started."

With just that little nudge from the agent in New York, the basic narrative took shape quickly, growing out of the canoe wreck with Al, from the scenery on the Coosawattee, from the life among the gray affable men in Atlanta—and all of it building to the climactic scene when a middle-aged man at the limit of his powers, Ed Gentry—Jim Dickey, climbs the sheer face of a cliff with his bare hands.

"I wrote 'The Ice Skin'—which is about you," my father had said.

I should have taken the book from him then, and read it, and reread it, because in fact it was about us and our whole lives, this poem about ice written on the sun-washed balcony in Positano. "All things that go deep enough / Into rain and cold / Take on, before they break down, / A shining in every part." I see us in an ice storm, like the ones that sweep through Atlanta every year, when the branches of the trees are weighted beyond their power to hold, "Until a cannon goes off / Somewhere inside the still trunk / And a limb breaks, just before midnight, / Plunging houses into the darkness / And hands into cupboards, all seeking / Candles, and finding each other." And the poem turns the ice skin of the trees to the ice skin of an airplane's canopy in war, or the glaze of death on a lost relative taken on like a mantle by the living, or the barrier of glass in a hospital ward: "Through the window of ice / I have stared at my son in his cage, / Just born, just born." And then:

> My son now stands with his head
> At my shoulder. I
>
> Stand, stooping more, but the same,
> Not knowing whether
> I will break before I can feel,
>
> Before I can give up my powers,
> Or whether the ice light
> In my eyes will ever snap off
> Before I die. I am still,
> And my son, doing what he was taught,
> Listening hard for a buried cannon,
> Stands also, calm as glass.

Years before he drove me away, I thought, he had always known I would come back.

BARNSTORMING

Portland, Oregon. On the last day of seventh grade, at the beginning of the summer of 1963, I was racing home for lunch on my Raleigh ten-speed when the cuff of my pants caught in the sprocket and stopped me dead. By the time I realized what had happened I was on the pavement. I could see I was covered in blood from a cut on my chin that was still flowing red, and my left arm, which hurt like hell, had an extra bend between the elbow and the wrist. The bone hadn't quite come out through the skin, but you could see where it was trying to. I walked to the nearest door and knocked on it, and the man in a bathrobe who opened it told me to lie down on his driveway. Other kids from school who were going to lunch, or coming back, passed me and stared at me, not sure what to do. And Officer MacBrier came and called an ambulance and my father. And my father arrived before the ambulance did.

It was my father who remembered MacBrier's name, more than thirty-three years later. My father had never forgotten any detail of the fear he felt that afternoon.

God, I was glad he was there. There had been times before, and there would be many times afterward, when he made me feel as if I were just an excuse for his overplayed emotions. But Jim Dickey was not putting on a show that afternoon in Portland as he sat on that stranger's driveway beside me waiting for the ambulance to come, or as he held my good right hand while they wheeled me on the gurney to the operating room. I still remember the gentle strength of his grip, and the strength it gave me.

When I came out of the anesthetic it was late afternoon, and in the recovery room around me there were adults just recovering consciousness. Some of them were groaning in pain and in fear of death in a way I had never heard. I couldn't speak yet, because of the drugs, couldn't even ask what was going on as a woman pleaded with God and cursed the doctors. I had been in hospitals before, for a tonsillectomy and such, but always in the protected world of the children's wards in Atlanta. Now I was surrounded by the agony of adults in a white-walled purgatory. After a few minutes I was wheeled back out to the corridor, to my parents, and taken home. And I had never been so happy to be there.

For most of that year and a half we were in Oregon, we lived on the edge of the wild. We rented a ramshackle mansion overlooking the wide, brown Willamette River, and for a while the adventure we began in Europe felt like it was still going on in the spectacular landscapes of the West. We had driven all the way across the country, from Atlanta to Los Angeles, then up the coast to Portland. My mother and Kevin were usually in the VW bus, my father and I in the MG, and there were times, as we rolled into the West Texas sunsets, when it really did feel like we were on our way to some All-American Promised Land. My father and I, convoying in the rear, would watch my mother drive over a rise that looked out on expanses of sandstone and saguaro cactus, and she would just spread her arms and wave like she wanted to embrace it all.

My father was still making my head. As I nestled in the black bucket seat of that blue MG, I'd listen to him tell me the Mars stories again, and we'd talk about Doc Savage. And now he started to make up verses and to pull me into that game, too. From somewhere around Baton Rouge until we rolled into Portland, we were making up a children's poem called "Kevin the Diver" in which a little boy—my little brother—discovers the ocean. The only couplet I remember is "Kevin the Diver whooped with glee, / As the mullet school took over the sea."

We drove coast to coast across the United States four times in the four years between my eleventh and fifteenth birthdays. We felt like Woody Guthrie claiming the land. We got to feeling familiar with wide-open highways and towns we'd never heard of before, like Tucumcari, New Mexico. "A town of nothing but motels—and swimming pools," my father remembered. "We came across the desert and came to that place with all those swimming pools." And even when we had our place in Oregon we kept rolling: west to the rolling dunes and haystack rocks of the Pacific shore, or up onto Mount Hood, or north to the prosperity of Seattle and the tranquillity of British Columbia.

But as much as we traveled together, my father was now traveling more by himself.

James Dickey had given some poetry readings before we'd moved to Oregon. There was the infamous encounter with the Pen Women of Gainesville, of course, and a nice little presentation before martinis and whisky at Edna Lewis's place in Positano. "The first reading I gave was in Houston, when we were teaching," as my father recalled. "I had published a few things in magazines, and a church group asked me to read. And a few people went to it, maybe six or seven or eight—ten? —in a basement of a church. And they had never had anybody address their group except ministers, I guess, so the lady who introduced me hardly knew what to say about what I was gonna do. I read other people mainly. I told Maxine I didn't have enough to read of my own. And she said, Well, read somebody else's and throw some of yours in somewhere as you see fit. So I said okay. But I was on sort of a death kick in those days. Death, war and mutilation, and all that. And I read those. After my appearance, there was a polite spattering of applause and the lady got up and said, 'We all want to thank Mr. Dickey for that nice message.' "

When he was in Atlanta, the few reading trips he made exposed his poetry to the world and the world of other poets to him. After his first book was published, he'd been invited to read at Hollins College in Virginia with Randall Jarrell and Katherine Anne Porter. "That was a big jump for me," he said. Jarrell had written about the war, he loved German poetry, he was looking for his own muscular, controlled, powerful voice. "Randall Jarrell was the most brilliant man that I ever conversed with for five minutes," my father remembered from his armchair in Columbia. "He knew everything and he knew it his own way. He was so learned and so quick and so opinionated. I mean, you talked to him, and any topic that came up, he was right on it. And he knew forty times more than you did about it. But he was not ostentatious at all. He'd talk about Browning. It was fashionable not to like Browning's verse. He says, 'Yeah, but people don't understand him. You know that poem where . . . ,' and he starts quoting from it. He says, 'Now, that's good, isn't it?' I say, 'Yeah, I didn't know about that.' He says, 'Now you do. That is good. Don't you think so?' Randall Jarrell was the only person I ever knew who was more interested in your work than he was in his. He was working on 'The Owl King' with me up at Hollins. He says, 'This is great right in here. Suppose you shorten this down and you cut this down.' And we were just— working on my poetry. He was so much more interested in it than he was in anything else. He never brought anything of his up. He was interested in mine. I was pretty well unknown at the time, and he was an extremely giving type of a guy."

It was only after we got to Portland that my father really began to tour—to perform. He called it barnstorming for poetry: "I made a hundred dollars a reading. I read all around the University of Oregon and Washington—and California some of the time. I had two and a half books by then. I remember talking to your mother. I said, 'You know, it's terribly arrogant to get up and read your own work and get paid for it.' And she said, 'Well, you are a teacher, you get up in front of a class every day.' I said, 'Yeah, but this is different from all that. I feel real self-conscious doing so much of it.' She said, 'Now, you go up there, Jim. We need the money.' I said, 'Okay, I will try to find a way to do it.' She said, 'Just get up there and be yourself.' Which sounded fine at the time, until I got to thinking about it. Be myself. Yeah. But which one? I never did figure that out completely."

He was quoting himself. Jim Dickey knew all along what was happening to him on those tours—"the living-up-to, the giving them what they want, or might be expected to feel entitled to from a poet" —and had written about it in a long, only slightly fictionalized tale, "Barnstorming for Poetry," about a swing through the Wisconsin winter in 1964–65. "The self he has become on this trip bears but little relation to the self he left at home in the mind, say, of his wife." The poet has taken to carrying a guitar with him and picking out a few songs at the inevitable parties given after his readings, "satisfied that he has done the something idiosyncratic that people are expecting and that, much more dangerous to psychological stability, he expects of himself." The tone of the piece was at once ironic and ecstatic, like many of his best poems. But also a little coy. The barnstorming poet "has never been lionized by anyone, not even his immediate family; but these small, repeated tastes of local notoriety are definitely agreeable, and he does his best to live up to them."

I used to read and reread this essay, as if its exegesis could tell me what went wrong, and partly it does. The poet is worried about middle age, about losing his talent, about losing his hair and teeth. "At the outset of the trip he had thought that the poems themselves would be enough; if they were good, and he read them well, he could collect his money at each stop with a clear conscience. But it is he who is not satisfied with *just* reading; it is not only poetry that is involved: it is the poet as well." The poet is drinking a lot, much more than usual, and enjoys it. Drunkenness gives him a divine sense of license, and, hell, Dylan Thomas drank. It's what poets do. Under the ecstatic influence, he says outrageous things at parties, and labors through the days with terrible hangovers. "Yet he has in some obscure way been a good deal better satisfied with himself . . . and is now looking forward to acquiring the courage to get drunk *before* the reading." He hitchhikes to one commitment. At another he finds himself housed in a monk's cell, left to contemplate a skull. At a girls' school a student asks if she can kiss him. "He agrees without thinking, and she does it with startling ardor." At still another snowbound college he has to read above the noise of a fraternity boy smashing a car with a sledgehammer in the middle distance, and the poems pick up the rhythm. He is always on the verge of exaltation—and silliness. But he has loved what he has become. "He begins walking with students trailing him as though he were a messiah or a Beatle":

> Everyone seems pleased by the way things have gone; there have even been some letters of appreciation from the schools. But he is still bothered by the difference between his touring self and his usual self. He has definitely been another person on this trip: more excitable and emotional, more harried, more impulsive. Yet he knows that these qualities will die out upon his arrival home and he is more than a little glad of it; they are too wearing, too hard on the nerves. He might live more vividly in this condition, but he cannot write in it. He must calm down and work. But on the aircraft aimed at last at his home, he feels also that such nervous excitement, such over-responsiveness to things, is probably the poet's part. Intensity, he murmurs, where have you been all my life?

The poet of "Barnstorming" seems to have thought that his wife and children (actually, there were no children for this fictionalized character) would miss the tension between the two selves, or that they wouldn't care. And when we lived in Oregon my father still believed, I think, that he could keep the two separate. As he had been an adman by day and a struggling poet by night, now he would be the wild man of the readings on the road, and the hardworking writer, loving father, and attentive husband at home. But the wildness started to settle in there, too.

It felt like a good time a lot of the time. The house by the river was so big, with fireplaces in just about every room, a brick terrace overlooking the water, and a big glassed-in porch with a Ping-Pong table, that my parents felt it would be a shame not to give parties. And just about every Sunday they did. Bacon and eggs and Ramos gin fizzes at eleven in the morning for a handful of students and favored members of the faculty: Ottomar, the Afrika Korps veteran now in command of the German department; and Sam, the Greek Jew who was head of the French department; and Fred, the literature teacher who played bass at local jazz clubs and did handsprings on the lawn after a couple of fizzes. There on the glass porch, table tennis was a game of unbridled passion, ferocious competition, surrogate revenge for everything from slights in faculty meetings to the outcome of World War II. And when the matches were over, and everyone was out of breath, my father would pick up one of the new guitars he'd bought himself, maybe one of the twelve-strings, and fit picks on his thumb and two fingers and bang out a few of the songs he'd learned from local folksingers: "Handsome Molly" or "Stewball" or a piece he'd heard played by a couple of guys named Mike Russo and Ron Brentano that they called "Dueling Banjos." Ah, intensity. It was good to be drunk. It was fun. And it was great to be living this kind of life in this kind of place. And Jim Dickey was starting to write the best poems of his career. And starting to work, seriously now, on *Deliverance*. What could be wrong with that?

But we all knew something was wrong. And we even knew the drinking was part of it. The alcohol kept flowing just the same. The first time I remember my father trying to quit drinking was the year before, in Europe. It was his idea. He didn't like what was happening to his body. And for a day or so he talked about how much better he felt. But he was tense and his patience disappeared. For any reason and no reason he would turn his anger on my mother, or on me or my brother. And after a couple of days we were pleading with him to have a drink. When he would go away on the reading tours, there was no reason to quit drinking, and in some obscure way he was better satisfied with himself. When he came back, he didn't want to stop, didn't see why he should. And he found my mother drinking, too. And drinking now steadily, almost conspiratorially. She didn't hide her drinking, but she didn't call attention to it, either. She just kept at it every night. And if my father said he was going to quit, she would offer him another Ramos fizz, or just a highball, or a beer. As a couple, they started to treat alcohol as a sort of necessary lubricant to ease the frictions between them, and, often, to fuel the rage they really felt.

"*Ass-man!*" I heard my mother screaming downstairs one night— really screaming, hysterical, raging, crying, not sure if she wanted to throw my father or herself out of the house, screaming so loud that anyone nearby could have heard—so loud that I could hear even if I was in my upstairs bedroom, even if I was on the top floor, in one of the rooms of the empty servants' quarters, where I would go to be alone. No matter where I went, though, I would hear her screaming. And she knew it. I couldn't make out most of the words, but I could hear my name.

The dialogue was one I knew well. At least since we lived in Atlanta, there had been times when my father would sit me down with my mother nearby and tell me that they were getting a divorce. And I would plead with them not to. And not only would they not—a day later, or even hours later, they would act as if nothing had happened. Now I was twelve years old. Old enough to know this game, old enough to think I was cynical about it.

"Show him the letter," my mother shouted at my father.

"I don't—"

"Show him the goddamned *letter!*" she screamed.

My father's teeth closed hard against each other, his lips pulled back a little, his nostrils flared, and he squinted narrowly, meanly, in that pig-eyed animal face that was frightening when I was little, but that seemed theatrical and vaguely contemptible by the time I was twelve. It had even less effect on my mother. He made a gesture of resignation, throwing his arms in the air. His face relaxed and saddened. He handed me a letter in an opened envelope.

I didn't recognize the name. "Who's she?" I asked.

"Your father's whore," my mother said.

I looked at the letter, but couldn't seem to focus on it. The young woman who wrote it (I remember my mother discovering, somehow, that she was only in her twenties, and this made all the hurt that much worse) was writing to Dad in the language of the road, that half-bawdy bullshit tongue of late, drunken nights and forced, faked ecstasy. I knew the tone even if I didn't know anything else about what had happened, and my mother knew it better than I did. And in the middle of it the girl says she knows he's "a real ass-man." Short of a straight-out reminiscence about fucking and sucking, it could hardly have been clearer. But—"I don't think you should blame Dad for this," is more or less what I said to my mother. She looked as if I'd hit her in the stomach. "This is what this girl wants to say," I tried to explain to her and to myself. "You know. She sort of thinks it's—" My mother looked like hunted prey, defeated and exhausted, as she turned and retreated to the kitchen. My father nodded, and maybe smiled a little. But I thought somehow that this was really what *she* wanted to hear. My mother didn't want righteous anger. She wanted desperately to be wrong, even if she knew—and we all knew—that she wasn't.

"What are we going to do, Chrissy?" my father asked me. I didn't know. And I didn't know why I *should* know.

"Did you—?" I asked him.

"No." He shook his head. "No."

The rage and tears went on for hours, but the dialogue was all the same. My mother's accusation, my father's denial, my scrambling to make it all somehow all right. Kevin was brought into it, too. He was four or five by then, and he came down the stairs sleepy and upset, and my mother held him and kissed him and pulled him to her side. He pleaded with her not to leave. "Nobody's going to leave," my father said. "Nobody's going to leave, honey," my mother said. And nobody did. Eventually we all went to bed in separate rooms. And the next day we acted as if everything was okay. But it couldn't be.

I saw that night, as I'd never seen before, that my father was living a life that wasn't about us and that threatened us as a family, because it threatened my mother's whole sense of what the family was and who she was, and that he thought he could just hide it and lie about it like a kid smoking cigarettes behind the garage. And I saw that my mother was getting hard, the kind of hard you are when your life comes apart in front of you and you look around and see you've got no one to depend on, no one who'll support you, not even anyone to talk to, and you just sort of shrug to yourself and say less and less to anyone and take another drink.

We still planned adventures as a family. We still went camping together in our aging Volkswagen bus and the tents we'd had in Europe. We'd drive deep into the mountain forests, which were so much bigger and wilder than anything we'd seen in the Appalachians. My mother, who never came with us when we were hunting in Georgia, would make it a point to come on these trips. She would pack deviled eggs and other picnic food, and help set up the camp, and she was good at it. Even in the wilderness she'd make a home. And my father would tell her what a good pioneer woman she'd have been. She would smile, and more often than not change the subject.

Elk wandered in the woods near our camps, and bear were close by, too. The enormous trees and the huge rivers boiling over homicidal rocks had an intimidating beauty. My father did not hunt these woods, did not canoe these waters, and never really did write about Oregon. At least not as such. I can remember one night in the forest in 1964 being truly terrified for no reason: just lying in the tent imagining, sleepless, all that could happen to us in this wilderness, and falling to sleep, finally, with the comfort of my father's strong hand resting on my forehead to let me know that he was, and would be, there. But that was the last time I felt that way. We were going through the motions of family. This land did not feel like our land; neither the sense of adventure nor the illusion of escape seemed complete. And we did not feel like we were together in it.

At the end of "Barnstorming," the poet settles down in his airplane seat to fly home and become again "an older and more dependable self," but he believes that, on the road, at the readings, among the admirers, "remembering the skull in the room, a plain girl's unexpected kiss," as the messiah-celebrity "for better or worse, he has been moving and speaking among his kind." We were not my father's kind any more. But we all wanted to believe, still, that we could be.

THE
NIGHT POOL

Jim Dickey had a recurring dream that made him happy. In it several friends would be sitting around a swimming pool and talking. There was nothing special about the pool itself. Nobody walked on the water. And he never told me who the friends were. Maybe he didn't want to say, or maybe he didn't really know. But what he took away from the dream was a sense of contentment, of being at ease with himself and the world, as if he had gotten a preview of heaven. He called that place "the happy swimming pool."

When I first heard my father talk about the dream, we were in Atlanta and I wasn't ten years old. But it came up again and again as it would recur, or he'd wish that it would recur. And sometimes I'd ask him about it, because just thinking about it seemed to make him feel so good.

My father loved the ocean, rivers, lakes. Wherever we went he was drawn to them, and if we could, we lived near them, and if we could not, he sought them out. "Shall We Gather at the River" was his favorite spiritual, and the phrase was a refrain in our lives and in his work; you'd think that for a white-water man like him a swimming pool would be a pitiful substitute, but it wasn't. A pool—even a public pool—was about a certain kind of community, about youth and beauty and ease, about nature contained and clement, about a certain time, a certain kind of life. "All your earthly debts are canceled while you are in a heated pool in the middle of a cold night," he once said. "You're in the warm, amniotic fluid of the pool, comfortable and protected, and the effect is superhuman. You never want to leave."

In the summer of 1964, we moved to Los Angeles, California, to the flat expanses of ranch homes, strip malls, and garden apartments that were Northridge. My father was taking up a new writer-in-residence job at San Fernando Valley State College; my mother and Kevin and I looked at houses perched on hillsides, we looked at Sheetrocked apartments decorated like haciendas and Roman atria, we dreamed about living on the beach in Malibu, on the far, far side of the city, but there was never really any doubt we'd get a place in the Valley with a pool.

The house we finally found was an old and slightly sad little cedar-sided bungalow set back from Balboa Boulevard, just across the street from a huge discount mart. The yard was spotty and dry, front and back; the cinderblock wall on one side was unpainted, and the wooden fence on the other was splintering; and there would have been nothing to recommend the place at all if it had not had a pool. But it did, and the pool is where we lived.

A lot of the time when we were alone we were naked. My father, even in the middle of the afternoon, would sunbathe in the back yard, and whenever we opened the front door to visitors we had to look over our shoulders to make sure he couldn't be seen visibly stitchless through the picture windows at the back. "Cover yourself up, Jim," my mother would shout, and he'd put a battered Frisbee over his genitals. There were afternoons when he'd come inside and all of his body would be a painful red except for the white circle that stretched from just below his navel to the top of his thighs. "Been playing with my Frisbee," he'd say on the way to the shower.

On a hot night after supper, my father would look at my mother and smile and say *"senza pantaloni,"* and sometimes she would demur, but often she would not, and the two of them would descend into the chilled water. Sometimes Kevin and I would join them. Swimming beneath the surface, I would see the blurred shapes of my parents in the shadows of the shallow end, but pay no attention. I would swim breathless into the deep, homing in on the shimmering spotlight like a cold moon, then turning and swimming, still below the water, back to the other end, erupting there at last with an explosion of breath to hear my mother and father talking quietly as they treaded water, and laughing softly.

My mother liked to swim at night, liked to be naked in the water in the shadows. She did not like to swim in the day, did not like to see her body as it was reflected in the picture windows, swelling now with the alcohol and the beginnings of menopause; did not like to hear my father tell her she had to lose some weight or have him shout to her and to the empty air of Balboa Boulevard, "Hath seen the white whale?" But you could never be sure when he would do that, and the dark was not protection. His tenderness could turn to cruelty with little warning and for no cause. And I remember nights in the pool when my mother would be laughing one minute, and leaving in tears the next.

I do not know if she knew then about the other woman my father loved.

Her name was Robin Jarecki, and I don't believe I ever met her, but I might have. My parents used to give a lot of beer parties around the pool, the place would be packed with students and their friends and their friends' friends, and she could have been one of those. She was in her late twenties, a little older than the rest. Some of them knew her. Later, he would say he first met Robin at the American Express in Rome, there by the Spanish Steps, and talked to her there. Maybe I met her then, and forgot.

A couple of years after we'd left California, when Robin was dead and my father wanted to draw me into his mourning, he showed me a picture of a woman with long dark hair pulled back off her face, her generous mouth smiling, her warm eyes looking straight into the camera. She looked intelligent, and happy. All he told me was that they had lived together in Milwaukee when he spent a few months teaching at the University of Wisconsin in 1965. And he told me that she had died in Los Angeles. "I loved that woman," he said. And it seems to me that I asked my father why he hadn't left my mother and married Robin. I was sixteen by then and thought I was mature and cynical. And he just said, "It wasn't meant to be."

There were a lot of little snatches of memory from California that didn't make sense until I knew that my father had had several lovers there, and that Robin, whom he adored, had been just out of our sight. My father came into my room one night full of energy to announce, "I must have fucked a thousand women in my life." And I, who had fucked none at age fourteen, couldn't figure out why he was telling me this. We weren't comparing notes. He was just feeling mighty good about that particular woman he'd been fucking that particular day, but he couldn't say that. Another time he brought back an old leather-bound book about hunting that he said he'd won at an archery tournament. But it had nothing to do with archery. It was an eighteenth-century treatise on foxhounds, how to breed and train them, and it included an amazing word-list of potential names for every member of the pack: "Passion" or "Celerity" or "Fidelity." It was a present from Robin, he told me years later. He couldn't part with it, but couldn't really explain it. So he told an easy, implausible lie and let my mother and the rest of us think what we would.

Students came to the house all the time to talk, to drink, to hold forth. But there was one, Michael Allin, who had come to our place in Northridge like a child adopting parents. He was an enthralled admirer of James Dickey, like a lot of others, but he was also an attentive listener to Maxine Dickey, who could talk to him in ways she could not talk to sons who were too young or too close to their father to understand. Michael began to accompany us on trips, ostensibly to take care of me and Kevin, but mostly because my mother enjoyed his company so much. Michael was wound so tight if you touched him it was like knocking a top off balance, you weren't sure which wall he'd bounce off of. He vibrated with nervous energy and fresh ideas, and he was always looking for a way to get close to us by impressing us with how much he understood about the least details of our lives. He shared our house, our table, and, with each of us individually, our secrets. Including, with my father, the secret of his other women, and of Robin.

One afternoon, as Michael remembered later, my father and one of his lovers had been together at a motel—one of those places where a cheap painting of an Indian welcoming the sunrise hangs on the wall above the bed—and he asked Michael to pick him up afterward at the Valley State library. Michael found him inside the entrance sitting on the stairs. By the time they got to our house it was already dark. No one was home. The lights were out. And that put my father into an eerie panic. Michael went around turning on lamps. My father was really worried and kept saying he had "a terrible feeling that something's wrong." A few minutes later my mother came home with Kevin and me, and my father grabbed her in his arms. Loving the affection, laughing, she teased him about worrying. "I don't like coming home to a dark house," he said.

Most of the James Dickey poems I know best are ones I have heard over and over again. When we lived in California, we started going to a lot of his readings. A few that were out of town would be made into family expeditions. And when James Dickey went back to Houston in triumph to read at Rice for the first time since 1954, even Michael came with us.

I got to know not only lines and stanzas by heart, but also James Dickey's introductions describing the people or incidents on which the poems were based. He was still writing at a phenomenal pace, and he had turned a corner in his poetry. It was weird, wonderful stuff, especially when he wrote—and read—about the power of sex. He'd use "Cherrylog Road" to warm up the crowd, the story of a motorcycle-riding kid making love to a cracker girl in the back of a junkyard car, then tearing away up Highway 106, "Wringing the handlebar for speed, / Wild to be wreckage forever." Like a disc jockey pacing his show, he'd work in poems with different moods, different beats, then spring something like "The Fiend" on his audience. Maybe he would cite the French poet Paul Claudel and say it was important to him that a woman be "the promise that cannot be kept," then, in the next breath, he'd talk about the vice-squad cop who supposedly wrote him to say, "I just want you to know that I've always had a lot of secret sympathy with you fellows." (Much later, in fact, serial killer Ted Bundy would correspond with my father from jail, but I think that was more about movie and book deals than about poetry.)

"The Fiend" begins in the branches of a tree outside the window of a girl seen chewing gum and talking on the telephone. A man in a seersucker suit and Panama hat (dressed, oddly, the way my father's father used to dress) watches and waits.

> . . . *She touches one button at her throat, and rigor mortis*
> *Slithers into his pockets, making everything there—keys, pen*
> *and secret love—stand up.   He brings from those depths the knife*
> *And flicks it open   it glints on the moon one time   carries*
> *Through the dead walls   making a wormy static on the TV screen.*
> *He parts the swarm of gnats that live excitedly at this perilous level*
> *Parts the rarefied light high windows give out into inhabited trees*
> *Opens his lower body to the moon. . . .*

The audience would titter, and fall silent, and love it. Or Jim Dickey would hit them with the weird, primal beauty of "The Sheep Child," which, he explained, is about the creature, half man and half beast, that farm boys warn each other may come from coupling with sheep. Most of the poem is told from the perspective of this little thing in a formaldehyde bottle on a forgotten shelf in a museum in Atlanta, and my father would always say that it might not be the best poem ever written, but you could not fault it for originality of point of view.

> . . . *I woke, dying,*
>
> *In the summer sun of the hillside, with my eyes*
> *Far more than human. I saw for a blazing moment*
> *The great grassy world from both sides,*

Man and beast in the round of their need,
And the hill wind stirred in my wool,
My hoof and my hand clasped each other,
I ate my one meal
Of milk, and died
Staring. . . .

Or he would just blow them away with "Falling," an inspired rush of mythical sensation as a stewardess accidentally plunges out of an airplane's emergency door toward the fields of Kansas, knowing she is going to die, stripping off her blouse, her skirt, everything:

Her last superhuman act   the last slow careful passing of her hands
All over her unharmed body   desired by every sleeper in his dream . . .

In the last stanza she lies broken-backed, embedded in the loam of a field as her clothes drift down all over the Midwest. She is not quite dead. She

Feels herself go   go toward   go outward   breathes at last fully
Not   and tries   less   once   tries   tries   AH, GOD—

Ah, God. At some readings James Dickey was triumphant, and the audience was on its feet. At some he was a spectacle of slurred words and awkward silences—and still he got a standing ovation. And I got used to that, more or less. But when he read the poems about himself and about us, I couldn't get over the idea that something was missing. My father was a better man, I thought, a braver man, more wise and loving and even more mystical than he would let on in public. His poet persona puzzled and angered and disappointed me. This half-drunk world he invented at the readings was less mysterious and exciting than the world as it was—or had been—his world, our world, the world that he had given us.

"Encounter in the Cage Country" was a great crowd-pleaser—one of those poems where he'd stop himself in the middle and shake his head and say, "Isn't that good?" and everyone would laugh and applaud—and it *is* damned good, but it was the first poem I heard him read where I thought he'd taken the easy way out.

I had been there. In London in 1962, we had gone to the zoo, of course, and we were just sort of strolling, as people do in zoos, through the building full of lions and tigers when the black panther saw my father in the crowd and dropped the bloody joint of meat he chewed and followed every step as we walked by.

At first my father didn't notice. "Daddy, look," I said, spooked. "Look."

Jim Dickey's eyes caught the animal's. Held them. Then, sensing the power of the moment, he walked back and forth in front of the cage. The big cat followed each move. My father looked at me and arched his brows. What was happening? Then he looked at the animal again, and the animal's eyes had never left him. Jim Dickey feinted in one direction, then jogged in the other like a broken-field runner, but he couldn't wrong-foot the panther. He moved out of sight of the cage. The cat waited, watching, his breath measured, his mouth open just enough to hint at the teeth within, his yellow-green eyes expectant, until my father came back into his view, and then, again, he followed him. Children and adults were starting to crowd around, curious and amazed. An old woman wondered if my father was an off-duty keeper, or if this were a trick. But nobody there, especially my father, had any idea what was going on. There was nothing unusual about what he was wearing, nothing at all. The reasons behind this moment were all in the panther's mind, more hidden than the spots beneath the black.

For the sake of the poem, Jim Dickey told the world and his audiences that he was wearing bottle-green aviator glasses that day we visited the big cats, as if that was the key. At the end of the poem is the voice of the animal: "... we know you / When you come, Green Eyes, Green Eyes." But my father wasn't wearing dark glasses that day. The connection between him and the animal was genuinely mysterious—and mystical. It seemed to me, an intolerant teenager, my father's son, better not to have written the poem at all than to have turned the handwriting of God into a plug for Ray-Bans.

James Dickey would tell how six-year-old Kevin panicked when a bee came after him near a busy road in California. I was there, too. Dad took a couple of steps, reached out, and grabbed Kevin to keep him from backing into traffic. That was all that happened. In the poem "The Bee," Dickey the wingback-poet-father has to summon up all the old discipline and drive shouted into him by the rough-mouthed coaches of Clemson. "If your knee action is high / Enough, the fat may fall in time   God damn / You, Dickey, dig...." But Dickey never wrote about—never even talked about—his sprint to the edge of the chasm and beyond at the ski lift in Italy, when he really had risked his life to save his son. And the remembered coaches really had saved him.

In some of my father's work he killed us off. I thought that was to be expected. But the poem was the poem, I thought, and what we lived was what we lived. We ought to be able to keep that straight. From my seventh-grade bicycle accident, Dickey extracted "The Aura," about remembering a dead teenage son whose transistor-radio music followed him around the house wherever he went, and "Them, Crying," about *the superhuman tenderness of strangers.*" He would say that I was hit by a car and spent days near death, and he would turn the whole tale into one about his loathing for hospitals—"charnel houses," as he called them. And that became a part of his script, a dose of righteous anger that was practiced and predictable. He would say that Kevin almost died of the flu in Positano, whereas, in fact, he was just a sick little boy for a couple of days. "For a doctor to tell me that the person I love has something that nothing can be done about makes me feel murderous," he told one interviewer. But when he said that, no doctor had ever given him that news.

We were living with the sad memories and impending threat of imagined tragedies, made-up illnesses: the first wife in Australia who never was and died of blood poisoning she never had; the diabetes that my father, who had not the slightest hint of the disease, announced would cost him his life; the minor back injury that almost paralyzed him; the plaster in his eyes that nearly blinded him. He was always just about to die of anything but what was really hurting him, the drinking. And it wasn't until we were together at the house in Columbia and he really was sick and really was lucid that I realized he never believed a lot of that shit himself. It was all a game. It served his needs, he said. But it didn't do justice to anyone my father loved: not Kevin or me or Bronwen, not my mother, or Deborah, or even Robin. Not even Dad. And it showed a part of him that was purely selfish. But, still, that was better than the part that was purely cruel.

My father wrote one poem in those days that my mother clung to as hers, "The Night Pool," about a man and woman swimming together in the chill of the evening. They step out of the water and it is colder still. They kiss "and her lips / Turn blue, sealed against me." And all that he can give her, all that he needs to give her, is to "wrap her in many towels." The image of nurturing care and affection is perfect, and my mother was proud of that poem. She used to talk to Michael about it, hold it up as a kind of vindication of my father's love. But when James Dickey had gotten famous enough, in 1968, to be interviewed about almost every verse he'd ever published, he said this one—about "when love is really love"—was about some other woman he didn't name.

* * *

The little auditorium at Rice University was not full. Maybe my father was disappointed by that. But I was in the audience, and Kevin, and Michael and my mother, and a lot of old friends who had been in Houston since the days when we lived there. My father was drunk onstage, and disoriented. It was difficult to watch him, but I knew the old friends would make excuses. They always did. We always did. He held the sides of the podium, partly to steady himself, partly to act as if he could control the audience, could steer it with that square slab of wood, could kick-start it with inspiration. Then he ran his forefinger back and forth under his broad nose and shook his head, and began.

I don't remember all the poems he read that night. There would have been a couple of war poems, an animal poem or two, a hunting or a canoeing poem. "Isn't that good?" The audience laughed, warming to him. I think James Dickey read "The Fiend" that night, or possibly "The Sheep Child." And then, I remember clearly, the poem he introduced as something new. He said the title was "Adultery." He looked up at the audience—all the audience, without focusing. He ran his finger under his nose again and smirked, a little like a teenager who's been jerking off and thinks you don't know. "Oh, don't," I thought. "Ah, no, Dad." And he began:

> *We have all been in rooms*
> *We cannot die in, and they are odd places, and sad.*
> *Often Indians are standing eagle-armed on hills*
>
> *In the sunrise   open wide to the Great Spirit*

(Dickey throws wide his arms. He *is* the Great Spirit. He is going to rouse the audience whether it wants to be roused or not.)

> *Or gliding in canoes   or cattle are browsing on the walls*
> *Far away   gazing down with the eyes of our children*
>
> *Not far away. . . .*

(I could not not look at my mother. Her eyes were slightly watery, but no more than they usually were in the evening. Her features sagged on her face. She just stared straight ahead.)

> *. . . There is always some weeping*
> *Between us   and someone is always checking*

> *A wrist watch by the bed to see how much*
> *Longer we have left.*

(A scene from a movie, I thought, hoping I could find a way to say he was making this up.)

> *Nothing can come*
> *Of this   nothing can come*
>
> *Of us: of me with my grim techniques*
> *Or you who have sealed your womb*
> *With a ring of convulsive rubber:*

(Ah, Jesus, Dad.)

> *Although we come together,*
> *Nothing will come of us.*

(Oh, come on.)

> *But we would not give*
> *It up, for death is beaten*
>
> *By praying Indians   by distant cows   historical*
> *Hammers   by hazardous meetings that bridge*
> *A continent. One could never die here*
>
> *Never die   never die*
> *While crying. My lover, my dear one*
> *I will see you next week*
>
> *When I'm in town. I will call you*
> *If I can. Please get hold of   please don't*

(Breathlessness on stage.)

> *Oh God, Please don't any more I can't bear . . . Listen:*
>
> *We have done it again   we are*
> *Still living. Sit up and smile,*
> *God bless you. Guilt is magical.*

(End. A thin smattering of uneasy applause. And fuck you, Dad.)

* * *

Robin died of a brain tumor, my father told me that day a year or two later when he showed me her picture and looked for me to console him. And apart from "Adultery," as far as I know he wrote only three other things about her. One was a work-in-progress called "The Indian Maiden" after the dirty song he used to try to teach me when I was a little boy. One was a poem called "Exchanges" which he delivered as the Phi Beta Kappa Poem at Harvard in 1970. He links his discovery of poetry and her loss and the blastoff of a Saturn V—"Apollo springing naked to the light"—but he does not name her. And then there were several brief journal entries that he decided to publish in a prose compilation called *Sorties* that came out in 1971, the year after *Deliverance* was published, when I guess he didn't much care what my mother thought, and didn't have it in him to do more for Robin.

She lies in Glendale, in Forest Lawn.

Will "The Indian Maiden" ever be written? I don't know. I don't know. Maybe there is too much there; maybe too much. I am terribly, terribly afraid.

This is the element of play, and fun and improvisation, and escape. No one can tell me that this is not important. This Robin Jarecki and I had. We were like children who had discovered sex and literature together, I at the age of forty-three, she at twenty-nine. I think of this as the true glory, at least for me. It was doomed, but not doomed in the way that it ultimately *was* doomed. I sat at my official desk at the Library of Congress, and Ruth Felt called me—a strange voice—and said, "I'm afraid I have some bad news for you. Robin died last Monday."

But we must not lose our dead.

Am I getting back into the terrible morbid nostalgia of the romantic poets, with all the emphasis on Robin now?

I don't know, and I don't care. *Es muss sein. Es muss sein.* It must be. It must be.

What matters is that Robin and I tried to make some kind of life, which was really outside of life. We tried to make something with the tools that we were allowed, and they were pitiful indeed. But we tried, and for a while we did. A very little while indeed, but that is what life tells us we must be content with. Why should this be? It must be. It must be.

My God, to hold that big sweaty body in my arms again!

She lies in Glendale, in Forest Lawn.

It is too late.

I saw Robin Jarecki in a dream last night—a long, long dream— but she was someone else and seemed not to know me.

THE CORVETTE

The Chevy salesman knew when a man was in a mood to buy a car, and Jim Dickey was in the mood. He was looking at a brand new 1966 Corvette Stingray, a maroon machine, the color of wine, with a 427-cubic-inch engine and about four hundred screaming horses under that feather-light fiberglass hood. "Want to go for a ride?" the salesman asked. "For starters, let's put you in the passenger seat." That was okay with Jim, for starters. They headed out toward the freeway. They were rolling slow on the on-ramp. The salesman put his pack of cigarettes on the dash. "Now, in a second here, I'm gonna ask you to reach up and get that pack for me. Got that?" Jim had that. The salesman put his foot to the floor in first gear. "Now!" he said. But Jim Dickey was pinned to the back of his seat like an astronaut on blastoff. Couldn't reach that pack of cigarettes for love or money. Sold.

It was time for a new car. My father's MG-A was a wreck. It had been around for so long, and been so badly used, it was falling apart. Before we'd moved to L.A. in the summer of '64 we'd swung all the way across the country again to Atlanta; then the morning we set off for the West Coast again, the MG's brakes were dragging. It wouldn't accelerate. The pedal felt flabby. Each night we tried to find somebody to fix it, but an MG rust-bucket was not something the good ol' boys in Mississippi and Texas could figure out. So they told us every morning it was going to be okay and took our money, and it wasn't. And then, just as we were coming out of the Painted Desert into a little no-'count town called Winslow, Arizona, the dragging stopped. "I think we're okay. I think the brakes are okay," my father said. But I could smell something burning. I looked out the side flap of the plastic window and saw flames jumping out of the wheel wells. "Daddy!" Now smoke was pouring in around us. My father's foot hit the floor. Nothing. He geared down. Third. Second. First. And rolled us just as nicely as could be into the very first filling station on the edge of Winslow. We were both a little shaky, but he was purely proud of himself.

In Winslow they couldn't fix the damn thing either, and it took us a day of knocking around town and calling parts suppliers to find that out. Finally we left the car there, and didn't come back from the Valley to the Painted Desert to pick it up for a couple of months. The cost of the repairs wasn't much. But they'd charged us storage for the whole time it was there. The bill my father was handed was hundreds of dollars, and he wasn't too happy about it. But the more he pushed, the more he and my mother demanded to see whoever was in charge, the messier the whole thing got. A middle-aged woman came. Turned out that her husband, the man who owned the place, had died. The station was tied up in probate. The MG might be caught up in the same legal wrangle. It sounded like Kafka among the cacti, or maybe just a scam. My father's nose was flaring and his eyes were getting narrow, and he was moving up into the face of the woman. "Now, let's suppose we just call the sheriff and ask him what he thinks," said Jim Dickey, sure that the threat of the law would put this woman and her probate and her goddamn filling station on notice. "Hi, there, Betty," said the sheriff when he got out of his car. "Hi, there, how you doing, George?" said the widow. "Just fine. Just fine. What seems to be the problem here?" He was real friendly with the widow.

Jim Dickey's face was flushed. He explained the situation with the car as he understood it. But the sheriff, well, he wasn't too impressed, and as my father got hotter, and moved in on the sheriff a little, the sheriff said, with his own eyes narrowing, "Why don't you just settle down," which was an order and not a question. And I think it was about this time my mother must have started to think that our lives were going to get a lot more complicated if my father was thrown in jail. She talked to him, half in tears, and he calmed down enough to keep out of trouble. We paid. We got the car, which still wasn't fixed right, and we drove back to L.A. with a lot clearer idea, if we hadn't known it already, just what it was like to be strangers dealing with a small-town lawman and his friends in the middle of nowhere.

The MG limped along for another year or so, taking my father to his classes, to the archery range, and to his assignations. And all the while he was saving up the money that was rolling in now from his reading tours. His fourth book of poems, *Buckdancer's Choice*, won the National Book Award. He was invited onto television talk shows. He *deserved* a new car, and he had enough money now to pay cash for the 'Vette. My mother took him over to the dealer to pick it up wearing blue jeans and a jean jacket and a knit cap, a forty-three-year-old teenager ready to roll.

Poetry! Jim Dickey just couldn't believe that poetry could buy him something like this. Easing up on the clutch was like setting a bear trap. The spring was stiff, the power outrageous. Get it wrong one way, you stalled. Get it wrong the other way: liftoff. But after a while he got the feel of it and, for the most part, puttered around the Valley like a man in a nuclear golf cart. He didn't have to show what he had. He knew it. He was—a star. And there we were, just on the fringes, literal and figurative, of Hollywood itself, and feeling like we belonged.

The movies were always part of his life, our lives. For as long as I can remember, my father talked about them as they appeared on the screen, as he dreamed them, as he reinvented them. He hid out in the cool of theaters. He threw himself into the fantasy of the screen. And he took us along.

In little diners in North Florida when he was teaching at Gainesville, waitresses would ask my father if he wasn't Marlon Brando. My mother would cringe a little. But he loved those moments of mistaken identity, and whenever the waitress left, he would launch into his imitation of Brando in *On the Waterfront* for the benefit of his little family. He could have been a contender, he'd say. We heard that over and over again. But if he'd been drinking he'd go on with it.

"Maxine? Maxine! Who's this?"

Brando? Or Wallace Beery? Apollo? Bacchus?

Now you could say, Hell, that's Jim Dickey the *poet* in his wine-red Stingray.

Movies had been a measure of time and its passage, from *Gentlemen Prefer Blondes* to *La Dolce Vita*, *Them!* to *Spartacus*. In California, documentaries became part of the movie fascination, especially documentaries about Africa. *Trader Horn* led us to *Serengeti Shall Not Die*, about the hunters of animals and hunters of men. And when the lights came up, we talked about when we would go there, when we would see those animals, those places for real. "Ngorongoro," my father would say. It was a word that sounded magical. The kind of place where we wanted to be. But it had been enough, in fact, just to see the film. Walker Percy had it just about right in *The Moviegoer*, one of my father's favorite novels in those days. It was "the peculiar reality" of movies and their stars that astounded him, their peculiar strangeness.

In California, Jim Dickey was being asked not only to write scripts (his first was a documentary for the United States Information Agency), but to have them written about him. There was a director, Jeffrey Hayden, who'd read "Barnstorming for Poetry" in the *Times Book Review* and wanted to make a movie out of it. He came to the little house on Balboa Boulevard to talk about the project, and brought his wife, the actress Eva Marie Saint, who had starred, as it happened, in *On the Waterfront.* (I do not think my father did his Brando imitation for her.) My mother was thrilled to have met a star, and later let on that she thought of Saint as a friend. But the deal never came down, and the friendship faded. It was Hollywood.

I was leading my own fantasy life by then, filled with pubescent obsessions and imagined lives mingling Ian Fleming and Henry Fielding, Frank Harris and Henry Miller. I wanted to be Tom Jones, so I started learning to ride; or James Bond, conceiving myself as a man of action, studying French because I thought that's what a spy needed to know, and poring over books on gambling, guns, and wine. For my fourteenth birthday I got everything I asked for: a movie camera, a trip to Disneyland, and a bottle of Dom Pérignon champagne. Our friend Michael went along, too, and remembers that my father, drunk, also humiliated me in front of the girl I'd asked to join us. But maybe because it was so painful, or more probably because it was just such a common occurrence by then for my parents to be drunk and us to fight and me to feel humiliated, I don't remember that particular incident at all.

My parents had, I think, a vague presentiment that I was homosexual, and normally did anything they could to encourage my interest in women. My mother bought me Henry Miller novels and *Playboys* and let me line my closet with foldouts. And my father gave me his much-thumbed copy of Frank Harris's *My Life and Loves.* But I needed no encouragement. I liked to be with women: touch them, smell them, feel them, taste them. . . . Ah.

Imagination and pornography were giving way so slowly, too slowly, to the real thing. I spent a lot of time at a local stable, and worked for a while as an exercise boy at a training track, not least because I had a ferocious crush on the woman who was teaching me to ride, and I loved being surrounded each day at the barn by girls who were, well, not quite as interested in discovering me as I was in discovering them, but close enough.

All I wanted, all I needed, I thought, was a decent car to get me over the edge from anticipation to consummation. A car like my father's 'Vette. All that flash and all that power. Sex appeal: raw and pure. I loved that machine. I washed it, polished it, waxed it. And waited for it.

In the summer of 1966, our time in Los Angeles ended and we made our last, long drive across the United States as a family. We were headed back east to Washington, D.C., where James Dickey had been named the Poetry Consultant to the Library of Congress, as close as you could get in those days to being poet laureate. We packed up the books in the house. And the new color television. And the old arm-chairs. Kevin and I and my mother and our dog, a little wild-eyed Australian shepherd I named Thunderball, crammed into the Buick station wagon. My father and Michael went in the Corvette. We were rolling toward Barstow, then across the middle of the country to St. Louis, and to Washington.

Sometimes we rotated our positions—Michael would go in the station wagon, Kevin or I in the 'Vette. But not often. My father could talk to Michael about all sorts of things—poets, novelists, women, Robin—that I didn't or wouldn't know about. Robin lived at 1275 Selby Avenue, my father told Michael. "You ought to go visit her." Up ahead in the Buick, we couldn't know what they were talking about, but we'd see the Corvette fading farther and farther back, until its form was almost lost in the shimmering heat rising off the concrete, as if my father had forgotten he was on a highway, or as if he wanted to be as far from us as he could and still keep any contact at all.

I wasn't comfortable being with my father any more. I was almost fifteen and it felt like we'd been fighting all my life. So I rode mainly with my mother and brother, and filmed the countryside with my Super-8 camera, and tried to keep the dog from jumping out of the window, and counted the days, hours, minutes until the trip was over.

Again we hunted for houses, and again my mother found some-- thing special: a big three-story antebellum box in the middle of Lees-burg, Virginia, with high ceilings and wood floors and fireplaces in the bedrooms. It was an hour-long commute into Washington, but my father's hours weren't going to be so regular. He made himself a little office in the attic. We settled in. We felt, again, as best we could, at home. But all I wanted to do, I thought, was get away.

"I'm going to teach you how to drive just the way my instructors taught me to fly," my father told me when I'd gotten my learner's permit. The first thing they'd said, holding up a model, was "This is

father, James Lafayette
ckey III, on the shoulders of
father, Eugene Dickey, and
h his mother, Maibelle Swift
ckey, at Sea Island, Georgia,
e summer in the early 1930s.

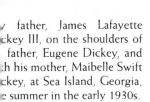

Jim Dickey, middle, had great form running
the high hurdles in high school and, later, at
Vanderbilt. He was the star running back of
Atlanta's North Fulton High School in 1940.

Jim, twenty, his father, and his brother, Tom, in the backyard of the house on Wes
Wesley, February 23, 1943. Cadet Jim Dickey in the cockpit of a trainer at Camder
South Carolina, where he washed out of flight school. Intercept Officer Jim Dickey i
Manila, 1945.

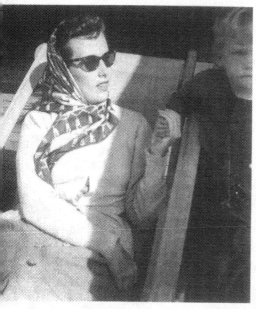

On our first trip to Europe in 1954, my mother, Maxine Dickey, and I; Jim and Maxine among the Greek ruins at Paestum (Laura Rispoli and my younger brother, Kevin, are in the shadows).

At five months old on my father's lap in the little house in Waco, Texas. In Southampton, England, 1962, waiting with him for the SS *France* to take us back to the United States. Kevin is on the right, I am at left.

A self-portrait on the street in Rennes, France, during my brief spell with Schoolboys Abroad in 1967. The photograph I took of my father in 1967 that was used on the jacket of *Deliverance*.

My son, James B. T. Dickey, reaching out to his great-grandmother Maibelle Swift Dickey in the summer of 1971.

m dressed up for a grave-digging scene
the set of *Deliverance* in 1971.

evin Dickey, sixteen, at Myrtle Beach
rport, summer 1975.

hn Boorman, the director of *Deliverance*,
the set with my father in 1971.

Robert Lowell and Jim Dickey on the dock of the house in Columbia, South Carolina, in the early 1970s. They had been called the two greatest poets of their generation.

Deborah Dodson and James Dickey on their wedding day, December 1976, two months after my mother's death. The photo appeared in *People* magazine.

My father and my sister, Bronwen, in 1981.

My father's funeral at All Saints Waccamaw, in January 1997. Capt. James B. T. Dickey, my son, is in uniform on the left. I am next to him, and Bronwen is on the right. Pallbearers, clockwise, are Ward Briggs (in glasses); Matt Bruccoli (his face obscured); Don Greiner, in dark glasses; Lewis King, with the striped tie; Al Braselton, wearing a striped suit and glasses; and Michael Allin. My brother, Kevin, and Deborah are in the background.

With my father one morning in 1986, on the campus of the University of South Carolina after the publication of my first book, *With the Contras*.

an airplane." Their technique was to tell you only what you needed to know when you needed to know it. Now my father was going to sit me in the driver's seat of the Corvette. I was going to turn the key. I was going to put my left foot on the clutch. I was going to put the stick shift into the reverse position so we could back down the little hill and onto King Street, Route 15, the main highway running through the middle of town. "But, Dad . . ."

"Just *do it*."

The engine roared deep and infernal as I gave it a little gas. I let the clutch pedal up off the floor. The car bucked like a colt—and stalled. "Give it more gas. Let the clutch up slower."

More gas. Clutch slower. The car started to move—backward. I was looking over my shoulder, twisting my body, trying to see where— The car was moving faster. We were going down the hill now, the gravel was spinning up from the rear tires, rattling under the car, the engine was roaring, faster, swerving, backward, right into traffic. We jolted to a stop in the middle of the road. Nobody had hit us yet. "First gear!" my father shouted. But he hadn't told me which gear was first gear. I guessed. I hit third. We lurched forward, the car heaving now like it had something rotten in its gut. The engine died.

"You do this, Dad. I can't. I can't," I said. I had dreamed about this and dreamed about it, and now, sitting at the controls, I could not do it. I got out of the car, and went to the refrigerator and got a beer, and went to my room and drank it and cried.

Leesburg was in Loudoun County: rough, luxurious rolling hills full of rednecks and Southern gentlemen, long-distance commuters living in cracker-box houses and Yankee millionaires hunting foxes across vast estates. I went to high school with prep-school dropouts and with boys who'd break each other's jaws in the parking lot outside of the bowling alley, and at least one of my classmates spent the occasional weekend going to visit a brother in the state pen. (He was there for shooting a black man hitchhiking on Route 7. Why? " 'Cause he don't like niggers.") There wasn't a hell of a lot to do in Loudoun County. A town boy from Leesburg might blast twenty miles over to Middleburg, or up to Purcellville, or even to Wheeling, West Virginia, on a Friday night. Depended who you wanted to see, what kind of trouble you wanted to get into. An exotic evening was one spent at Dulles Airport watching the planes land and take off, spaced far and few between, making you think about all those other places you could be.

There were high-school sports, of course, and sometimes there'd be a shooting in the bleachers. ("I told that bitch if I ever saw her

again I'd kill her.") Basketball got really important when Loudoun
County High School integrated and took all the best black players
from the colored school. We got to the state championships that year.
And there were the rich man's sports: hunt races and horse shows.
There were a lot of guns, a lot of fast cars and lonely highways, and a
lot of people who died young. And the one thing everybody did from
the time he could hoist a Budweiser was drink. It seemed perfectly
natural to me.

But, as much drinking as I'd seen and done by the time I was
fifteen, I was still learning from my father and mother and their friends.
When the poet Jim Wright came to stay with us, he was such a
rapacious drunk that my mother hid the whisky, gin, and vodka. But
when she came downstairs to make breakfast in the morning, she
found he'd already knocked back most of a fifth of Cointreau.

My father was persuading some of the best writers in the world
to come read at the Library and we'd go to hear them in Washington,
and a lot of the time I'm not sure how my parents managed to drive
home. Leesburg was about fifty miles out, most of it on two-lane roads
unless you detoured over to the expressway that ran from D.C. to
Dulles Airport. It was four wide-open lanes, and there was almost
never anybody on it, because it was supposed to be restricted, in those
days, to the few cars that were going to the airport. My parents went
that way often. Maybe that's why they weren't killed.

One night that first year, we all went into Georgetown to a party
at Carolyn Kizer's house. She was a poet we'd known when we'd been
living in Portland and she'd been living in Seattle. Her daughter Jill
was more or less my age, and beautiful, and I tried to make sure I went
to any party I could at Carolyn's. And when we got there I'd be so
busy trying to impress Jill that I wouldn't pay much attention to what
my mother or father was doing. So I hadn't noticed, toward midnight,
that my father could barely stand up. My mother, who was pretty
drunk herself, called me down from Jill's room to help him to the car.
He leaned against the side of the Corvette, his eyes closed. "You're
going to have to drive," my mother told me.

I didn't want to, but she didn't want to leave the car here. Didn't
want to leave him here. Didn't want to give him an excuse to come
back here. I didn't know what had happened and didn't know what to
do except what I was told, but I was scared. I hadn't been at the
wheel of the Corvette but once since the near-disaster in the Leesburg
driveway, and that hadn't gone much better. Now we were going to
have to drive in Washington, in traffic, and then on those long roads
home in the middle of the night. And I'd had a couple of beers myself.

"I can drive," my father said, and gave a little laugh. But he slumped into the right-hand seat of the Corvette and, as far as I could tell, he was out. We inched out of the little side street where Carolyn lived. Don't stall, don't stall, don't stall, I kept telling myself. We got to the first stoplight. I pushed the clutch to the floor and waited for it to change, concentrating on my mother up ahead. Green. I revved the engine and eased the clutch out and the engine roared but the car didn't move. I looked at the gears. My father was slapping the knob back and forth. "Put it in neutral when you stop," he said.

"Please don't do that."

His head lolled back to one side again. I put the car in gear and started catching up with the Buick, which was crawling along through the Georgetown night toward Key Bridge. Another light. I put in the clutch and saw my father reaching for the gear shift. "DON'T DO THAT!" But he did it anyway.

I don't remember what I screamed or for how long. I remember that he said he'd drive, and I told him no. And all the shouting may have lasted for a few seconds or a few minutes. Then he just faded away again—"Just drive," he mumbled—and we were on the George Washington Parkway running along the Potomac, and the Beltway, and the Dulles road, driving into that long dark night.

And something was bothering my mother. She slowed down. She was beside me. She was rolling down the window and I was just trying to hold the Corvette straight. She was shouting at me to dim the lights. But I didn't know how. My mother drove on ahead, the Buick's tailgate floodlit by the Corvette. We headed into the home stretch. On Route 7 I blinked against the oncoming high-beams punishing me for not knowing this basic thing: that there was a button on the floor that you had to hit with your foot to lower the lights. But my father was out. My mother was losing me in the dark. There was no one to ask.

The gravel under the tires had the sound of home. I pulled up the hill and stopped the Corvette and turned the key—OFF—in the ignition. My father was shaking his head. "Here?"

I heard my mother's voice, still slurred and angry. "Why didn't you dim the goddamn lights?"

It was during that year I was fifteen that I made a kind of pact with myself. I had spent so much of my life being scared that I just couldn't be scared any more. So I gave myself twenty years to live, until I was thirty-five, and I told myself not only that I would be ready to die at that age, but that somehow I would not die until that age. It was not a solemn vow to anyone else. There was no ceremony. It was just something I told myself one afternoon on the front porch above the boxwoods at the house on King Street. And like a thousand resolutions taken at the New Year or on a birthday, it might easily have been forgotten. And mostly it was. But, still, I started to live as if there were only twenty years, eighteen years, five years, two years of tomorrows. I just couldn't be scared any more. At least not so scared.

First *Life* magazine made it public, then *The Atlantic Monthly* made it official. James Dickey was a god. We'd only been in Leesburg a few days when *Life* hit the stands with its article about "The Unlikeliest Poet," this "athlete, pilot, ad man and fresh, emerging literary voice." There was the Dickey myth brilliantly told for all the American public to read. He might have been a professional football player, but he'd fallen in love with poetry and made it his unexpected life after he started reading seriously during the war. The critical moment was when Okinawa was devastated by a hurricane and the base library was blown all over the island, he told *Life*. He just picked up books and started reading anything that came to hand. It was a wonderful image. A new way to say that all the island had shivered into flowers.

   The *Atlantic* piece, a little over a year later, was by Peter Davison, himself a poet, and it aimed to answer the question of who might be the likely successors to Robert Frost, Wallace Stevens, William Carlos Williams, and Theodore Roethke as the new giants of American poetry. Robert Lowell, the aristocratic New Englander, was one, said Davison. And James Dickey, the Southern populist, was the other. A collection had just come out, *Poems 1957–1967*, that defined the best my father could do. And Davison felt blown away. What he had to say about Jim Dickey's earlier works, the influence of poets like Edwin Muir, the searching for a voice, the monotony of the dactyls—all of it rang true, but all of it was just setting up what Davison really wanted to say. The new stuff by Dickey was amazing. "If American poetry needs a champion for the new generation, Dickey's power and ambition may supply the need. His archetypal concerns are universal to all languages and will no doubt carry over into translations; his sense of urgency is overwhelming; his volume, his range, his style, his technique, his process of maturing—all might supply W. H. Auden's five categories [for what makes a major poet]." But Davison got it right, too, when he ended with a note of caution. "Such writing as Dickey's requires a vast fire to keep the caldron boiling. If he were to encounter a slight recession of energy . . . Dickey's value as a poet might easily enter into decline just at the moment when his reputation . . . has reached its apogee."

· · ·

The month the *Atlantic* paean appeared, I was living in the provincial French city of Rennes, in the home of a retired French sergeant with his wife, his old-maid schoolmistress daughter, and his teenage son, having made my escape from my parents just long enough to start missing them.

My father wanted me to go to Harvard and to be a Rhodes Scholar. It was an idea that was as important to him as his own Phi Beta Kappa key, which he carried in his pocket on a chain all his life. When Kevin and I were both well grown, and I had written books and Kevin had collected numerous honors as a physician at Yale, and both of us were working in our own ways to try to save his life, my father would say, still, with that lilt of disappointment in his voice that came so easily to him and so painfully to us, "In some ways I was sorry that neither one of you boys was a Rhodes Scholar."

"Well, I know that you wanted us to."

"It turned out better this way."

"It has turned out okay." I didn't know what more I could say as we sat there among the walls of books in Columbia. "Well, maybe Bronnie will be a Rhodes Scholar."

"Yeah, maybe. That's not really important," my father said. But of course he thought it was.

The plan in 1967 was for me to repeat my junior year at one of the important prep schools in the Northeast, then go on to Harvard. So, when my father gave a reading at Exeter one snowy week early in the year, he took me along. I sat in on classes. I talked to professors and students. I thought, Yeah, I could make it here. And I drank a lot with my dad. That trip was the first time I remember going to sleep beneath a spinning ceiling.

Exeter and Andover were just starting a program called "Schoolboys Abroad" in France, and I was accepted. So I finished eleventh grade in Leesburg in June, spent a summer on the drunken roads of Loudoun County, and sailed for France to do eleventh grade again in Rennes, Britanny. I had just turned sixteen when the *Aurelia*, an old troopship full of students and hippies, pulled out of New York Harbor. And I had only been in France a couple of weeks when I started thinking of all the time I'd waste by repeating a year of high school.

The letters I wrote home strained to convey some sense of excitement. I was trying hard to be my father's son, writing about the poetry and novels I was reading, and reading mainly the things that I had heard him talk about for much of my life. But as I woke early each morning in the chill house of the sergeant, I felt as if I were in exile. Each letter from home told me the world of the Dickeys had become hugely exciting. Suddenly, since I'd been away, we'd rented an apartment on Capitol Hill as a pied-à-terre. My mother had traded in her station wagon on a convertible Firebird 400. My father had gone hunting in West Virginia, to the same woods and cornfields where the two of us had gone the year before, and had come up against two big black bears. The State Department was going to send him on a tour of Asia. A publicity campaign was launched for a record of him reading his poetry, and he was booked on the Johnny Carson show. He'd returned to Atlanta, he wrote to me, "as a kind of principal in a Roman Triumph of the Arts. I suppose every man who ever lived would like to come back home under such conditions. I thought all the time of the functionary who followed the Roman Conqueror during his triumphal processions, assigned to him to repeat in his ear, 'Thou art only a man.'

"The proportions of 'fame,' or whatever it is, have simply shot through the roof, the sky and everywhere else since the appearance of the Davison article in the October *Atlantic*," my father wrote by way of apology for not having sent me a letter in a couple of weeks, "(I now don't even *look* at reading offers of under $1500), and I must move where the currents of cash are flowing for 'there is a tide in the affairs of men.' Anyway, I am holding up pretty well under it all, and gave up drinking not partially but fully and finally, for it (pleasure, at least, of that kind) was simply too much of an added drag on my faculties. It is better this way, though a great deal less exciting, and I'm told I will last longer under such (rather tame) conditions."

"Have you really stopped drinking?" I wrote back. "I haven't. I just can't pass up the chance to buy a beer when I go in a bar. It's so easy. But I never even get mildly drunk. It's so expensive."

"Beer, wine and aperitifs will upset your stomach," my mother wrote to me. "Be careful."

In early November, I got a letter from my father telling me he didn't approve of my new plan to spend this year abroad only to get a diploma in the summer from Loudoun County and go to the University of Virginia in the fall. He didn't want me going to college at "such an early age," and he was worried about "the Vietnam situation," thinking I'd be fodder for the draft that much earlier. So I must stay in the program, he said. "Don't rush, and don't overmatch yourself when you don't have to."

A few days later, I quit "Schoolboys Abroad" and flew home to Leesburg. Recriminations were brief. My mother welcomed me home. My father made his peace with it. They went back to fighting among themselves, and I got on with my life. In the course of a few days, I had my driver's license, lost my virginity, and met the woman I would marry.

Her name was Susan Tuckerman and she was a student at Foxcroft, a girls' school in the heart of the Virginia hunt country, near Middleburg, Virginia, where young women could see a lot of horses and very few boys. For the months of November and December 1967, I didn't go to school at all, but worked in a little Middleburg camera shop. Susan used to come in to complain about her processing. She had a mane of auburn hair, hazel eyes, a splash of freckles across her face, and a confident wildness I thought was wonderful. There sure weren't any girls like that at Loudoun County High, especially not the one that I'd slept with. When my father gave a reading at the school, I went to bask in the glow, and to get to know Susan better. She loved his poetry, she told me, especially "Cherrylog Road." And, ummmm, did I think I could get her out of this place over the weekend?

I borrowed the Corvette and roared through the Foxcroft gates in the crisp morning light. Susan was just where she said she'd be waiting. The green school smock that served as a uniform was gone. If memory serves, she was wearing a velvet mini with net stockings.

On the Dulles road, the speedometer needle quivered erratically as it edged up over 120 miles an hour. "I've been this fast on a motorcycle," Susan said. The whole car was starting to vibrate like the fiberglass shell was going to peel off that monster engine. 130. Now the needle was really shaking. "Hm," said Susan, cool. My foot was on the floor and the engine was whining loud, the roar becoming a throaty scream. 140 . . . 145. "That's pretty fast," she said. And at just that second the carbon blew out of the engine with an explosion that did nothing, in fact, to the motor, but just about stopped my heart. It didn't matter. By then, I thought, I was wild to be wreckage forever.

In the late spring, reconciled to the academic plan that I'd imposed on myself, my father got me my own car. A cobalt-blue Jaguar XKE roadster.

All from poetry.

And *Deliverance* was still to come.

APOLLO

The night before liftoff, we ate at a long, loud table in Cocoa Beach. The columnist and commentator William F. Buckley was at one end, running his tongue along his teeth like a lizard waiting for a fly, my father at the other, leaning into the table and the people around him, ready to take on the world, the moon, the blackness of space, or Norman Mailer if he showed up. My mother was there, and Michael. Across from me sat Buckley's wife, Pat, and scattered around were friends from *Time* magazine. All of us were drinking hard and picking over our surf and turf. In a few hours we were going to go out to the launch site for Apollo 11 and watch it take off for the moon, and none of us could really believe this was happening, or that we were here. But we deserved it, I figured. We were here because Jim Dickey was a god, and so we were pretty goddamned godly, too.

Pat Buckley started talking about what brave men the astronauts were, what great men. And I interrupted her. I didn't think so. They were going to be put on the moon by machines, and they were like the machines themselves. Why didn't America send up somebody who really was brave, really was extraordinary, really had the power to tell Earth what such a journey was like. Like Jim Dickey, I was half thinking. These guys, Armstrong and the others, they were technicians. They were—ordinary. I looked over at my father and could tell he was listening. He gave me a little signal with his head, like he'd do when he was watching a football game on TV and wanted to encourage the quarterback. Pat Buckley said something dismissive, more or less on the order of "Children should be seen and not heard," and I could feel the color rising in my sunburned face. I thought to myself,

"You dried-up old bitch." I didn't say it. Even though I was on my third or fourth beer, I didn't say it. But the tone must have come through. She flushed, and I could see my father smile. He'd made my head.

By the time we hit Cocoa Beach, the summer of 1969 was already a long, overheated dream. I'd finished my first year at the University of Virginia, then set out in the XKE with a sense of freedom like I'd never had before. Susan graduated from Foxcroft, and for much of the month of June we drove from one debutante ball to another, gypsies of the party tents, familiar with the nuances of omelets and champagne served at 2 A.M., the comparative virtues of bands that normally filled stadiums but were playing now for a few hundred of the debutante's closest friends; living out of the trunk of the Jaguar, never knowing where we would stay, but sure we could find someone on the dance floor with a mansion that could accommodate us, or, failing that, knowing we could just pass out on the lawn beyond the glow of the big house and get enough sleep so we could get in the car at dawn and drive from Piping Rock to Peapack. Then Susan had gone to summer school in Switzerland (her parents were anxious to get her away from me), the Gatsby reverie ended, and I headed south to the house by the lake in Columbia, South Carolina.

My parents had made their last move. In 1968, when his time at the Library of Congress was coming to an end, my father was offered a job at UCLA. My mother, Kevin, and I all wanted to go back to California, but my father had this idea that he'd like to go back to the South. He wanted to be someplace "where the action isn't," he said. Maybe he could feel the fire beneath the caldron starting to cool, the energy starting to wane—already. Maybe he was just homesick for a place where people were supposed to care about each other, and take care of their heroes. The University of South Carolina might not have known much about poetry, but the administration did have a feel for celebrity. Jim Dickey was a hell of a fish to land in the Columbia pond, and that's how they made him feel, and that's where he decided he wanted to be. So we packed the books, the guitars, and the bows for the last time and moved in our Stingray-Firebird-Jaguar convoy to a low-slung suburban house on a little man-made lake on the fringes of the city, back to the shallow heart of the suburban South that we thought we'd left behind years before, 4620 Lelia's Court.

In 1969, there were a lot of people who'd make a pilgrimage to see James Dickey. Some were on business, like Jacques de Spoelberch, the editor from Houghton Mifflin, going over revisions on *Deliverance*; or Larry Du Bois from *Time* magazine, who was talking about putting my father on the cover; or Rollie McKenna, a photographer who was working on a series about American poets. Others just came to be near the great man: to sit out on the dock and drink and talk poetry, or hunting, or the war, or space. *Life* magazine had called him the unlikeliest poet three years before, but had now made him its own laureate. "The moon-shot poet." It had commissioned a poem about Apollo 7 and about Apollo 8, the first manned mission to orbit the moon, and published the latter one across six pages in its special issue on "The Incredible Year '68." It would ask him to write again about the landing. And eventually even about the death of the Green Bay Packers' coach Vince Lombardi. He was becoming a poet for all seasons, or at least for all occasions.

My mother set about making the house her own. She had a decorator in, and suddenly the furnishings were all designs we had admired for years in the pages of our books on architecture: Wassily chairs by Marcel Breuer; Barcelona chairs by Mies van der Rohe. And in the kitchen my mother, who had stood in front of the refrigerator to get cool in Waco and waited for the blocks of ice to be delivered in Antibes, installed a large machine that coughed up pure, clean, copious little cubes of ice—so many of them that you could never run out. She was as proud of it as of anything in the house. It was so— convenient. She kept a quart of Cutty Sark next to the sink, and if I was awake early I could hear the ice rattling into her glass while she made breakfast in the morning.

It had become a privilege, a source of pride, even arrogance, and an irresistible temptation to be my father's son. I was proud and wanted him to be proud, too. I wanted to do well for him, be the best for him, go to bat for him. Was he surrounded by admirers? I wanted to admire him more than any of them could ever do, and God knows I wanted to believe him when he said he admired me for whatever it was he claimed I'd done well. But every bit of praise was just that bit off target, as if he were talking about somebody else. "You've got more guts than a burglar," he liked to say. And nobody knew better than I how scared I was of everything. "You're going to be taller than six feet," he'd say, and I'd just laugh. That wasn't going to happen. My father didn't damn with the faintness of his praise, only its irrelevance.

He would get excited about a riff on the guitar, or something he'd read, or written—or something *you* had read or written—and the exhilaration was contagious. You felt brighter, more interested and more interesting, than you had ever imagined you could be. He was just the way he remembered Randall Jarrell, able to talk about almost everything, anxious to talk about *you*. Then, when he was drinking, or sometimes when he hadn't drunk enough, he'd turn on you. And all that energy, all that excitement he'd generated would be sucked out of you, and then some.

He was talking more and more, my father. It was getting so easy. He was talking to his students, talking to his fans, talking into tape recorders with his paid assistants or earnest graduate students to press the buttons, and his ramblings were getting turned into books: first *Self-Interviews*, then *Sorties*. "Don't tell 'em, show 'em," was a motto he liked to repeat. But now he was talking his poems, his books, his big projects into existence, when there was little or nothing on the page. He was telling the tape recorder about his grand passions and petty hatreds. He was telling it about Robin Jarecki in Forest Lawn. He was telling it about me, how I was "born for controversy," how "in Chris I have produced a son who can *think*." But he was talking with me less and less.

There were vast numbers of things that we both thought about but could not talk about. Vietnam was one. My father didn't want me to go, but at the same time he wanted me to live up to his past. He wanted to keep me alive, but he wanted me "to have my war." Hell, I didn't know what he wanted. I just didn't want to get drafted. We fought about it, and then we just didn't talk about it. We talked about sports, but without much enthusiasm. Kevin was growing fast, and growing very athletic, and as he got older he was given the mantle as the family athlete. I was supposed to reflect the intellectual side of my father, Kevin was supposed to reflect the physical. Kevin and I would joke about this notion, but that didn't make it any easier on us.

My father and I almost never talked about my mother. We never talked about her drinking or his, at least not as a problem, unless he announced that he was stopping, or that he had stopped, and we'd all know it was a lie.

But we still talked about movies: the ones we'd seen, and the ones we'd like to see. My father said he hoped, and it seemed perfectly natural to me, that we could make a film together, and there were ideas that he played with and we made notes on and I tried to write scenes for that sustained us through the last of our days in California, and Leesburg, and even Columbia. He loved—we loved—the epic Technicolor costume dramas of the day. My father wanted to make one about Thermopylae. He liked the history itself, the idea that, when a Persian envoy threatened to turn the sky black with arrows, the Spartan said, "We shall fight in the shade." He loved the poetry that had been written about it, including a line by Lowell about Leonidas and his men getting ready for battle by combing their "golden Botticellian hair." There had already been films made about the battle, of course. But they had not touched on the society of Sparta as it was, so cleanly obsessed with killing, so totally centered on the male body. They had no vision of war as my father had imagined it from thousands of feet above the surface of Earth in the night sky over the Pacific: a vision of the many men so beautiful. The scene he would always talk about was one where the Spartans were arrayed in the tight confines of the pass at Thermopylae like football players defending their goal, and we did talk about this history as easily as another father and another son might talk about the Packers or the Colts. We were talking, I realized later, the way my father had talked with his father about Horatius at the Bridge, the lone man against overwhelming odds.

Another imagined film was based on a novel by Allan Seager called *Amos Berry*. Amos works as the business manager of a chain-link fence company in the Midwest. He murders the man who is his boss and his best friend—and he gets away with it. But his son, who wants to be a poet, figures out what his father has done, and finally confronts him. "The father and son have a magnificent meeting together," my father said. "It cannot be called a reconciliation—they have never been kindred spirits at all, but now they are."

The father saw the killing as revenge on the insignificance of life, and the son tries to help the father rationalize the decision he made. The son has long philosophical talks with Amos, and gives him books of history and philosophy to put it all in perspective. But in the end Amos kills himself. In the note he leaves behind he says:

> Dear son,
>   I'm sorry there was nothing for me in those books you told me about. History is only what I can remember. I must submit to something. I have to make my escape good. I hope this will be acceptable.
>   Love,
>   Dad

"I have been unable to come to any conclusion," the son writes at the end of the book. "The one comfort was that we had come to love each other before he died. He had signed the note, 'Love.' I could hear the sound of my own breathing there in the empty house. He was gone. There was nothing to stay for."

My father loved that book, which must have reminded him of himself as the son-poet. But when my father and I talked, even when we talked about this book, we were not reconciling. We were just biding time. I could not stand to be around him or at his place in Columbia for more than a few days.

The house on the lake was never really my home. I left for college soon after we moved there, and when I went back on vacations, it felt like a prison to me. My parents' bedroom and my father's study looked out over the water through expanses of glass, but my room and Kevin's, on the driveway side of the house, had narrow windows beneath low eaves behind thick bushes that allowed in only the most sepulchral light. I'd lie on my bed for hours with headphones listening to The Doors, whose grim, rebellious chants exactly fit my mood, or I'd drive for miles out of town through the hills and the pines listening to the radio as if it could put me in touch with another world. As soon as I got back to Columbia that summer of '69, I started looking for ways to escape.

Rollie McKenna, the photographer shooting my father among the bushes in our back yard, mentioned she needed someone to paint her house in Stonington, Connecticut, in August. I volunteered. But that was still weeks away.

Michael saved me. He was back on the scene, staying at the house in Columbia, soaking up as much love and genius as he could get. He'd gone over to Atlanta with my mother and Kevin and seen Grandpapa—"the Colonel," as he called him—and they'd even driven up to North Georgia to meet Wha-cha-know Joe Underwood, keeper of fighting cocks. Grandpapa wanted to show him "every feather on the place."

"Lord, Columbia was intense even before you arrived," Michael told me when we were long grown, and far away from there. "Anticipating Jacques de Spoelberch's arrival to edit *Deliverance* was the only time I ever heard Maxine really ugly-angry at Jim (or at anyone else, come to think of it). Mornings, he'd work back and forth from his office to the kitchen, always strumming the curtains, preoccupied, along the front windows. We'd meet in the corduroy chairs and he'd read me sections of *Deliverance* —'amateurish,' was his constantly worried response to any reaction I had—and it had all changed so much since the spring day in '65 when he and I were alone out under that palm tree in Northridge and he went in and got his novel and read it to me. I particularly remember that early version of Drew being actually instead of maybe shot and how obviously it was JFK's assassination —'And then the back of Drew's head flew off.' But, like the book, so much else was changing in Columbia that summer. I had been blessed into your family, loving you all, individually and together; but in Columbia, three years after California, you were all separate, and sides were being taken."

Michael was thinking he'd like to go down to Key West, visit Hemingway's house, and Audubon's, and soak up some sun and atmosphere and some drinks at Sloppy Joe's. And I thought that sounded great. Within a couple of days, we were rolling south through Georgia and Florida and along the long causeways to the Keys. And at every stop I was trying to get phone calls through to Switzerland, to Susan. This summer ramble around the East Coast was a short-term escape, but she was my real liberation. I was desperate to be with her and, as my father would say, with "her people." I loved the self-confident decadence of their lives, as recorded in the cryptic entries of the Social Register's dilatory domiciles. I liked the patina of history that seemed to lie on libraries of dusty leather-bound books, walls covered with faded hunting prints and the slightly musty heads of foxes. I reveled in long walks beside stone walls in the fields that slanted down to the estuarial Westport River on her family farm in Massachusetts. Susan, I thought, was that whole other world I wanted. But I couldn't get through to Montreux, and when I did, she was asleep.

From Key West, Michael and I drove back up to Cape Kennedy a day before the launch. Before our scheduled dinner, *Life* magazine was giving a party in the afternoon, and we got there just in time. Except for my family and the Buckleys and Larry Du Bois, I didn't know anybody. Then a short, quiet man—he would have wanted you to think "dangerously quiet"—came in. Norman Mailer. The whole room tried not to be quiet. Mailer was walking up to Jim Dickey. The diminutive macho novelist-journalist and the oversized, overpowering poet were face to face, sizing each other up. Most of the rest of the people there kept their distance and let them talk. I heard Mailer asking my father how he stayed in shape. I heard my father say he ran, yeah, nodding, ran around the lake where he lived. How far was that, Mailer wanted to know. About four miles, my father said. He'd clocked it. "Yeah," said Mailer, real quiet now. "And about how long does that take you." "Twenty-five, thirty minutes." Mailer nodded like a lawyer. "So you run a mile in about seven minutes." Mailer knew he couldn't do that himself. Knew my father couldn't either. "That's right," said Jim Dickey, squinting a little.

And then we'd gone to eat our surf and turf at our long table, and I don't really remember how that evening ended. I was too young to go to the strip joint when Michael went with my father and Buckley after the meal, and I was too tired and drunk anyway. I slept for a couple of hours, and woke long before dawn to go to the launch site. Buckley and Dickey between them had a whole collection of press credentials. Michael became the second Buckley on the scene, and I became the second James Dickey, for *Life* magazine. "The youth angle," is what I told people I was working on. In 1969, that sounded plausible.

When we got off the press bus we were far, far away from the Saturn V rocket, but as close as it was possible to be. The spotlights on the gantry made a white hole of light in the night sky. Liquid-oxygen fumes sifted out of the tanks like the dry-ice smoke on a theater stage. A lake or an inlet lay between us and the rocket. As the sun came up, you could see birds there, unaware or unconcerned about what was about to happen. The air around us was softly warm, earthy and green and damp, and every so often I breathed it in like history. I felt I had swindled somebody to get to this place, and I had. I wasn't a reporter, I wasn't working for *Life*, I wasn't James Dickey. But I was happy as hell to be here.

The spotlights had dimmed and the sun was high by the time the countdown ended. There were pauses. Fears of disappointment. Then it started again: four, three, two, one. We could see the flash of ignition, and then the birds on the lake taking flight and a weird pattern of small waves coming across the water, and then the sound was on us, a noise as deep as space that hammered our ears, heads, bodies, until some people fell on their knees and others, shielding their eyes, looked as if they saw God Almighty rising from the swamplands of eastern Florida. We watched the Saturn quiver in its own flames, and rise, and then just disappear into the sky.

In the parking lot afterward, a reporter caught Buckley on his way to his car. "Mr. Buckley, you've always been an eloquent man with words," the reporter said. "How would you describe what you just saw?"

"With silence," Buckley said. Which was glibly good; maybe better, even, than Buckley knew.

My father went to work on his lunar-landing poem. The *Life* deadline was approaching. That part of this fantastic experience, the writing of the verse, in the service of journalism, in the service of fame, was becoming a kind of routine. But it made him uneasy. Months later the whole business would be something he looked back on with a confused sense of regret, as a moment he had lived through but somehow failed to experience.

"I think with terrible sadness of the evening spent with the astronauts a couple of nights before Walter Schirra's lift-off," Jim Dickey told the tape recorder for what became *Sorties*, thinking about an encounter with the Apollo 7 crew. "I was drunk out of my mind, and could not focus on anything that happened, but simply sat in a corner in a drunken stupor attempting conversation with one or another nice young fellow who drifted by, doubtless out of a sense of duty, or of some kind of obscure loyalty to the *Life* people I was with. That opportunity will not come to me again, that is certain. And yet if I had been cold sober what would I have done? Would I have been an eager-eyed middle-aged fellow, terribly receptive to all their personalities, and so on? No; if I had it to do again, I would be a drunken poet among the astronauts. And, by God, I was a drunken poet. I remember them; now let them remember me."

Twenty-seven years later, my wife Carol and I were into our second day trying to make order in the Columbia garage, still hoping somehow that doing so would help us make some order in my father's life, which was not so well remembered any more. We were stumbling, sweating, straining with the weight of garbage, wading deeper and deeper into the deteriorating memories of a quarter-century. Here were yellowed copies of the *New York Times Book Review* with "Barnstorming for Poetry" in it; and the special issue of *Life* with the Apollo 8 poem. Here was a little chest of drawers that my mother had found at a Goodwill store in Portland, Oregon. She and I had painted it in bright colors for Kevin's room when he was four years old. There were boxes of hotel brochures and letters, even a program from the Folies-Bergère, collected on the trips we took to Europe. In one corner of the garage sat the old ice machine that had once seemed such a marvelous badge of success, now filled with trash and stranded in a dried puddle of rust. Here were stacks of clippings about the movie *Deliverance,* and there were boxes and boxes of photographs.

Among the pictures we found in the garage and in the house were a few of those taken that summer of '69 by Rollie McKenna. They are funny. Charming. My father mugged for the lens from behind the back-yard bushes, or smiled gently over a chord he'd made on his guitar. He was still so young then.

After the moon shot I drove up to Kennedy Airport to meet Susan when her plane came in from Switzerland, then went to work in Stonington painting Rollie's house. It was a good job, well paid, and right on the water. I had the run of her house, a wonderfully comfortable and practical place with spare, carefully chosen furniture. Whenever we got tired of scraping or sanding, the other painter and I would just go for a swim. When the day ended, I sat and read in an Eames chair that looked out through picture windows to the sea. I went to New London to register for the draft. I drove to Susan's farm on

weekends. I wrote a few letters home. Very few. And on the last day
of the month I turned eighteen.

Rollie gave a party in my honor. It was her big end-of-summer
bash for just about everyone in town, and I didn't really know anyone
there, but it was the best birthday I'd had for as long as I could
remember. We ate paella and drank wine and talked about what
seemed like important things. I felt I was on my own, but not alone. I
was in love. I was the son of a great man I didn't have to see or to be
with, at least not that night. I was looking forward to a life of wide-
open possibilities. After a while I just sat in the embrace of an Eames
chair looking through the picture windows at the sea. Rollie had put
eighteen candles in paper sacks out on the rocks and, one by one, the
tide came in to extinguish them.

Three months later Susan and I were married, and by the summer of
1970 our son was born. Our parents did not like any of this, but could
not stop it, and in the end both Susan's folks and mine decided they
would keep supporting each of us as they had done before. We had
been so indulged that there was plenty of money left over to support
the baby, too. Still, my father was bitter. None of this had been part
of his plan. He came to our wedding on the hills above the Westport
River; he even played a little guitar for the guests. But the first time
that Susan and I went together to Columbia, when she was still pregnant, he could not bring himself to sit at the same table with us at
dinner. "You have thrown away your youth," he said between his teeth
with a ferociousness, and at the same time a tone of despair, that I had
never heard.

Looking back as a man, now as old as my father was then, I can
easily imagine the anger and disappointment a father would feel. But I
thought then, and believe still, that my father thought I'd thrown away
his youth, deprived him somehow of his second coming.

AT THE RIVER

The plot was simple and strong: Four Southern suburbanites decide to go canoeing in the last remnants of the Appalachian wilderness. They are Lewis Medlock, a survivalist determined to master Nature single-handed; Ed Gentry, a friend whose only real acquaintance with the wild is what he sees reflected in Lewis's fierce excitement; Bobby Trippe, a soft denizen of sales meetings and country clubs who's just along for the ride; and Drew Ballinger, the conscientious family man who, like the rest, has no idea at all what he's getting into. These four plunge into a wilderness populated by few and brutal inhabitants—a terrifying place where one of them is sodomized at gunpoint, one is killed, one almost loses a leg, and all of them learn, of necessity, to murder.

I'd been watching that plot, the book, the script take shape since the days when my father took me onto the mild rapids of the Chattahoochee in an aluminum canoe, when I was hardly big enough to see over the gunwales. I'd never forgotten that night he and Al and Lewis King came back from the Coosawattee hurt and scared. I'd seen the arrow tremble on its rest as the tension of the bowstring grew too much to bear, and the silent flight of deer over fences as we staked out frozen cornfields; seen the young men climbing cliffs above the Italian sea, seen the narrow-eyed sheriff send us on our way at the edge of the Painted Desert. My father had sat in our living room in Atlanta in the fall of 1962 and talked the plot into that first Grundig tape recorder we'd bought in Germany, and we had all felt the fear of the wild among the dense, dark forests of Oregon. And all the while that he'd been writing the book, he'd been thinking of what the movie might be.

The novel hit the stands in the late spring of 1970 and climbed the best-seller lists quickly. Only the phenomenal success of Erich Segal's *Love Story* kept *Deliverance* out of the number-one position. I watched from a distance. Jim Dickey was really on a roll, and all I could do was stand aside, amazed and amused, proud and a little appalled, as he loomed larger and larger in the book reviews, the magazine articles, on talk shows and publicity tours; combative and funny, drunk and outrageous and ruthless, in fact—and even more outrageous and ruthless in the stories he told about his experiences. Talk and testosterone were taking over, with heavy hits of Jack Daniel's to keep things going. At a book-and-author luncheon with Erich Segal and Pauline Kael, Segal told the little old ladies that in his novel the only four-letter word was L-O-V-E. When the luncheon was over, and the three of them had crowded into the back of a limousine, somebody turned to Segal—my father would sometimes attribute this remark to Kael—and said: "Listen, you little cocksucker, what do you know about L-O-V-E?" It was a story that Jim Dickey liked to repeat on any and all occasions.

When I talked to Columbia on the phone, I would tell my mother what I was doing, and my father would tell me what he was doing. But his tales, exciting as they were, didn't lure me home the way they had before.

I was happy now not to be there. I had my own family to tend to in Charlottesville. We'd bought a big dog and rented a little house in the country. On warm days we swam in our own lake; when it was cold we had our own fireplace. I got a four-wheel-drive Ford Bronco and gave the Jaguar back to Big Jim. I went to my own classes and wrote short stories and started seriously to take photographs and study film, trying to cobble together my own primitive little documentaries. I liked the distance from my father. It made it so much easier for me, in my way, to try to be him.

Jim Dickey was only beginning to learn how little he'd have to say about the way his book was made into his movie. But he would always talk about who *our* director was going to be, and our stars. To play the role of Ed, who narrates the book, Jim Dickey wanted Gene Hackman. But Hackman wanted to play Lewis. Or so it was said. To direct, Dickey liked Sam Peckinpah, who made his mark on Hollywood with the relentless violence, horribly literal and beautifully stylized, of *The Wild Bunch*. Peckinpah, an ex-Marine who specialized in Westerns, had a feel for the society of dangerous men in dangerous situations. His "misogynist heroes experience passion only in slaughter," said a British critic. Well, you could find worse sensibilities for the story at hand.

They met in London, my father remembered when all of this was coming back to us from the distant past. "We talked almost the whole day long, Peckinpah and I, and I really thought he was going to be good. He had everything down in his head just like he wanted it." My father smiled beneath the oxygen tube. "We were talking about certain scenes and he said, 'You know, Mr. Dickey,' he says, 'I am famous for what they call my blood ballet.' " And now my old, sick father erupted with laughter. "I said, 'Well, we've got plenty of room for that in this movie.' "

Peckinpah said that what the two men had in common, and not just because it was the end of a long hard-drinking day, was their desire—Dickey in his poetry, Peckinpah in his films—"to create images people cannot forget." My father thought that was so right that more than a quarter-century later he could even remember where and when Peckinpah said it, in the late afternoon standing there on Regent's Street saying goodbye. "I never did see him again."

The director, in the end, was John Boorman, who was British and had done two action films with Lee Marvin: *Point Blank* and *Hell in the Pacific*. The last film Boorman had done was an embarrassing romp with Marcello Mastroianni called *Leo the Last*. No one we knew had ever heard of it. But the studio liked Boorman, and Jim Dickey learned to live with him, and said he thought he was great, at least for a while.

The making of the movie brought me back to my father of course. How could it not? Movies, remembered or imagined, had become our last common language. This, at last, was the real thing. None of us wanted to miss it.

It was May of 1971 when Hollywood moved to the little town of Clayton, Georgia. My father, my mother, her mother, my twelve-year-old brother, myself, my wife, and my child all followed. In a Toyota Land Cruiser, which was my father's second car (along with the XKE), a Cadillac Sedan de Ville he'd bought for my mother, and my Ford Bronco we left that suburban house in Columbia and headed up into the hills, across the Chattooga River. My father took with him his bows, arrows, guitars, and tape-recorded music to show Boorman just what he wanted. We were headed into the mountains of *Deliverance* thinking we were pioneers, but thinking, too, that we already knew our way around. This was coon-on-a-log and corn-liquor country. Grandpapa's stomping grounds. Wha-cha-know Joe's neck of the woods. "The country of the nine-fingered people," as it says in *Deliverance*, because there's so much inbreeding and so many bad accidents that everybody's missing something. This was a place we knew about, and knew enough to fear—but it was ours. The British director, these Hollywood crews, they wouldn't have much of a feel for North Georgia. But we Dickeys were ready for the backwoods boardinghouse where the toilet would be down the hall, if we were lucky, and the screen doors wouldn't quite keep out the mosquitoes.

When we got there, we were put up in A-frame chalets around the golf course of the Kingwood Country Club. Clayton, it turned out, was a burgeoning resort area, an outpost of Atlanta. Within the confines of the club, at least, Hollywood was right at home. And we were no longer sure what to expect.

The evening the Dickeys arrived, Boorman gave a party for the author, to introduce him to the cast and crew. Boorman's German wife, Christel, was with him, and his four blond children. The whole scene was supposed to feel "like family." But things had started to get a little sullen and ugly already in the afternoon. My father had been handed the shooting script that he thought he'd approved. But this one started with a terse note: "Scenes 1–19 omit." This was going to be an action movie that began and ended on the river. Real clean. Real simple. Really not what my father had in mind.

On the way over to Boorman's $1,000-a-month cottage, we had to squeeze the Cadillac by a big car headed out the drive. Burt Reynolds was at the wheel, his shirt a little too small so it showed off his biceps, a wide-brimmed Stetson on his head. It was the first time we'd seen him. "Afternoon, ma'am," he said, doffing the hat, and then he drove on. He was going to be Lewis.

Boorman greeted us at the door of the house. My father had been working with him for months, but I'd never seen him before. Long hair, gapped teeth, ruddy complexion, a British accent and manner that had nothing to do with this place or this story. He was going to be a spectator here, I thought. He didn't know these people. But, then, I wasn't sure any more that we knew them either.

Jim Dickey stalked into Boorman's living room like he would have done when he was creeping up on a bear in West Virginia. Or as if he were the bear. I'd forget sometimes what a big man he was, what a huge presence, but when he'd been drinking, as of course he had this night, he lumbered dangerously through the fragile auras of strangers in small spaces. Boorman followed behind him to make introductions —and to watch. Dickey was introduced to Ronny Cox, who'd play Drew. Tall but ineffectual, his hair bleached blond at the time, Cox resembled Rod McKuen, whose book of sentimental verse, *Listen to the Warm*, was a best-seller. This did not enhance his image in my father's eyes. Jon Voight came to the party a little later. He still wore the

credulous look of Joe Buck, the baby-faced gigolo in *Midnight Cowboy.*
He was beginning to grow a mustache to give his features a little
maturity, but he seemed way too young to play Ed. Someone told
him, "Dickey has arrived." He fixed himself a drink from the bar near
the door. Would he like to meet Dickey now? Voight stood up to his
full height, took a deep breath. "I guess now's as good a time as any,"
he said, and into the living room he went. He'd heard tales about the
way Dickey came on, the way Dickey could get to you.

After a while my father worked Cox and Voight over to a table
by themselves. He was uncomfortable with most of the others at the
party: moneymen, secretaries. They were Hollywood's version of gray
affable men. They were Boorman's people. It was the actors my father
wanted to talk to—to perform for—and so he did.

"Do you really want to play Drew?" Dickey asked Cox.

Boorman listened from across the room.

Cox looked scared, but managed to say finally, with overintense
sincerity, "I really do."

Dickey paused for effect, let the anxiety linger for a second, then
slapped Cox's knee and smiled. "Good," he said, "because I want
you to."

Cox and Voight grinned. Boorman let out his breath.

For the next few days the actors were rehearsing, waiting for Ned
Beatty to arrive. The crew was getting used to working in the mountains and on the river, running tests, sorting out equipment. Cox and
Beatty were theater guys, not movie people. But Beatty's reputation
impressed everyone. He was late coming to Clayton because he was
finishing the run of a new play by Eugène Ionesco. He was serious; or
supposed to be. But the first time I met him he was wading around in
his tennis shoes and pants, fat, playful, childish, and funny. "I like to
get my feet wet," he said with a well-honed grin.

Boorman would invite small groups of people over to his house
in the evening to play Ping-Pong and have drinks. Boorman was trying
to build that sense of informal family, full of confidence, where people
trust their emotions and reveal their secrets, and where he was the
only man who understood it all and made it work. But as long as Big
Jim Dickey was there, nobody was going to believe that.

After a few days my mother, her mother, and my brother left. But
my father stayed. He said he thought he was needed for the music—
he'd heard that song called "Dueling Banjos" at a folk concert in
Portland seven or eight years before and he'd brought the tape and he
could pick it himself for anyone who wanted to hear. He wanted it as
the theme. For *his* movie. And it was so right, in fact, that Boorman

took the idea. Then Dickey stayed for the actors, he said. Boorman was still rehearsing them in semisecrecy, but they were coming on the sly to see Dickey for background on the characters, even voice coaching. Voight recorded hours of Dickey accent.

I was slated to stay on as a stand-in, a warm body around whom lights and camera angles are positioned so the actors will be able to come on fresh for the actual shooting. It's about as lowly a position as you can get on the set. But you're on the set. You see what goes on. You learn. And I was taking notes the whole time. Later, my father told interviewers he worked on the movie himself partly because he wanted me to get that job. It was the kind of thing that he'd say that always left me uneasy. There was no question he'd gotten me the job. But there was no question he was anxious to work on his movie whether I was there or not. "We need to have a very long script conference, I need to see the locations and a lot of other things," he wrote in his journal a couple of days before we drove up. "It is going to be an awfully hard-working summer, but I am really ready for it, and will not give down. It is going to be one hell of a film."

My father, my wife, my little boy, and I were settling in for the long haul when Boorman asked Dickey to lunch at the Kingwood Club. In the late afternoon my father was back, knocking on the door of my room. Our year-old son, Tucky, was napping. We were watching soap operas.

"I'm leaving," my father said, as if his world had crumbled. Boorman had said he was interfering too much. Said the actors were upset by his presence. Boorman had said, "Jim, if you want to direct this picture, fine." Dickey had said of course not, John was the director; John was the *auteur*. And John had said in that case he thought it would be best if Jim left.

Dickey took a long sigh and shook his head. "So—I guess I'll be going sometime this evening."

"I think it was largely Burt," my father said when we were going over this ancient history one day in Columbia. I thought that by looking back on that summer I could distract him from his sickness, and I thought that I would find more clues about us.

"You think it was Burt?"

"Yeah. Do you remember that publicist up there? He gave me to understand that I made Burt nervous."

I think my father made everybody nervous in the end. Cox, Beatty, Voight, and Boorman, too. Especially Boorman. But it was true that Burt seemed the most fragile. The making of *Deliverance* was a big break for everybody connected with it. It meant more money, more work, more fame. But Burt was looking for respect. He wasn't coming from the stage, like Ronny or Ned, or from an Academy Award-winning film like Jon. He was coming from one ludicrous television series after another, most recently an uninspired detective show called *Dan August*. Ned and Jon were accomplished actors, but Burt was a former stuntman who wanted to be a star. He was made by and for the screen. The question was whether he could make it from the little one to the big one.

Burt was sharp, funny, self-deprecating, taking shots at himself before others could get them in. But he was excruciatingly sensitive about his height, supplemented by lifts in his boots, and his hair, which was disappearing fast. And if he was going to make it in this movie he was going to have to act. He was going to have to concentrate. He was going to have to feel just about as sure of himself as he ever had in his life. And Burt sure as hell didn't need Jim Dickey, who really was big, who'd played a little football, too, who could be the redneck in the morning and the intellectual in the afternoon—who was half Lewis Medlock himself—to tell him anything, anything at all.

"I just couldn't handle his act—his Jim Bowie knife on his belt, cowboy hat, and fringed jacket," Burt wrote in his autobiography.

"The contacts I had with him were amiable enough," my father said, a little wistful, disappointed, and angry even all these years later. "We rode back from one of the locations together a long, long ways out, and he and I talked for a while. And it seemed all right to me. I don't know anybody else's version."

I was left alone in Clayton. The Dickey. And Boorman probably would have gotten me off the set, too, if it had been worth the trouble. I wasn't quite right as a stand-in: too short to be Jon or Ronny, both of whom were over six feet; too skinny to be Ned. I was the right height to stand in for Burt, but Burt, playing the star game, had to have his own personal stand-in. So I just went wherever I was needed whenever I was needed, walking through the moves of one actor or another, especially the rednecks. I kept a low profile. I knew how to do that. I was nineteen years old and wasn't going to intimidate anybody. Keeping me around was an easy concession.

Boorman simply stopped paying for my accommodations. When Jim Dickey left, none of the Dickeys had a room at Kingwood any more. I didn't have the money to pay my own bill staying with the stars, or even at the Heart of Rabun Motel, where most of the blue-collar crew were housed. So we found a little bungalow in a local low-rent motel and moved out of Hollywood onto a kind of border-land between movie fantasy and redneck reality. And I liked it. More and more of the friends we made were local hires: trailer-park girls who worked as waitresses; good ol' boys who thought they'd had a fun night if they saw a knifing at a roadhouse. My old Southern accent —lost long ago, when we moved to Oregon—started to come back. I started to feel, at last, like I did have a claim on this place.

Warner Bros. got some of its extras that summer out of local jails. One was released into the producer's custody every morning and went back to bed behind bars every night. A lot of them had never seen a job that paid so well. "I found out a long time ago I could make more money raisin' children than raisin' hogs," as one of the older ones liked to say. But even by mountain standards the work could get boring. "Ain't had so much fun since I cut my toenails," you'd hear them say. When those first scenes were being shot, there was plenty of time to sit back, chew on a blade of grass, and talk.

One of the locals I liked a lot was a reputed moonshiner named Randall Deal. He swore up and down he'd reformed his ways. Problem was, the police just wouldn't believe him. Randall was built solid, with heavy arms and a barrel chest, and a look in his eye about as mean as you could find in those mountains. In the movie he plays one of the Griner brothers, paid to drive the suburbanites' cars down to Aintry, where they're supposed to pick them up when they get off the river. But it's clear the Griners don't think much of these city boys who seem to have trouble even finding the water. "It ain't nothin' but the biggest fucking river in the state," Randall says in the film, and you do get the feeling he'd kill you as soon as look at you.

"How come you was in jail?" I asked him one day as we were lying around in the sun near some of the shacks the prop people built.

"Well, it was like this," says Randall. "I wadn't doin' nothin'."

"Unh-hunh." I wasn't sure how far I wanted to push this, but I got my question out. "How come they arrested you, then?"

Deal looked at me like I'd just missed the biggest fuckin' river in the state. Why, he was just driving his car minding his own business when a state trooper pulled him over for no reason at all. "I wadn't doin' nothin'."

"Unh-hunh," I said again.

"And this trooper, he commenced to beatin' on me with his stick. I just sat there and he kept beatin' and beatin'."

"But I heard you was in jail for assaulting a . . ."

"Well, finally I just had to get out of the car and unconscious him."

"Unconscious him?"

Randall just smiled.

Other mountain people used in the movie weren't so tough, and in fact they were terribly vulnerable. The face that you don't forget when you see *Deliverance* belonged to a backward boy of fifteen named Billy Redden, who had the role of a retarded banjo player. His thin-lidded eyes and simple grin are haunting on film, and they were just as disturbing to see on the set. Billy seemed so lost. He went around bumming cigarettes, proud of himself for smoking in public, more interested in his Marlboros than almost anything else that was going on. And he did try to do as he was told, but some things were beyond him.

The movie opens with a sequence at a backwoods gas station, where Drew on the guitar and this boy with his banjo start out just sort of picking a few notes, then take off into a burst of bluegrass virtuosity: "Dueling Banjos." Nobody ever expected that Billy could play that piece, or any piece. The music was all going to be dubbed. But Billy couldn't even fake it. He could make his right hand strum more or less convincingly, but he couldn't imitate the fretwork with his left hand at all. In the end the scene was set up with Billy sitting on a kind of swinging bench, and another little boy hidden beneath it, whose left hand up Billy's sleeve was faking the fingerwork for the camera.

In that same sequence, Ed looks through the window of a little shack and sees an old woman whose face is covered with skin cancers tending a spastic child whose head lolls pitifully to one side. The little girl was thirteen, but you would have thought she was five or six. Of course Hollywood paid these people and treated them as gently as it knew how to do, but it was hard to get over the feeling as the lights went on and the cameras rolled that souls were being stolen here.

THE CUTTING ROOM

Most movies are shot in what seems a random order, and the various scenes are assembled later into a whole. But *Deliverance* was filmed in sequence. Each day moved the cast and crew a few more pages into the story, farther along the river, deeper into the woods. All the horrors were foretold.

At the beginning, because we knew what would come later, simple accidents somehow felt like omens. The first day on the Chattooga River, the camera crew and actors set out early in the morning in a flotilla of rafts and canoes. They barely made it a mile downstream. They broke one of the canoes in half. They ripped the bottom out of a raft and spilled thousands of dollars' worth of camera-and-sound equipment into the water. No one was hurt, but everyone was soaked, tired, worried, and maybe a little scared. The characters in the story had gotten too far into these woods, too deep into this river. The fact was, you didn't know what might happen up here.

On that first day of the story, the four men run a few mild rapids, then set up camp in the late afternoon. Lewis, played by Burt Reynolds, goes out in a canoe to see if he can shoot a trout with an arrow. Ed, along for the ride, lies back and has a beer. They talk about their lives. Lewis talks about how civilization is going to fail. He takes a shot at a trout and misses. Ed says he doesn't think his own life is as shitty as all that. He *likes* his life. Lewis takes another shot and skewers the trout that they'll eat for dinner.

Since I was James Dickey's son and I was supposed to know how to shoot a bow, one of the assistant directors asked me to shoot one of the trout they'd put in a little makeshift pond at the edge of the

river. They needed a close-up miss and a close-up hit. I'd never shot a
trout. But, hey, this was going to be like—this *was*—shooting fish in
a barrel. Just to get the feel of it, I took aim at one of the trout,
steadied the shaft, aiming low to compensate for the refraction of
light, and released. The arrow went right into it, just the way it was
supposed to. Now the cameras rolled. And rolled. And rolled . . . and
rolled. I could not hit another fish. We joked. We laughed a lot. I
made excuses. The sun was going down and we were losing light.
This whole little sideshow was turning into an embarrassment, then a
humiliation, as people came over to see why we were taking so long.
"I thought you knew how to do this?" said the assistant cameraman.
Even fish in a barrel are hard to hit with an arrow. Anyone might have
made an equal fool of himself. But I was Jim Dickey's son, and I wasn't
able to do what he could do—or, more precisely, what the characters
he created could do. The arrow splashed into the clear water another
time. Now the trout wriggled in agony. Finally. Good enough. I should
never have said I'd do this, I thought. I was Jim Dickey's son. Yeah.
But I was only his son.

At the end of the first day in the story, there is a long scene by
the campfire, where the men, now drunk, let themselves get spooked
by the sounds of the forest. In the book, Ed hears something hit the
top of the tent. "The material was humming like a sail. . . . The cloth
was trembling in a huge grasp." He shines a flashlight directly above
his head and sees "a long curving of claws that turned on themselves."
The owl—a very big one—flies away, then comes back. "From some
deep place, I heard the woods beating." It perches again above Ed's
face and he reaches up slowly, gently, until he can touch the claw, feel
it tighten, feel the strength that "had something nervous and tentative
about it." I always thought it was a wonderful scene, and it meant
something special to my father, and to me. This was the owl from our
tent by the lake; and the Owl King of his poetry, the symbol of
fathers, the teacher of the blind child. "All night the owl kept coming
back to hunt from the top of the tent. . . . I imagined what he was
doing while he was gone, floating through the trees, seeing everything. I hunted with him as well as I could, there in my weightlessness.
The woods burned in my head. Toward morning I could reach up and
touch the claw without turning on the light." But in the movie there is
no owl. Nobody would know what it meant. The imagery wouldn't
work in Boorman's spare film. There is just the dark, the four men, and
their fear.

The next morning, Ed wakes early. He's got nothing on but his
long underwear as he takes his bow into the woods, thinking maybe

he'll get himself a deer. And he does see one, a little spike buck just visible through the mist. "The ghost of a deer, but a deer just the same." He draws down on it, steadying the arrow, trying to steady himself. But at the moment of release, he loses control. The deer turns and runs. The chance is lost.

To shoot that scene, a little deer was brought in from an animal park, and heavily tranquilized so it could be easily controlled. There was never any question of shooting it, or hurting it in any way. But it died. It had been given an overdose. Boorman and his assistants were in a quiet panic. "This is all we need," I remember one of them saying. "The fucking SPCA will crucify us." So the death of the deer was treated as a terrible secret, and those of us who knew about it were admonished to say nothing to anyone. And we didn't. But the death of this little animal, like the exploitation of that tiny thirteen-year-old girl, so vulnerable, so lost in the machine, filled me with doubts about everything we were doing.

Among the chalets and cottages of the Kingwood Country Club, Boorman and the actors returned each night to lives of quiet domesticity. Boorman's wife, Christel, went on shopping expeditions to buy chenille quilts, and took under her wing not only her four small children, but some of the actors' wives and girlfriends: Jon's Marshalene, whose long straight hair and winsome beauty still seem to me a kind of paradigm of the time, and Ned's Belinha, who was very smart and very pregnant. I don't remember Ronny's wife. She kept her distance from the set and from Christel, I think. But I do remember that Burt's women (there was decidedly more than one) never really seemed part of the Boorman scene. Early in the shooting, Burt was with "Numero Duo," as he called her. She was polite, good-humored, had too-black hair, long nails, and large breasts, and looked like she was as tough a cracker as ever waited tables at an all-night truck stop. But by the time the filming was halfway down the river, she'd been replaced by Numero Uno. Her name was Miko Mayama, she was from Japan, and before she came to the set in North Georgia, Burt was like a little boy waiting for his mama to pick him up at school for a party. It was part of his charm that, as much as he was fucking around—and wanted to be seen to be fucking around—he was so obviously in love with this woman.

The young Dickeys didn't get invited much to the Boormans'. But Ned and Belinha and Burt and Miko had us over to their cottages a couple of times. Ned was getting into cooking, and liked to try wild foods—literally wild. Euell Gibbons's *Stalking the Wild Asparagus* was a best-seller in those days, and Ned was a disciple of sorts. So one night he whipped up a wildflower tempura. It was purely awful, but we drank enough to kill the taste.

Burt put on a different kind of show. The food was ordered in, and he would sit and talk in a big armchair like he was sitting on a throne. Miko would sit at his feet, as if there were no other place for her in the room, but also as if she were keeping an eye on everything he did from as close as she possibly could be. They both seemed happy enough with the arrangement. And when conversation flagged, he pulled out his secret party surprise. I don't know what I expected. He'd been talking a lot about how Miko walked on his back. But the surprise, in fact, was Skittles. I'd never seen it before: a wooden top spinning its way through a wooden maze knocking over little bowling pins.

Whatever happened on the river, life was deliberately, almost desperately tame at the Kingwood Country Club.

Every couple of weeks, my mother and father would come back to Clayton, and Big Jim Dickey would start to try to impose himself again, but the movie was out of his control, and everybody knew it, maybe even him. He'd had a partial reconciliation with Boorman, but my father was still resentful, and still drinking hard. He took to calling all the actors by the names of their characters. "Lewis! Come here, boy!"

One night at the buffet at the Kingwood Country Club, I was talking to Belinha Beatty and we were watching Jim Dickey do his thing. He was acting out one of the scenes he'd written, but having trouble keeping his balance. He was drunk, obviously drunk, but everyone seemed to be enjoying the show. Belinha knew I was upset. "When you're a star, you can do anything," she said. "Yeah," I said, "and when you're a poet, people *expect* you to do anything."

That was what I was trying to convince myself by the time I was nineteen. It was the people around my father who were really to blame: bored people looking for a way to be in touch with Jim Dickey's effusive, effulgent, half-mad energy. They wanted him to dare to do the things that they would never do, and maybe make them dare a little more, too. So they would drink with him until he was falling-down drunk, hoping he would say something brilliant, or outrageous, knowing they could say to themselves and others that they'd lifted a glass—a lot of glasses—with Big Jim Dickey. And they would watch him move in on a woman, any woman, in a crowd, and wish they had the balls to do that. Or wish that they were the woman.

It was their fault that he was like this, I thought—the spectators waiting for the spectacle, they seduced him with his own show. It had been bad when he was barnstorming for poetry, and worse when he was a best-selling novelist, and now, if the film was a success, all restraints, all that was left of him that I loved, would be gone. It was a premonition that stayed with me the whole time I was on the set.

My mother was there, too, and I was starting to watch her more closely than I had before. Her face was bloated, and in it her eyes had grown narrower, and more liquid, and very often they were mean. She talked more and more about the things my father had given her: the Cadillac; a mink coat; a few bits of silver jewelry from Georg Jensen; and the house and its furnishings. She was clinging to it all, still trying to be a wife and make a home even as the people she was making it for were leaving. She had no real friends to talk to—really talk to—about what was happening. Her mother had followed us to Leesburg and then Columbia, and the two of them would sit together at the house on the lake and drink in the late afternoon. But that was always a grim scene: my mother's mother chain-smoking Tareytons, slurring her words, inciting my mother, but never giving her any idea what she could do to change her life except hate my father more and have another scotch. And there was Kevin, who wasn't even a teenager yet but had to try to understand all the resentments, and all the pain.

On those quick visits to Clayton my father started to spend time in the editing room at the Heart of Rabun Motel. It wasn't just the process of assembling the film from the strips of celluloid that fascinated him, it was the editor himself; who he was and how he happened to be there.

Jim Dickey loved the power of coincidence, the way it defeated logic and created a sense of magical surprise in his life—in anyone's life. And he was even more intrigued by the power of dreams to defeat time. He liked to cite a line from the French poet Gérard de Nerval, who said the dream is a second life, and liked to believe that this second life was where the best poetry could come from. My father wanted to believe that in your dreams you could travel backward and forward in time, and the phenomenon of coincidence was somehow part of that. He first got excited by the concept when he was on a troopship coming back from the Pacific in 1946 and picked up a copy of J. B. Priestley's *Midnight on the Desert* to read in his bunk. Priestley, a British novelist and dramatist, used the movement forward and backward through time in the lives of a family in some of his plays, and wrote about the phenomenon at length, and Lieutenant Jim Dickey had been hooked.

The editor of *Deliverance*, sitting day after day in his room at the

Heart of Rabun running time-coded strips of celluloid back and forth and back and forth through a Moviola machine, was Tom Priestley, who was J. B. Priestley's son, and when Jim Dickey found that out he was just blown away. A long time later, even just a few days before he died, he would still be telling his students about the book he read on the troopship, the man he met in Clayton. "The roots of coincidence, plus the dream," he said in his breathless voice, enthralled by the possibilities.

Priestley showed my father a rough segment of the first scenes from the film, where Voight looks in through the window of a shack and sees the spastic child, then another segment where they first see the river and Voight says, "Looks good. Looks good."

"I thought, God, sounds like me," my father remembered. "That sounds very much like me. He got it. 'Looks good.' "

Of course Voight's accent was not coincidence, that was the tape recordings and practice and the actor's craft, and Jim Dickey knew it perfectly well. But, still, the effect was strange. During the making of *Deliverance* it was hard to know, really, just where the dream left off. Or whose dream it was.

RESTING PLACE

W arner Bros. had built a dirt road to a dark laurel thicket by the river. It was a rough, steep track that got slicker and more dangerous every afternoon, when rain poured from the skies. The trees were enormous, forming a thick canopy hundreds of feet in the air. It was a rain forest, right here in the mountains of Georgia. Its floor was so shadowed that small plants found it impossible to grow in the thick loam of the rotting leaves. The mountain laurel was not shrubbery but a collection of trees twisted like gnarled fingers reaching for the light. The whole effect was beautiful and threatening. This was where the rape scene was going to be filmed. The script called it "Resting Place."

It is the second day of the story. Ed and Bobby in one canoe have gotten separated from Lewis and Drew in the other, and they pull over to the side of the river to wait for the others to catch up. Coming at them out of this dark forest they see two mountain men, one of them carrying a double-barreled shotgun.

One of the mountain men, the smarter of the two, was played by Bill McKinney, a serious character actor whose main obsession off the set seemed to be looking after his body. Each morning he swallowed dozens of vitamin and mineral pills, and when he talked to you he'd study with casual fascination the veins and sinews standing out on his own forearms. Burt claimed he saw Bill running naked through the Kingwood golf course in the early mornings.

The other was Herbert "Cowboy" Coward, who had worked with Burt a few years before at one of those Wild West shoot-out shows in a rickety amusement park in the Smoky Mountains. Cowboy was no

actor, but the script called for the character to be missing his front
teeth, and Cowboy looked like his had been knocked out with a
ball-peen hammer. The character had to seem at once terribly stupid
and terribly frightening. Cowboy could do that. He never left character. But when he talked, he usually stuttered, and when he tried not to
stutter, words would come out in weird orders. "You ain't a'goin any
damn wheres" was a line that stayed in the movie. "I'm g-g-gonna lay
a b-b-big long dick right in your mouth" was one that didn't.

For the first few days at Resting Place, a full crew was on the set.
There were some problems with new lights that the cinematographer
brought in. The preparations were slow, conditions uncomfortable. A
lot of people were getting sick in the constant damp and the changing
temperatures. A couple of the gaffers who'd been working in the water
day after day were getting lesions like jungle rot. Others were busy
spreading calamine lotion on poison ivy, chigger infestations, mosquito bites. At first there were a lot of jokes about snakes, but there
were a lot around, and soon they were taken seriously. We'd see
cottonmouths in the water and big rattlers sunning themselves on the
higher, drier stretches of the road. One day, as I was walking with the
hair stylist from the set to the riverside mess tent for lunch, talking
about the tensions that were growing around the scene that was coming, and not really thinking about where we were putting our feet, I
saw a shape in the middle of the path just in front of us. It was fatally
still. Its back was patterned like leaves. "Freeze," I said, and touched
the hair stylist's shoulder. Her foot stopped in midair, inches above
the copperhead. The snake's sullen, slow-moving skull lay like an
arrowhead in the black compost, its body thick and passive. One of
the lighting men decapitated it with a shovel and skinned it. We knew
there were others around, waiting.

The stars rehearsed, memorized lines, or practiced canoeing. All
of them were getting pretty good at it, and out on the river, most of
the day anyway, at least there was sun. But at Resting Place the mood
was getting darker. Ned Beatty no longer played the happy fat boy
around the set. He was getting harder to talk to, brooding, concentrating.

The day of the shooting, Burt and Ronny weren't called. The
press, even the studio's photographer, was barred from the set.
Donoene the hair stylist and Cindy the nurse were asked to go watch
the river.

There is a full rehearsal that tells us what's to come. One of
Boorman's great talents is the way he orchestrates the movement of
his actors through the frame, and the movement of the camera around

his actors. His cinematographer, Vilmos Zsigmond, sets up a master shot in which the actors go through the entire scene, and the camera takes it all in. Ed is pushed up against a tree and strapped there by the neck with his own web belt. McKinney takes a big hunting knife Ed carries and asks him how he'd like his balls cut off, then cuts a line across Ed's chest just to watch him bleed. Bobby is standing at a distance. McKinney tells him to drop his pants. Cowboy points the shotgun at him and gives a big grin that is no less horrifying for being so ludicrous, so hungry. When he's stripped to his jockey shorts, Bobby panics and tries to run. McKinney chases him; Bobby is trying to scramble up a steep hillside on all fours, but the earth and leaves slip away beneath him. McKinney grabs him, pushes him up the bank for a few feet, then follows him, pawing him, squeezing Bobby's ass and his breasts, sliding and falling back down into the rotting leaves. He grabs Bobby by the ear and the nose like a pig and half drags him, half rides him to a decaying log, forces him to lie over it, and rapes him.

One of the assistant directors called me from the sidelines and had me follow the actors through the scene. I was going to stand in for Ned while they set up the lights and the track for the camera. I didn't have to take off my clothes. All I had to do was go through the general motions, standing on the marks set up during the rehearsal, crawling as if in slow motion up the steep bank covered with leaves. No one led me by the nose, or rode me like a sow. But I had to lie down over the log, with the wood pressing into my stomach, and there were no jokes that could be made, there was nothing for anyone to say, that could keep me from feeling humiliated. I couldn't wait for this day to be over. But it was only beginning.

Jon and Ned, McKinney and Cowboy come back onto the set. They've been looking for a way to match dialogue to action, and somebody has the idea of making Ned squeal as McKinney forces him over the log. "Squeal like a pig. . . . Squeeeeal! . . . Squeeeeal!" And Ned does, in terror at first, and then, slowly, horribly, the squeals become groans of pain. And finally Boorman calls, "Cut." Then the action is run again, and again, each time growing more grotesque.

At lunch there were several nervous, risqué jokes. There was some kidding about McKinney's getting carried away. Ned tried to snap back out of character, to relax. But it wasn't working. And that day, and for the rest of the time he was in North Georgia, he seemed to have changed, as if whatever sadness or insecurity he'd covered up before as a man, as Ned Beatty, just couldn't be contained any more.

In the afternoon there were more shots of the same scene, but now from different angles. I wanted to go somewhere else, but I had to stay available to stand in, or lie down, or kneel for every new camera setup. I didn't watch the shooting any more, but I couldn't get away from the sound.

That night I called my father. I was sick of the film, sick of the whole story. And I wondered why the hell he had to have this homosexual rape. "I had to put the moral weight of murder on the suburbanites," was what my father told me. It was what he always said. He had to portray the mountain men as such monsters that the suburbanites would decide not only to kill, but to try to cover up their crime. Lewis can shoot McKinney in the back with an arrow, and look around at this forest about to be inundated by a dam, and say, "Law? What law?" and every man watching will think, Yeah, bury the son of a bitch.

I understood that was the way it was supposed to work. But I didn't think my father understood what had happened that day filming by the river. In the book you can read the rape scene and know it happened, but you get around it and go on, and get other things out of the novel. In the movie—it was becoming what the movie was about, it was the thing everybody was going to remember. "Squeal like a pig!" Not Lewis's survivalism, not the climb up the cliff, not Ed's conquest of his own fear. It was all going to be about butt-fucking.

"You're wrong, son," my father said.

There was something else that I wanted to tell my father on the phone, but I couldn't bring myself to say it. We were starting to hear from our trailer-park friends that there were a lot of people in these mountains who didn't like this film we were making. And you didn't know who might get it into his head to teach some of these movie people a lesson. There were plenty of real mountain men out there, with real guns. The director and the stars were all secure up at Kingwood; the rest of the crew were together at the Heart of Rabun. But I was here at this bungalow motel with my little family. We were all alone. And I was the son of the man who wrote the book.

I was scared. Scared enough to leave. But I stayed, because more than anything else I was afraid to admit how scared I was.

Each morning we struggled and slid down to some part of the Chattooga, and each evening we crawled back to Clayton. But the lingering depression that started in Resting Place grew worse. The work was no longer new. People had gotten to know each other too well. Even the river seemed to have run out of surprises.

Then we changed rivers.

On the mythical Cahulawassee there is a deep gorge not far

downstream from Resting Place. The four suburbanites bury McKinney and head back out on the water with no idea what lies up ahead. The sound of the rapids is rising in their ears when Drew, in the lead canoe, looks like he's been hit by something. Without any warning he tumbles over the side. Now they are all caught up in a rush of white water too powerful for any of them to handle. One of the canoes is broken in half. The other tumbles through the falls. By the time they reach still water at the bottom of the gorge, Lewis's leg is horribly broken. Drew has disappeared. And Bobby and Ed think he was shot. The other mountain man must be up there on the cliffs above them, waiting, they think. It's up to Ed now to save their lives, and the only way he can do that is to climb the side of the gorge at night. He puts his bow over his back with the razor-sharp arrows in a quiver attached to the handle and starts the long ascent through the dark.

The actual Chattooga didn't have a suitable location for this action. But Tallulah Falls, not far away, was perfect. There was a hydroelectric dam about a half-mile upstream with gates that could adjust the ferocity of the torrent pouring through the gorge to suit the needs of the shot. The flow could be reduced to a trickle if need be. But it was still a dangerous place. The first half of the falls ended in a deep pool that you could swim or paddle across easily when the current was turned down. But the only way to walk to the other side of the gorge was on a slick, slightly submerged retaining wall twelve inches wide, with the pool on one side and a ninety-foot drop on the other. Everyone used the wall, holding on to a little rope for security. I still don't know why no one slipped when the water was low, or was washed over the precipice during filming when the river swelled across it in heavy waves. Maybe it was the luck of people who'd started to quit caring.

Burt, the former stuntman, wanted to take his own risks, do his own "gags." For the breakup of the canoes, special-effects man Marcel Vercoutere devised a catapult to launch Reynolds thirty feet in the air, hurling him toward the pool. He was well padded, but he was still pretty badly beaten up on the rocks. Jon Voight took to climbing the lower levels of the cliff without any safety equipment. One day Jon was about twenty feet above the crew when he lost his hold and tumbled back off the rocks. A prop man was able to break his fall, barely, but stood frozen for a few seconds before he let Voight go. Everybody was frozen. The exposed blade of a hunting arrow on Jon's bow quiver was a breath away from the prop man's throat.

It was like the whole film was becoming some kind of macho gamble in which each man was out to prove he could take the risks the characters were running, characters that James Dickey had only imagined.

At the top of the gorge, 150 to 250 feet above the rocks, the risks were even greater, and everybody played. As they searched for the best camera angles, Boorman and Zsigmond leaned way out over the edge of the precipice, and only rarely put on safety harnesses. Lives were risked to position lights, or to saw off a twig that blocked the lens.

In the story, Ed reaches the top of the cliff just before dawn. He sees the mountain man, rifle in hand, peering at the river below. Ed draws down on him. His hand starts to shake, just as it did with the deer. The mountain man sees him. Ed's only going to get this one shot. The mountain man fires, Ed releases, and you're not sure for several seconds if the arrow has hit him or not. Then the mountain man turns. You see the arrow in his chest and he falls to the ground. But Ed doesn't leave him there. All this killing, all these crimes have to be buried by the river. He uses a rope to lower the mountain man's body down the cliff and sink it in the pool.

The special-effects men thought they'd use a dummy for the scene of a corpse dangling and twisting at the end of a cord high on the side of the cliff. But the dummy looked too much like a dummy. "Would Cowboy do it himself?" someone asked as the mannequin was dragged back up over the ledge. Cowboy took a look at the drop. It was about two hundred feet at this point. He fingered the thin rope that would hold him. He shook his head. He took a swig of the Pabst Blue Ribbon beer he always had close at hand, and sighed, and nodded toward the dummy. "Well," he said, "I g-guess if he c-can do it so c-can I."

Members of the crew and the artificial family at Kingwood began to go home. An assistant producer, both assistant directors, a camera operator, and two nurses left for reasons of health, or weariness or frustration. Burt's Numero Uno left, too, during the most dangerous part of the filming. But it was so important to him to be seen with a woman, even if no woman was at hand, that one day he came to the set in Tallulah Gorge with a handful of love letters written to him by women who'd slept with him. He passed them around to the crew for their reading enjoyment. One collection was from a pair of girls who called themselves Franny and Zooey. Another, more depressing set of letters was from an exotic dancer in a Newport News service club who was trying to launch her son's career as a musician by having him play backup during her routines. Burt was going to be her ticket out of all that, she thought.

The filming moved back to the Chattooga for a last sequence on the roughest section of the river before the four surburbanites arrive on the still waters of the lake that is rising behind the fictional town of Aintry. One morning everybody arrived on the set to word that someone had been shooting at the trucks the night before. No one was hurt. Everyone was a little spooked. It added to the sense that the whole production was racing against time, against some impending disaster. But we were on the homestretch, and almost too tired to care.

When the shooting was on the river, the stand-ins were usually left waiting at pickup points to meet the actors and camera crew when they came in off the water. We'd been most of the day at one of the roughest sections of the Chattooga when a heavyset kid everyone called Chicago borrowed a raft from the prop department and suggested we try shooting the rapids. It was midsummer now, and the only place you could see that was cool was in the water. We watched a couple of other members of the crew bounce downstream in inner tubes. They dropped over a ledge of about ten feet, twirled around for just a second in a whirlpool, then bounced out and headed on down the river. It looked like a safe enough thrill.

Chicago and I got into the raft and kicked out from shore. We hit the current and started to twirl slowly, picking up speed as we approached the drop. Now we were over the edge. And down. And the raft filled with water and we started to spin. It wasn't sinking, but it wasn't moving out of the whirlpool either. It was agitating and banging like a tennis shoe in a washing machine. One of the boys onshore threw us a rope, and Chicago grabbed it and went over the side. I saw him resurface downriver and get pulled in by the others like some enormous salmon. I was gulping water under the falls, and the raft was spinning and shaking too fast for me to think of anything now except how I was going to get out of it. I knew I couldn't make it swimming. I knew the hydraulic tumbler would drag me down to the bottom. I had to have the rope. The boys onshore were shouting and signaling. They were going to throw me the line, but I was supposed to tie it to the raft so they could pull it out. They threw. After a couple of tries, I caught. They left the line slack. But as the raft spun, the rope wrapped around my chest, my arms, my neck. I struggled to get it off, tried to find someplace to tie it, but it looped over my head and neck again. The water pounded from above, boiled up from below. The raft felt like it was going to tear apart. I freed my neck of the rope again and wrapped the end around my hand and went over the side. The current pushed me straight to the bottom, banging my body on the rocks, twirling me at the end of the cord that tightened like a noose around my hand and wrist. And then I was back on the surface, and being pulled in to shore. I guess I looked like hell: as gray as the rocks by the riverside. "We thought we'd lost you," said Chicago. "Me, too," I said.

It was about as close as I'd ever come to dying, at least at that point in my life, and that evening I tried to tell my father all about it. But he seemed to have other things on his mind. He was back on the scene. Back in the movie.

The shooting was almost over, and he'd been given a part to play on screen. He was going to be Sheriff Bullard, who doesn't really believe the story these city fellas tell him about what happened on the river—"How come you boys to have four life jackets?"—but lets them go anyway.

My father had never acted before. Not as such. And it embarrassed me then to watch him on the set. When I watch the movie now and see those scenes I think he was just about perfect: he is big and menacing, and there is a little of the Winslow sheriff in him; but there is also this genteel insecurity as Bullard tries to cope with the hinted atrocities taking place in his county, and there are several times in his brief appearance when he is just so much like my father, even the best of my father, sober and thoughtful and picking his words with real care, that I am glad just to be able to see him.

We were into the last days on the set. There was a last scene to shoot in which my father and I appear together, although it was later cut from the movie. Ed and Bobby and Lewis are called back up from Atlanta to the dam at Aintry. Lewis is on crutches. All of them are wearing business clothes, all have come to see a corpse on a stretcher covered by a sheet. Sheriff Bullard reaches down and lifts the shroud to show them the body of—you're not sure. It could be one of the mountain men. It could be Drew. You don't know and you never do see. Ed wakes from the dream.

I was the corpse under the sheet.

Everyone was counting the hours until shooting was over. Some read scripts for future films, some wondered where their next jobs would come from, and a couple looked forward to retiring soon. The stars spent much of their time playing golf and gambling together, competing and performing still, but taking fewer risks. Voight and his girlfriend, Marshalene, were over at the Boormans' a lot. Ned and Belinha awaited the birth of their child. Ronny spent his evenings picking and singing for the country-club set at Kingwood. I had the impression Burt was picking up any woman who came to hand. He also went around buying property. Tom Priestley, the editor, secluded himself with a Moviola at the Heart of Rabun to turn out a rough cut from thousands of feet of film.

Then, when my father had finished his part and was getting ready to leave, he and I were very cordially invited to Boorman's house one morning to see what there was to be seen in the makeshift basement projection room. We were alone as we watched the product of three rugged months of work thrown on the screen. We drank beers, one after another. We took breaks between reels, and after the first couple Jim Dickey was ecstatic. By halfway through the movie he was shouting out loud; then, at the climax on the cliff top, he went completely quiet except for two brief moments when, his hand over his mouth, acting awestruck, he breathed, "My God. Oh, my God."

He was faking it, I thought. Trying to convince himself. He had lived with this story—we had lived with it—all these years, and then it had all been taken over by other people and made into something else. Jim Dickey wouldn't let anyone change a line of his poetry, and he'd been ferocious defending every comma in the manuscript of his novel. And now this. It was a good movie. Very good. But it wasn't the one he had had in his head.

The last reel over, the last beer drunk, we stumbled from the dark recesses of Boorman's cottage into the glaring Georgia summer light. We said goodbye to Boorman's family and walked up to Kingwood's desk. My father asked for his check, flirting with the pretty receptionist. She soon found the bill. "Warners is going to pay for this," he said. "I don't want to see the total." The girl laughed and slapped her hand over the sum as my father signed. Her little finger was missing.

Outside, I helped my father fit his tape recorders, bows, and typewriter into his car. He was smiling. "I think we've really got something in this film," he said a couple more times as he climbed into the driver's seat. He drove out past the golf course, onto the highway, and home to Columbia. A few days afterward, I followed, leaving behind Clayton's Hollywood-in-residence, its country clubs, dirt farmers, mountain men, and white water, leaving behind the country of the nine-fingered people.

Deliverance did not hit the theaters for another year. There were technical problems with the scenes where Ed climbs the cliff. They were shot in the day, but were supposed to look like night. They did not. In the final version there is a weird, solarized halo around Voight throughout the sequence. There was also a dispute about the script. Boorman had changed so many lines during the shooting—"Squeal like a pig!"—that he wanted to share the writing credit, and the writer's money. The conflict went to arbitration, and James Dickey won. He got to keep all of the credit, all the cash.

When at last *Deliverance*, the film, was at hand, I had to realize that James Dickey had not made this movie, he had let it make him. This man, this father-poet-god, who had always demanded of himself, and of me, such perfection, had settled for artistic compromises that he would never in his imagination have tolerated—or forgiven—in another poet, in a student, in his child. And he was not only settling for less, it seemed to me, he was reveling in the result.

The tremulous sense of uncertainty, the inchoate anger that I'd felt all through my adolescence began to focus now on the idea of betrayal. I felt the righteous fury of any young man whose ideals have been sullied, and, added to that, the ferocious intolerance that came with being James Dickey's son. And all of it was turning on him. Yet I could not get away. The attraction was too strong. I was drifting like a satellite in an erratic orbit, circling close, circling at a great distance, circling always within the pull of his enormous gravity.

I would go with him, in the end, even to the theaters where *Deliverance* was showing. He would wear his purple fringed leather jacket and his big Stetson hat with the pheasant-feather band. Sometimes the long strands of hair he combed over the top of his balding head would come loose and drop down over one ear, giving him the look of a cowboy who'd been half scalped. The smell of alcohol would ooze from his pores. And he would stand in the long lines—even walk up and down the lines—as people waited for tickets. "You see that?" he'd say. "That's my movie."

ENEMIES

The best of all wives is the country girl, and the next best
is the prostitute who manages to get married, and who
must work hard all the rest of her life at recovering the
love and the sensuality that she spent a number of years
losing for money.

—Sorties

THE CANOE
BENEATH
THE HAMMOCK

July 1996. I took a break from cleaning the Augean garage in Columbia and wandered to the back yard along the edge of the lake, looking for air. Ivy and pine needles had taken over. The archery target that used to be at one end of the lot had long ago become compost. And at the other end, not far from the wooden dock, an aluminum canoe lay upside down, as immobile as a sculpture. Beside it dangled the rope threads of a hammock that had rotted, fallen, and partly turned to mulch in the damp pine-straw. My father bought the canoe in the days of the movie *Deliverance*, when he was used to buying anything he wanted, and buying it *now*. The hammock came from Pawley's Island, near the house at Litchfield that he bought in 1973. Years later, long after my mother died, the next-door neighbor in Columbia found the canoe drifting in Lake Katherine with some empty beer cans and a skeletal Christmas tree inside. The neighbor dragged it ashore. The hammock fell out of use, and its wide weave slowly came apart, and it came down.

I was twenty-two years old and a thousand miles away in Massachusetts. I was living on the North Shore, commuting to Boston a few times a week to study documentary filmmaking, trying desperately to feel like my own man but trying, still, to be my father's son. I was writing constantly in my journal. The entries are full of my father as I thought about him, and as he thought for me with this head he'd made. There are notes for scripts, for short stories, for novels, all interspersed with readings from critics and poets favored by my father. On one page are the closing lines of "Dover Beach," on another an adage from William Blake's *The Marriage of Heaven and Hell*—"The eagle never lost so much time as when he submitted to learn of the crow"— which my father would quote to me whenever I had differences with my teachers.

I clung to the idea that my father and I were very different, but I was living a pale, strained imitation of his life. I drank a lot. I started to have quiet, guilt-ridden affairs. My marriage was coming apart, but Susan and I were too stubborn to admit it. These were, I realize now, the worst years of my life.

My father was able to pass on to me, now and again, writing assignments he didn't want. But people came to my father for his genius, and to help them create myths. I was not a genius, and de-mythologizing was becoming my obsession. *Life* magazine commissioned a piece from me about the making of the movie *Deliverance*, then decided what I wrote was too negative. A group of architects in Boston assigned me a documentary script for a film to be shown at the visitors' center they designed for Philadelphia's Independence Hall, but my script was too bleak, too obsessed with the fighting and the suffering, the bad judgment and the dumb luck that made the revolution happen. Eventually I managed to get a short story published in *Playboy* explaining why a much-heralded comet, one that was supposed to appear in the night sky like the Star of Bethlehem, had been such a fizzle. As the contributors note described it: "Chris Dickey—in all likelihood the only son of a *Playboy Interview* subject (James Dickey) ever to write for this magazine—checks in with *It Came to Pass.*"

My father and I talked on the phone about his work, my work. He revived the idea of making *Amos Berry* into a movie and persuaded a producer named Elliott Kastner to buy the rights from Allan Seager. My father hoped this would be *our* work, like "Kevin the Diver," or the Sparta film, but this time for real—for money. In November 1972, he decided to come up to our little house in South Hamilton to talk about the script. I thought maybe I had been away long enough, and far enough, to accept that. But just barely.

That first night my father was in Hamilton, we invited John Updike over from Ipswich, a couple of miles up the road. Jim Dickey had been reading Updike since we lived in Atlanta. He knew the man, knew his work, and liked both. There were no fights, no scenes that I recall. But the evening became more and more incoherent as my father slid away from conversation toward drunken performance. "Dad is in terrible shape," I wrote in my journal that night. "He is seriously, obviously alcoholic and he undergoes terrific stress when he doesn't drink. The whole picture is disconcerting, especially since he seems to perceive it without really wanting to change it." The next day we went into Boston and talked about the *Amos Berry* script on the long drive back to Hamilton. We recorded hours of ideas. But that night my father was so drunk that he broke a chair in the kitchen.

Still, he thought he had the out-of-control under control. "I don't make a very good madman," he'd say. He talked with contempt about "the drunken-poet syndrome" among other writers, and seemed not to see how enormous his potbelly had grown, how his massive arms had turned to flab, how his body shook when he needed a drink. The pattern of strained sobriety and the drunkenness that alternated surly and ecstatic had become grimly predictable. In February 1973, I took my son down to Columbia to see Fun Man—which is what my father insisted his grandson call him—for Fun Man's fiftieth-birthday party. There was a big crowd, and I listened as Jim Dickey declared for all the world to hear that he had given up drinking. But three days after his birthday he was off the wagon, and drinking harder than ever. There was always so much drama when he quit. So much relief when he started again. So much drama around Jim Dickey.

My mother was now starting to die. And none of us seemed to notice.

Susan and I were lying in our bedroom in South Hamilton watching public television. This night, by coincidence, the film was Jean Cocteau's *Orpheus,* with Jean Marais as the middle-aged poet torn between creation and complacency who descends into a Parisian underworld to encounter a younger, wilder, more intense poet-self, and to bring his pregnant wife, Eurydice, back to the land of the living.

The film was just beginning when the telephone rang. My mother was on the line in tears. "I'm going to leave him!" she screamed. I knew she was drunk, and I thought I knew this whole conversation already, by heart. But as she went on she sounded so angry, so desperate, so determined, that I thought maybe this time she would do what she said she was going to do. She was going to have him served with divorce papers, she said.

My father had been away on a reading tour, speaking at Washington and Lee University, and she had gone to pick him up at the Columbia airport. He had missed his plane. She waited. He caught another, and when he came off he was falling-down drunk. He'd been drinking like crazy, my mother said, ever since he'd gone to the doctor a few weeks before and been given a clean bill of health.

I never knew how clean those bills really were, but if they said he wasn't diabetic, and he never was, then they were good enough for him. My father had the idea that he was going to die of diabetes the way his grandmother had; that he would be whittled away by gangrene and the doctor's knife; that he would lose his sight, and his mind. For years he told people he had the disease, and he almost believed it himself. When he imagined he had some symptom, he would quit drinking for a few days, and that was always difficult. So, the minute he was told by a doctor that he did not have diabetes, he'd begin drinking again with a vengeance. And then, belligerent as an old bull, he'd start to attack my mother. Or just ignore her. Or taunt her. My father was a master of the taunt.

At the dinner table in Columbia that night, she'd tried to talk to him about the drinking. About the way he was living and acting. And he'd started to quote one of Lewis's speeches in *Deliverance*. Whenever he started re-enacting *Deliverance*, you knew you'd lost him. "It is a question of SURVIVAL!" he'd shout, nostrils flaring, face reddening. He'd play out the whole scene. "Law? Hah! What law? Do you see any law around here?"

My mother told me there was another woman, or women. She told me again she was going to leave him. And I just listened. I felt as if there were a huge wave of misery bearing down on us. But the only way I knew how to react during these scenes was not to react at all. I listened for a while longer, and told my mother I loved her, and hung up.

I tried to go back to watching *Orpheus*, but I'd lost the thread of it.

Susan called my mother back, then I got on the phone, and for well over an hour the three of us talked. We were trying to get her to get the hell out of Columbia. She said she had too much to do. Nothing would work without her. No bills would get paid. "Your father doesn't even know how to write a check." Kevin was in school. There was just no way, she said. But there was no way, I said, that she could go on like this. She didn't have to stay away long. Just take a break. She could come stay in Hamilton, see Tucky, who loved her, and in the meantime I would go down to Columbia and arrange for an accountant to take care of the check-writing, and I would take Kevin to school, and I would see if there wasn't some way to talk to Dad about survival—for all of us.

She agreed. I called the airlines, booked her ticket north and mine south, and felt at last we were getting somewhere. But by the time I called her back, ten minutes later, my mother had decided she couldn't leave. She had talked to my father. And now he got on the phone, his voice heavy with sleep and alcohol. "Now, you just let us worry about this," he told me. There was nothing to be done.

The next morning I called Columbia. My mother's hangover weighed on her, and she said she didn't remember a lot of what we'd said. Things were better, she said. Better.

Kevin called in the evening. He'd been visiting a friend and had only come back in the afternoon. Mom and Dad had been screaming at each other most of the night. Kevin, who was fifteen by then, was in tears.

My mother got on the phone and interrupted Kevin. "You two don't have anything to say to each other," she said. "You stay out of this, Chris."

"I'm trying to help—"

"You're not," she said, and she said her mother had warned her not to call me. She said my uncle Tom's wife, Patsy, had told her not to call me. I wasn't helping. I didn't understand. "And I'm paying for this phone call," she said, and hung up.

I waited a few minutes and called Kevin back. He was still in tears. "Mom says you don't know what's going on down here," he said. "But you're the only one who knows what is happening."

I told him that if he really needed me I would come down to Columbia. We would talk again in the morning. But in the morning, again, there was enough quiet to allow us all to think we could go on with our lives.

In the early spring, I went to Atlanta to make a documentary about Tom Dickey, who was my father's younger brother, and his passion for collecting Civil War artillery projectiles. I'd gotten the idea years before, when I was given a tour of the Library of Congress and saw the Mathew Brady stereo cards of the great Civil War battles. In black and white, but in three dimensions, corpses lay bloating where they'd fallen near Little Round Top; or stacked like cordwood after Shiloh; or reaching out with skeletal hands through the leaves and pine straw of the Wilderness. They were more graphic than any other pictures of war I'd ever seen, and I thought it would be interesting to put those images together with what Tom did, searching through old maps of the battlefields until he could determine where most of the shells would have landed, then sweeping them with an old mine-detector he'd bought at a surplus store. He'd made war a hobby, I thought, and reduced all that suffering to a collection of excavated curiosities on built-in shelves around a pool table in his family room: hundreds and hundreds of howitzer rounds, mortar rounds, cannonballs, all lovingly cleaned of as much corrosion as possible, then coated with varnish and numbered and catalogued.

My father had written a poem, "Hunting Civil War Relics at

Nimblewill Creek," about watching Tom's face as Tom listened to the sonarlike beep of the detector, then falling to the ground to dig up the history that lies beneath, "Like a man who renounces war, / Or one who shall lift up the past, / Not breathing 'Father,' / At Nimblewill, / But saying, 'Fathers! Fathers!' "

So I went down to Atlanta with another student, David Goldenberg, thinking we'd make a very serious—disturbing, negative, demythologizing—film. But Tom wouldn't let me. He was just too easygoing, too charmingly crazy, as he talked his way into people's back yards in Atlanta, or slogged through swamps worrying about rattlesnakes, or defused a fifty-pound shell in his basement with nothing but a hammer, a screwdriver, and a sponge—only to look up and realize that Dave and I had abandoned the camera and tape recorder and retreated behind a wall. "You know, I do worry sometimes," Tom said. "If this house ever caught on fire, you'd hear the last shots fired in the Civil War."

It was good to be back in the South, I thought. Good to be doing this film about my charming uncle, and good to be surprised by what I was discovering. Atlanta was at its best. The dogwoods were in bloom, the light was gentle and clear. And Grandpapa and Grandmama still lived in the big house on West Wesley. I ran up the stairs, I remember, and picked her up and twirled her around, and she laughed like a girl.

It was a good trip, but it was only an interlude.

After my father bought the Litchfield house, my mother spent more and more time there alone. What he was doing in Columbia she didn't want to know. None of us did. He wanted his freedom? He could have it. Jim and Maxine Dickey were liberated from each other at last. But my father didn't want to be alone. He didn't want my mother to escape. And Jim Dickey's cries for attention were always the first to be heard, and always the loudest.

My mother was down at Litchfield when word of the crash reached her. My father had been drunk, real drunk, in the late afternoon, and headed over to the Columbia house of a dreary little admirer he'd been fucking when he lost control of the Jaguar XKE and wrapped it around a telephone pole. He was in jail, my mother told me. But otherwise he was okay, she guessed. "What a jackass," she said. "What a jackass!"

"How's the car?" I asked, knowing my father's pride was the worst thing he'd hurt, and thinking about the machine that I'd loved.

"I'm going to leave him this time," my mother said. She was

crying and drunk and getting ready to make the three-hour drive up to Columbia to bail him out. "I can't get away from that bastard," she said.

"Leave him, for Christ's sake!"

"I'll take care of it," she said. "I'll take care of it." She'd just called because she wanted me to know about the crash before it appeared in the papers, she said. And it did appear, in all of them. The next week the crash even made it into *Time* magazine.

The two Columbia cops who were first at the scene that afternoon were named Mooney and Swisher. Mooney had noticed the Jag with its top down and "this older guy driving it" but paid no attention until a few minutes later, when he got a report a sports car had crashed. Sure enough, it was the Jag. The driver's head and face were bleeding, but he was conscious. Mooney started to help. The driver told him he could go fuck himself. He didn't want any help. Didn't need any help, goddamn it. There wasn't much question this driver had been drinking. The ambulance team arrived, but the driver didn't want them to touch him either. Mooney told him they were going to take him down to the station. They were going to cuff him.

"You ain't taking me nowhere," said Big Jim Dickey. "You ain't putting those cuffs on me." My father swung at Mooney like he thought he could unconscious him with a single punch, but it was a drunk's roundhouse that landed on open air. Mooney and Swisher were used to bigger, tougher, and younger men than my father. They pinned him. They cuffed him. They shoved him in the back of the squad car.

By now, they'd figured out who he was. Columbia was a small town; everybody would know who he was. When Mooney called in the license and registration, he didn't have to spell the name. "James Dickey," he said. "You know, like the man who wrote *Deliverance.*"

RE-ENACTMENT

Everybody moves around so much in America that, when people talk about where they're from, usually they mean wherever they went to high school. I had moved more than most. The Washington area, especially Loudoun County, was the only place I knew where I felt that little rush of excitement and self-assurance that means "home." So, in 1974, when at last I had to look for a job, I thought that was the only place I wanted us to be.

I was willing to take any job. But the only permanent offer I came close to getting was in the audiovisual department of the United States Chamber of Commerce, and finally even that fell through. The one and only job I could get, in the end, was a temporary slot at the *Washington Post*. An editor was working on a *Washington Post* guide to Washington, D.C., and I got a renewable one-month contract to work as her assistant. Then I helped pull together the instant paperback on Nixon's resignation. William MacPherson, who edited the book section, gave me a slightly less temporary job as a copy editor with a chance to write occasional reviews. My pay was just barely enough for us to scrape by in a little wreck of a house in Middleburg. But we were on our own.

I'd been married for five years. I had a four-year-old son. I was twenty-three years old. I felt like I was already behind the curve. I thought I was ready for the independence, the responsibility I'd accrued so quickly, and then some. But the sadness of being an adult, the losses that came with it, caught me unawares. I had been thinking about death—imagining it, romancing it—since I was a child. Now the real thing was moving into our lives.

Susan's father, who'd been in his sixties when she was born, held on into his eighties. He held on so long, in fact, that we thought he'd never die. And then he did. And I remember people coming up to her at the funeral to say that maybe it was for the best after all, these last twenty years he'd only been a shadow of himself. And Susan, who was only twenty-three, said that was the only way she'd ever known him, and she'd loved him as he was. Then, in early 1976, Bill Costin, the father of one of my best buddies in high school, died of cirrhosis. He was sixty-two. And my father and my mother were drinking just the way he drank. But they were younger, I thought, and stronger. They'd hang on for a long time, I thought.

The week after Bill was buried, my parents flew me out to California for the "premiere" of *The Call of the Wild*. The Hollywood concept was James Dickey meets Jack London; sort of *Deliverance* in the Klondike. My father wrote the script. He'd even composed a little country-and-Western song for the bar scene. He loved to talk about all the stars who might be in it. But in the end it was never meant to be more than a made-for-TV movie, and the star, playing John Thornton, was a long-since-forgotten television actor named John Beck.

Some of the people who had gathered at the river came to the hotel in Beverly Hills to say hello. Ned and Belinha Beatty; Jon and Marshalene Voight, who had gotten married, stopped by briefly. Michael Allin, whom I hadn't seen since the summer of the moon shot, showed up, too. Al Braselton paid his own way out from Atlanta, just for the hell of it. But the reunions were strained. Every time the old friends came to the door of my parents' suite, I could see how disturbed they were by my father's appearance, and my mother's. His body was a withered caricature of the Big Jim Dickey who had stalked the set of *Deliverance*. My mother was forty or fifty pounds overweight, maybe more. It was all from whisky. She almost never ate anything. Since 1972, she'd been talking about being sick, but never saying exactly what was wrong. She'd been passing blood, she said in the summer of '72. But the next time I asked her about it, she'd said it was taken care of. Now her arms and legs were covered with large red marks, a rash or hives of some sort, and her voice was sounding increasingly weak. "I'm doing what the doctors tell me," she'd say. Once again I thought that there was nothing more to be done.

That night, after the screening of *The Call of the Wild*, I don't think any of us knew what to say. Even as a TV movie it was mediocre. But there was no way to tell that to Jim Dickey. He'd started bluffing, bullshitting, bullying about everything he wrote, some of which sounded like a parody. *The Call of the Wild* was supposed to become a television series. "Who *is* John Thornton?" asks James Dickey's proposal. "He is a man, in the first decade of the twentieth century, who wants to have the *whole* of human experience for himself." And a dog at his side, of course.

Jim Dickey was more famous than ever. But there were so many works in progress, and only the worst of them seemed to get done. We had entered the era of James Dickey coffee-table books, lavishly illustrated overpriced tomes published by the same company that did *The Progressive Farmer* and *Southern Living* magazines. They were marketed by junk mail like trinkets from the Franklin Mint. The first was *Jericho: The South Beheld*, with tempera illustrations that were Southern-sentimental knockoffs of Andrew Wyeth, and the books got worse after that.

The booze and bluster were carrying over into everything my father wrote, everything he did. The obsessions of the poetry—the whole voice of it—changed. Ecstasy and creation gave way to masturbation and menstruation. The wild, passionate, overwhelming, mystical tirade of "May Day Sermon" becomes in *The Zodiac* the self-described "story of a drunken and perhaps dying Dutch poet who returns to his home in Amsterdam after years of travel and tries desperately to relate himself, by means of stars, to the universe."

By the time *The Zodiac* came out, his reputation was already in decline, and he called me at the *Washington Post Book World* and ordered me to get a good review for it.

"What?"

"What's good for me is good for the family," he said, "and good for *you.*"

"C'mon, Dad, that's why I can't—"

"Don't give me that shit. Just see that you do it—if you want those checks to keep coming in every month."

"You mean checks from you?"

"That's right," he said, like he had me by the balls.

"Dad, you haven't sent me a check in two years."

"I haven't? Well, I'll be damned."

We both laughed. But somebody else assigned the review, and when it appeared it was very brief.

Jim Dickey's biggest work in progress in 1976 was a pair of novels that he claimed to be writing simultaneously. "If I can bring this off, Tolstoy will seem a minor writer," he declared. The first, which he started out calling *Death's Baby Machine*, then *Alnilam*, follows a blind father's search for the meaning of his son's death in a flight-training accident during World War II. It was based on his experiences at Camden, and he'd been making notes on it since the late 1940s. The second would be *Crux*, about the air war in the Pacific.

He published a chapter from *Alnilam* in *Esquire* magazine in early 1976—and got his face on the cover. He was wearing one of his cowboy hats on his head and an aluminum life-mask over his features. That metal face had become an important symbol to him. When the mold was being made, some chemicals had gotten in his eyes, and for a couple of days his eyes had to be bandaged. He would say he was almost blinded. The superficial injuries in the XKE crash had become legendary, too. And he was convinced, once again, that he was diabetic. So, in notes and interviews, he contemplated what it would take to finish the two novels. "If there is anything seriously wrong with me, and I am told that I won't make it for more than, say, a few years, I will . . . write *Crux* as a much shorter book in brief scenes, something like Joan Didion's *Play It As It Lays*. If time is *very* short, I will do them both that way. It would be easier to do, and I could get them both done, even if I had only a couple of weeks to live."

It was another decade before *Alnilam* was published, and *Crux* never developed further than those few dozen pages of notes I read twenty years later at Litchfield. The problem my father had with both was that they were supposed to involve a mystical conspiracy devised by the cadet named Joel Cahill, who has died, or perhaps just disappeared. My father thought there would have to be some sort of vision of the future that the others in the plot would find compelling. "The society would depend very heavily on *role-playing*, and on *lying*. Joel believes that lying exercises the creative and imaginative faculties, and, when indulged in on either an individual or a group basis, raises the consciousness of the party or parties concerned." He is looking to "create a new human consciousness where there is really no difference between the actual world and the transfigured world." It was an idea that Jim Dickey tried to live, but he could never make it work in the novels, and in 1976 it started to fail him and everyone around him in his life.

I didn't understand why my mother was in the hospital. As I listened to her doctor, I had trouble grasping the significance of this "condition common in alcoholics" that I'd never heard of before. Her liver had hardened, and that had caused a narrowing of some of the veins that fed into it. They had swelled in her esophagus—"Do you know what varicose veins are?" "Yeah. Yeah, I guess." "Well, that's sort of what we're talking about"—and they had started to bleed—to gush blood—and she'd had to be taken to the hospital, where a balloon was inflated in her throat to stanch the flow.

"But she's going to be okay."

"We hope so. But—"

"You think I should come down to see her."

"Yes, Chris, I do."

I did not recognize my mother in her bed in the intensive-care ward. She used to spend so much time on her hair, blowing it and teasing it the way middle-aged women did in the South in the seventies. Now it was flat and close to her head, damp from the sweat of pain and fever. Her skin was the color of cheap paper. An oxygen tube was taped under her nose, and her lips were parched. Her arms were covered in patches of yellow-brown disinfectant, where intravenous drips were needled into her. "Oh, Chris," she said. "Oh, Chris. I'm so glad to see you." I hugged her and kissed her, trying not to disturb any of the tubes. She had put on some of her perfume, Femme, but underneath it she smelled like sickness.

"You're going to be okay, Mom."

"I know, honey. I know." She looked toward her mother. "Momma? Can you get that box?" Her mother pulled a shoe box from under the bed. In it were bills, and a checkbook. "Some of the bills need to be paid," my mother said.

"I'll take care of that," I said. She went over some of them with me. "I don't know who's going to do it while I'm in here," she said.

"I'll get it done," I said. "We'll find somebody who knows about these things."

She looked at me and at her mother, and what I saw in her eyes was suspicion. She didn't want to hear that somebody else could do this, the running of the house, the paying of the bills. It was all she thought she had left.

For two or three days I stayed in Columbia, going to the hospital as often as they'd let me in. She didn't want to see my father so frequently, so I had to try to find excuses to keep him away. I don't remember any more what they were. I didn't make any notes, and there is a lot I've erased from those days. But I thought whatever I was saying was working, I thought he was so terrified of what he saw when he saw my mother in that bed that it didn't take much convincing for him to stay away.

Finally, we all thought she was getting better. I didn't leave until I knew she was being moved out of the intensive-care ward into a regular room. I felt like I'd done what needed doing, and all that I could do. She was going to be fine. I went back to Washington. I believed in God back then, and I prayed every day, sometimes in church and sometimes wherever I was when the spirit moved me. She was going to get better. I knew it.

It was a few days later—a Friday, I think. I called my mother from the office and started to talk to her. But she sounded like she was in pain, and she handed the phone back to the nurse. And I heard my mother moaning, calling out. And the nurse said, "You're gonna have to call back, Mr. Dickey." I called again a few minutes later and they said she couldn't talk just then, I should try the next day. Susan was coming into town that night so we could go to a party at Kramerbooks & Afterwords. By the time we got back to Middleburg, the message light on the answering machine was blinking frantically. And one message after another was from my aunt Patsy, Tom's wife. She didn't say why I had to call her, but there was only one thing she could want to tell me. There were no messages from my father.

By the time I met my prospective stepmother, I was glad to see her— and I thought probably that was just the way my father planned it.

It was December 1976, not quite six weeks since my father and brother and I stood together at All Saints Waccamaw and saw my mother's coffin lowered into the ground and listened to the lines from Robert Penn Warren that my father chose for the service: "Tell me a story of deep delight. . . ." It was not quite six weeks since I had held my father's head next to my chest as we lay on the bed that looked out on the lake and he shivered from alcohol withdrawal. He had quit drinking then, for good. And so had I. We would face the future together, and sober, and with love. It was not quite six weeks since he had seen a girl he claimed he didn't know standing at the back of the crowd with a single tear dropping from her eye. But that, of course, was just something he told people later, one of those lies he thought would raise his consciousness, or appease his conscience.

Deborah Dodson was in one of his classes. She was twenty-four years old (about three months younger than me), and the first time he saw her in the hallway at school he put his hand over his mouth and said, his eyes widening, "My God! Robin Jarecki come to life!" They had lunch at the end of September, complete with her first martinis, and a week later he asked her to go with him to New York on a trip planned for later in the year. Not long after that, in mid-October, he told his class that my mother was in the hospital and dying, and after that class he asked Deborah to marry him. She was "light and warmth," he told her. It was the phrase he'd used for my mother, Maxine, on the dedication page of *Helmets*. So Deborah was Robin. Deborah was

Maxine. Deborah would be Mrs. Dickey. But my mother's condition started to improve, and Deborah didn't know what she was going to do. And then my mother died.

And now my father, for some reason, wanted me to approve.

All I knew, because his secretary, Shaye Arehart, had warned me, was that he was thinking of getting married. She asked me to try to talk him out of it. She didn't tell me any of the rest.

He was scheduled to arrive in Washington on Thursday and be on the *Panorama Show* with Maury Povich on Friday to talk about *The Zodiac.* Shaye organized everything the way my mother used to, giving me airplane numbers, departure and arrival times. I expected my father to land in Washington at eight in the morning. I would call him at the Georgetown Inn when I got to the office, we'd have lunch, and he could see my end of things at the *Post.*

He didn't check into the hotel until after one-thirty. But by then I'd given up and decided to go to lunch with someone else. When I finally got in touch we said we'd have dinner at seven. I'd meet him at the hotel.

When I called up to his room from the lobby, there was no answer. I sat down to wait. I read the paper and some notes. I called the room and waited some more. And called, and called again. It was well after seven-thirty. I asked the clerk if I could stow the gift books and the big wooden airplane wrapped in red Christmas foil behind the desk, and if I could have the key to the room. "The bell captain will open the door for you, sir," he said.

There were no signs of violence or panic. A few clothes were scrambled on the dresser, there were books scattered around the bed, and sprawled among them was my father. His face was puffy and slack as he slept on his side, all the lights in the room on, his head about a foot from the phone. He looked dead, but I knew he was just dead drunk. I let the bellboy go. Maybe I thought of walking out, too, but what I did instead was go over to my father and softly, as if I were rousing Tucky on his birthday morning, squeeze and move his shoulder until his eyes opened.

"Ah—my son." And he threw wide his arms with a grand gesture of embrace before saying, "Where am I?"

"*How* are you? I've been trying to call you."

His features looked out of place when he looked up—skewed, as if shaped in sagging putty. "Mmm."

"You look like you might have had a little somethin' to drink," I said.

I don't remember what he said then, only that he could not get to his feet. He sat and lay on the bed. He fell off the bed and onto the floor on his knees. He grabbed me around the waist, holding me. "Don't leave me, son. Don't leave me." I wasn't leaving him. But I was having trouble following what he was saying. He would giggle, then suddenly yell out that no one loved him, then simper again. He'd say he'd seen *The Missouri Breaks,* a film with Brando: "Worst movie I ever saw in my life." And he told me he was already married.

I asked my father why his wife hadn't come with him. "She thinks I'm a bum," he said, giggling, then put up his hands to frame an imaginary shot in some movie, talking about John Beck, saying how lonely he was. Then talking, and talking, and talking about my mother —how he would raise her from the grave if he could, and how she had gone there: "She *exploded* in my *arms,*" he said, and started to imitate her voice. "Oh, Jim, oh, Jim, help me, help me, oh oh oh aghhhh." He pretended to throw up blood, the way she had. "Buckets of it," he said. And then he told me he would put Deborah in the grave at Waccamaw if it would bring Maxine back. And then he flared his nostrils and said, "Thirty years I was married to that woman. THIRTY YEARS. And I killed her."

"No, Dad. Not really."

"Yes I did. I killed her. If I hadn't fucked around. If. But—and I loved her dearly—but if only there had been some good, natural sex at home, I—"

"You would have fucked around anyway," I said, as gently as I could.

I was sitting quietly in an armchair now, feeling too formal, too reserved in my three-piece suit with my hand alongside my chin and my fingers framing my face for support. My father was still on his knees and leaning against the bed. Tears were rolling down his cheeks as he talked about how lonely he was in the house. And, again and again, how he'd killed my mother.

"She could have left you, Dad. She could have left you any time."

"Yeah, except"—and he paused as he always did, waiting for whoever he was talking to to fill in the blank. I had stopped doing that long ago, so he went on—"she loved me. I killed her."

Then he told me again how he would raise her from the grave in Waccamaw. "She's under the water," he said. And how he would be buried beside her. And then he told me how much I'd like Deborah, about how tough she was. "Rougher than a night in jail."

At some point I asked him how he'd gotten in such a state, but I didn't find out. At another point he told me that he'd been in a fight downstairs, and that the woman named Tammy he had seen that afternoon had said he was a bum, and that Deborah thought he was a bum. "And I am a bum," he said.

"Yes you are," I said.

We laughed a lot. We laughed just as much as I could stand. In fact, I don't think I ever quit smiling except when he went into one more very long, graphic description of my mother's death and told me that near the end she had said, "Jim, I love you, but let me see my mother."

"She didn't want me," he said, as if she'd betrayed him.

I wrote down all of this a couple of days after it happened, but felt even then that there were rhythms to the evening I couldn't convey, as my father went back and forth from talking about John Beck as a great actor to nobody loving Jim Dickey to my mother exploding to *The Missouri Breaks*, giggling and crying, yelling and mumbling, and burying his head in my lap. For a while I ran my fingers through his long, thin hair, putting it back in place, telling him for the most part what he wanted to hear; telling him, also, that I was scared that he'd die the same way my mother had.

"You're strong," he said. "But I'm weak."

I felt very tired.

Eventually I called Deborah at her job at a telephone-answering service and I talked to her and my father talked to her and the two of us, with a little coaxing, convinced her to come up to Washington as soon as possible. I congratulated her on her marriage. She paused, and thanked me. I realized they were not married yet. Another lie. I handed the phone back to my father. He promised her they'd be getting married soon. He had the license, he said.

The call over, he seemed to be sobering quickly. He had what he wanted.

"You're gonna like her," he kept telling me. At dinner, he told me that she thought from my pictures that I was very handsome and that really she was interested in me, not him. I wasn't especially flattered. He was really anxious to have new children, he said. He really wanted a little girl, and he was going to have one if it killed him and Deborah trying to make her. That's why he wanted to get married right away, he said. To have a daughter.

So I spent the night sleeping on my friend Peter Mikelbank's sofa in Georgetown, as I'd planned, and the next day Deborah flew into Washington and met me at the *Post*. She was neither so beautiful as he described her nor so ugly as I expected. Tall and big-boned, she wore a green suit with a skirt a couple of inches too short. Her hair was long and a lustrous dark brown, falling straight and flatly plain to below her waist. Her features were fine but set in a face that was too wide and round. Her voice was Southern and pleasant, and sounded less fatuous in person than on the telephone. We drove out together to watch my father on *Panorama*, and he was better, I thought, than I'd ever seen him, fielding questions about *The Zodiac*, alcoholism, and suicide smoothly, easily, intelligently. Deborah said she wasn't in any rush to marry, but she told me several times how much she loved him. I did not ask her why. She said, "He is never dull."

All of that night at the Georgetown Inn, and for days afterward, I had contained my anger. Back at the house in Middleburg I wrote down what had happened, I even talked it onto tape, hoping that I could control it some way, turn it into material, shape it. My father claimed a writer should use everything he knew, and dreamed—everything he felt. Well, I had never felt like this. And part of me, the survivor in me, saw that this anger—so hot, so defining—could give me at last the strength I needed to escape my father's orbit. Yet there was still no clear break, no moment when I said once and for all, I'm gone. Like my mother, I guess, as much as I wanted to get away, I still had no idea where to go. The anger was only a beginning.

I did not see Deborah again until the inauguration of Jimmy Carter, a few weeks later, and by then I'd read about her marriage to James Dickey in *People* magazine. Shaye, who'd asked me to persuade my father to wait, had decided to serve as maid of honor.

My father the Georgia poet had been asked to write a poem for the Georgia president. He thought, and led us all to believe, that he'd be reading it on the steps of the Capitol, just as Robert Frost had read for John F. Kennedy. But Jim Dickey was put on a different program, reading instead as part of the inaugural stage show in the Kennedy Center. He was shaky behind the lectern. He'd been drinking beer with Paul Newman backstage, and had a few too many. The poem, "The Strength of Fields," went on too long. He tried to work his drunken-poet magic on the crowd, but the crowd was waiting for someone else—Chevy Chase or Shirley MacLaine or whatever act was next. "Isn't that good?" No one knew what he was talking about.

Most of his appearance was edited out in the videotaped broadcast of the gala, including what happened during the chorus at the finale. All the stars were lined up singing onstage—"God Bless America," I think it was—and Jim Dickey dropped out of line and walked across the stage and whispered something in Paul Newman's ear. Newman didn't break his smile or his song for a second. But nobody knew what the hell Jim Dickey was doing up there.

All night long, whether she was outside or inside, Deborah wore her cloth coat bundled around her. If she was intimidated by all the stars, she was making a show of it. She said almost nothing. When, finally, we caught up with my father, I asked him what he'd said into Newman's ear. Jim Dickey gave me a six-pack smile. "I asked him if he'd ever taken it up the ass." He looked around. "Debba," he said, "let's *go*."

WOMEN

The morning I woke up in the bed of one of my father's forty-something lovers was the morning I realized revenge was not what I wanted. She'd gone to fix breakfast and I was alone, naked and hungover, upstairs in the big Northwest Washington house she'd gotten from her ex-husband. It was a peaceful room decorated in gentle pastels. The early-morning light filtered in through the trees outside. In my memory, at least, I smell lavender sachet. I wanted to cover myself with the sheet and roll over and sleep forever. I felt like a perfect fool.

All my life my father had taught me to compete. He had taught me that I was smarter than anyone; taught me to be the eagle who never learned from the crow. I competed with everyone I knew and at every level I could find, and if I couldn't win, I didn't want to play the game, and wouldn't. I was like an attack dog, taking on all comers by instinct, and he loved that. He would watch my ferocity with quiet pride and amusement, whether I turned it on schoolmates or teachers, a dinner partner or a drinking buddy, my brother or my mother. And I think for a long time he was pleased even when I turned the rage on him. Because he'd taught me, most of all, to compete with him. I was conceived "the parricidal vision from the loin." But he always won. That was the essence of his father-son game.

Why did I play it, I wondered, listening to his lover move in the distant kitchen. Why would I want to be him? There were certain givens, certain things I would never have, whether his genius or his height. But I was young. I really was young. And, yes, I might die tomorrow, or in nine years, when I was thirty-five. But maybe not. Maybe there was time to have my own life, learn my own secrets, write my own books, and have my own women. I just didn't know how.

I had thought that marriage would be my escape, but all I had done was put a few more threads into the complicated skein that linked me to my father. Now the marriage was unraveling, and I was still tied to the man who had said, for effect, that he had killed my mother. And who would have had me, in my way, kill her, too. We were in it together, he and I. When she wanted to talk, when she needed help, when she needed to be saved, there was no way for her to turn to me. I was too much my father's son. I was always ready to attack. No wonder people warned her not to call me. And now she was dead. "No, Dad," I thought, "this isn't one of your fucking games." And as his lover and I undressed the night before, I thought, too late, that *this* was not the way I wanted to play. Not any more.

It had been so easy to get here. She gave a party and invited me. I was a columnist for the *Washington Post Book World;* I was the son of her friend. Then the rest of the guests had left, and I'd just stayed. Compared with other women I knew who had been with my father, she was attractive. So many of them were grimly plain; and one of them, one of his favorites, was plainly ugly. This woman in Washington had very pretty, very pale skin. I remember being startled by the whiteness of her in the dark of the bedroom. But she was so much older than I was, closer to my mother's age than mine, and I knew as we got into bed that there was no way I could do this. I told her I was drunk, too drunk, and lay awake for hours feigning sleep. Then I had slept, and now it was time to go down to say goodbye. But I didn't want to hurry. I stepped into her shower and let the water pound on my closed eyes.

"Guilt is magical," my father wrote. Was it? Had it been magical for him to be in this house with this woman while my mother was far away and dying? Had it been magical for him to be with Deborah when my mother was close at hand and dying? Had it been magical for him to tell my mother about all of the other women and make her live with some of them working in her house, or on the phone in the middle of the night, or in his poems, or in his imagination? He had loved guilt, my father, because he loved to demand forgiveness—and get it. That was the magic. "Don't leave me—forgive me—love me—bless me. No matter what I did. No matter who I hurt." But guilt held no magic for me. There was too much of it in my life already: my own, and now my father's. So I was glad I had done nothing more than fall asleep with this woman, and I was sorry only if I'd embarrassed her.

No one would know I had been here, no one else would be hurt, there was nothing, really, that I needed to regret. If I could live a life without any guilt at all, that would be magical.

I tightened my tie and put on my jacket and went downstairs, feeling my head throb a little at every step. "Would you like some breakfast? Some coffee?" I heard her say in a cheery voice. She was running some water in the sink. She looked up at me, then looked quickly over to the kitchen table. "I want you to meet my two girls," she said, setting a place for me and making brief introductions. Her daughters were about nine and eleven. They looked at me over spoons of cereal they raised slowly, very slowly, to their mouths as their mother left to get dressed.

"Where did you sleep last night?" asked the older girl.

"On the sofa," I said.

She looked at her sister. "I didn't see you there," she said.

"I went upstairs to take a shower," I said.

"In my mother's bedroom?"

"Yes," I said, surprised at how easily and quickly I lied, but feeling now deeply, deeply hungover.

The last time I saw my grandmother Dickey, she was dying of cancer, but sitting upright in a chair in the living room of the West Wesley house serving tea.

Grandpapa had died in 1974, and barely a ripple had passed through the family. Or, at least, none that I could feel. My father had built such a screen of contempt around his own father that he barely talked about him in life and seemed to forget about him in death. No reason he ever gave me could tell me why. As with so many people in his life, he was more interested in the abstraction than the man: "Not breathing 'Father' . . . / But saying, 'Fathers! Fathers!' " And it was strange now to discover how little the aura of the place on West Wesley had changed with his passing. He was no more missed than a piece of furniture that had been moved to storage. But Grandmama, her body hollowed out by surgery, skeletal but erect, still filled the house.

"Oh, Chris, we are all so proud of you," she said.

"Thank you, Grandmama."

"You have really made something of yourself."

"I'm tryin'."

"Not like Tom here," she said pointing to my uncle Tom, my father's brother the relic hunter, who was sitting on the sofa beside me. "Tom, when are you going to get a job?"

"Now, Mom, you know I have a job."

I couldn't believe it. She was almost ninety years old and dying and still she was busting Tom's balls. He would come over to visit her every day—for years he was coming to get lunch money—and he would sit and take this from her, and all he could do was laugh like he was doing now. Every day. Every damn day.

Tom's job was to manage the few real-estate holdings Grandpapa had acquired over the years. Basically, Tom collected rents. Now that my mother had died and there was no one left in the house in Columbia who knew how to write a check, I was trying to put some order into my father's life, albeit from a distance. I had come to Atlanta to take a look at the properties in which he'd inherited an interest, and Tom had spent the morning driving me around from one dreary building to another in rough corners of downtown. Some of our properties we got out of the car to look at, some we thought it wiser to observe through locked doors. There hadn't been that much to see.

We sat and talked with Grandmama for an hour or so before I started trying to break off the conversation. I wondered if it wasn't time for her afternoon nap. That seemed to me as much a part of the rhythm in this house as the clanking of buttermilk bottles delivered to the back step in the morning, or the whispering blades of a push mower on a summer afternoon. But of course those were gone, too. In fact, Grandmama was not at all fatigued. She was enjoying saying exactly whatever she wanted to say. I was the one who was tired, worn out by her ferocious energy.

"I love you, Grandmama," I said, putting my arms around her and feeling her ribs in my hands. "I'll be coming back again in a few weeks. I'll see you real soon."

"No, darlin'. You're never going to see me again," she said. "This is going to be the last time."

She died a few months later, in the summer. She lay in an open coffin in the funeral home, her soft skin now waxen, her smell some perfume chosen by morticians. At the graveside, my aunt Maibelle fainted and my father shouted and clung to Deborah's hand, and when the service was over I went back to the airport and back to Washington. It wasn't until a couple of days later that Deborah called to say my father had been hospitalized. "He's been trying to quit drinking. Doing real good," she said, but he'd had a seizure and bitten deeply into his tongue. He could barely talk. It was really scary, she said, but she was taking care of him. And I thought, "You do that."

In the space of a year, from the end of October 1976 to the end of October 1977, I lost my mother and my grandmother, my father remarried, I was picked by the newly appointed editor of the *Washing-*

ton Post Magazine to be her managing editor, she then walked into the propeller of her boyfriend's airplane, I was passed over for the top slot, and I wrecked my car.

My marriage fell apart over Thanksgiving. My father and Deborah were going to come for a visit, and I called Susan from the office to see how dinner plans were developing. We talked about turkeys, stuffing. She hung up. She called back. I would have to figure out dinner for my father and his wife myself, she said. She wasn't going to be there. She was going home to the farm in Massachusetts. I canceled Thanksgiving. A few days later Susan and my son came back; she and I confessed to what separate lives we'd led and loves we'd had, and screamed and cried, and started a halfhearted, half-denied, but finally definitive separation.

It was about that same time that my father's agent, Theron Raines, and his best friend, Matt Bruccoli, started calling me about Deborah. The stories they were hearing, the things they were seeing, were hard to believe. There was a lot of violence, mainly her attacking him. She was supposed to have stabbed him with a broadhead arrow. She was supposed to have beaten him with blunt instruments.

"That's terrible," I said. "If it's true, that's really terrible. But what do you want me to do?" When I called and talked to my father, he'd deny that anything had happened. Debbie would say there might have been a few problems, but they were both on the wagon now and doing really well. "There is," I said, "nothing at all I can do." I think it was Theron who said I should never underestimate the importance to a father of his son's respect. I thanked him, but "Not this father," I thought, "not this son."

Jim Dickey, as far as I was concerned, was on his own. And so, at last, was I.

I moved into a little apartment in Georgetown and started to work sixteen and eighteen hours a day. I commuted out to Middleburg to see Tucky on weekends, but if he was away with Susan at a horse show or in Massachusetts I worked the weekends, too. Howard Simons, the managing editor of the *Post*, had told me that if I wanted to make a career there I'd have to spend time reporting for the Metro section. I thought Howard was dooming me to covering sewer moratoriums in Prince Georges County, and I dreaded the assignment. But once I was out on the streets—literally out on the streets—I loved it, and him for making me do it. The work, for me, was about escape and about identity. "Christopher Dickey the *Washington Post*" was a single uninterrupted phrase.

All my life, whether in the suburbs of Atlanta or in the VW bus in Europe, and even, when I moved to Boston, at the end of long, overheated phone lines, my world had been enclosed by my father's wishes, dreams, visions, obsessions, abuses, confessions. Everything I tried to do was firmly tied to his range of experience. When he talked about me he'd tell people proudly, "I made his head, now he's making mine," and no one believed the latter phrase, of course, least of all me. But that wasn't the point. He defined me as his mirror, and everyone believed that.

On the Metro beat, words were my medium. Sure. But reporting was something my father knew absolutely nothing about, and the world—the worlds—that I reported on were all beyond his ken. They bored him. Utterly bored him. If I started to tell him what I was writing about—Salvadoran immigrants in Washington's slums, intrigues on Embassy Row, Vietnamese boat people in Arlington, an Indian indentured servant turned murderer in Maryland—I'd lose him in a matter of seconds, and that was fine with me. God bless his boredom, I thought. It meant we had nothing to talk about, and less and less reason to talk at all.

For that first year, even the women I slept with were part of the work. They were pretty and intelligent, but they were never wild to be wreckage forever, they never aspired to be poets, they didn't care about *Deliverance*. They were reporters and editors. The affair that lasted the longest was with a woman on Metro who was recently separated from her reporter husband. Her working hours were as long as mine and her life outside the office was almost as empty. We were the first into the newsroom in the morning and the last to leave, long after shifts had changed, every night. So, when we started having dinner together, then sleeping together, then having breakfast together—listening to the news to see which of our stories had made radio and TV headlines—no one knew. No one at all. The guilt was not magical, but the secrecy was fun in the face of all the newsroom gossips. We were colleagues and lovers, comfortable together, and it all seemed, to me at least, comfortably controlled.

Then, on October 5, 1978, a young immigration lawyer who was one of my sources opened his own law office and gave a party. I walked up the stairs, saw the woman he was talking to, and fell in love with her—the shape of her shoulders and the color of her hair, the way she held herself, vulnerable and elegant, and all of that before I saw her face, her honey-brown eyes, and her smile that was beautiful even when it was only, and barely, polite. She was not very interested in me. But I did not leave her side for the rest of the evening and would not leave her alone for the rest of the week. The month.

The year. Her name was Carol Salvatore, and she came from an Italian-American family in Philadelphia that had remained more Italian than American.

Our courtship—her reticence and tenderness, my obsession and confusion—is the stuff of another book. But it existed, unlike any other relationship I'd had, on its own terms. I was passionately, dangerously, absolutely in love with her for reasons I could not begin to articulate then—or now. We were constantly trying to get away from each other, and to be together. We had, by any measure, almost nothing in common. I thought I could change her, and she thought she could change me. And we just kept at it, fighting and reconciling and fighting, as if our fingers had touched across a chasm and neither of us knew how to get to the other side, and neither of us dared to let go. The passion was delicious and it was, in a way no other passion had ever been in my life, all mine. Carol had never heard of James Dickey, as it happens, and for a long time there was no reason James Dickey would know about Carol. She was not his affair.

You could hear echoes of the Nicaraguan war on the streets of Washington's ethnic neighborhoods. You could feel the fear creeping up from El Salvador to the dreary brick tenements where illegal immigrants slept in shifts. I was moving through the shadowy edges of a city where revolution and murder were all around, but no one knew or saw. The busboy clearing the table at the Madison Hotel came from a small town in Salvador terrified by death squads; the Ethiopian cab driver was a refugee from the genocidal Dergue in Addis Ababa. Survivors of all the killing fields in the world, Cambodians and Vietnamese, Guatemalans and Afghans, were living as if invisible, seen but unseen, in the nation's capital. They were my subjects, my beat, my friends, and they were drawing me toward places I'd never been before, and never imagined going.

Carol and I lay on her big bed in the summer twilight watching the evening news. The lead story again tonight, June 20, 1979, was the combat in Nicaragua. An American television reporter, Bill Stewart, had been killed by one of the soldiers of dictator Anastasio Somoza Debayle. Here it was: Stewart walking toward a checkpoint. We can't hear what he's saying. We see the soldier pointing his gun. Stewart's arms are spread, are flung wide to show he's got no gun, no weapon at all. The soldier is saying something. Stewart doesn't understand—what is he doing? Stewart is dropping to his knees. Now the soldier is over him, shouting something. Stewart is down, face-down on the ground, and the muzzle of the soldier's M-16 is at the back of his—*JESUS! He shot him! JESUS!* Carol hid her eyes. "Tell me when it's over," she said. I watched and felt a chill of fear ripple through me, and wanted to watch it again at eleven, and again on the morning shows, and again, and again, hoping I could understand what had happened, or numb myself to it. Because that was where I was going to be going, and soon.

The progression from being a reporter in Washington writing about foreigners to a foreign correspondent reporting to Washington seemed natural at first, then inevitable, then inescapable. The war in Nicaragua ended a month after Stewart was shot, but the terror in El Salvador was growing. Through the last months of 1979 I was counting down to the new assignment, exploring in my own mind for the first time the real possibility I would be killed, trying to imagine what life would be like if I survived.

One night at Carol's parents' house outside of Philadelphia, as I sat next to her at a long, rowdy table of relatives and friends and we watched an eighty-year-old distant aunt sing Neapolitan love songs she'd learned as a girl, and everybody was joining in, I thought, "This is the way family should be." I turned to Carol and asked her quietly if she would marry me—no, if she would think about marrying me, think about it long and hard. I didn't want to set a date. I didn't want her to feel trapped. We had been together for a year, but I was going off to war. She could come halfway there—to Mexico, where I'd be based—but there was no way of knowing what our life together would be like, or if we would be together much at all. Our future was uncertain and dangerous. And she had yet to meet anyone in my family. Anyone at all.

Over Thanksgiving, to introduce her to my son, I took them both to Italy. I had not been back in seventeen years, but the tumbled ruins of Rome, the heavy mists of Venice, and the Renaissance-haunted alleys of Florence were all places I knew. I took my son to the place where Caesar was killed and had him stand just . . . there. We looked at the agate beads in the jewelry-shop windows of the Ponte Vecchio and Perseus's fingers tangled in the serpent curls of the Medusa. By memory I found my way through the little maze of stalls in the straw market to the boar with the shiny nose. And in the Medici Chapel I showed my son the tomb of the beautiful Giuliano and wondered if, because I remembered so intensely, my child would preserve this memory, too.

On the first day of 1980, a couple of weeks before we were leaving for Central America, I introduced Carol to my father and Deborah. They had come up to Washington. I don't remember what for. They were staying at the Georgetown Inn. We met them in the restaurant there for dinner. We did not go up to their room. Debbie said that my father had just about quit drinking, but he was drunk no less than usual. "Tell me about your people," he said to Carol, his voice deeper, his Southern accent more mannered than I ever remembered it. She started to tell him about her mother, who had gone back to college to study art history—

He broke in. "Do you want to marry my son?" Jim Dickey asked, leaning toward Carol. She looked puzzled. She looked at me. "Yes," she said. My father paused. "Good," he said, "because I want you to."

When we got up to leave a little later, Carol was near tears. I had tried to warn her that this would be a difficult evening, but she had expected, or at least hoped, to meet in-laws who would welcome her into their family. Instead, all she'd seen was this strange, mannered performance by an actor so tired of his lines he only half bothered to remember them. I was angry and ashamed. Carol and I fought as we walked up Wisconsin Avenue, and in a fury I took the slim volume of poems he'd given us, *The Strength of Fields*.

It was autographed, of course.

> *To Carol and Christopher Dickey*
> *—at the beginning—*
> *from*
> *James Dickey*
> *New Year, 1980*

The dedication was perfectly formal. The sentiment—"at the beginning"—was the one he used for perfect strangers. I tore the book apart and threw it on the street.

THE
SUDANESE DAGGER

In July 1996, in the house in Columbia, I came across the machete with a leather sheath and dangling leather tassels that I had sent to my father from El Salvador fifteen years before. It was hidden away gathering dust on a high shelf in his study.

Knives were the gift of choice among the men in our family. We gave them as presents on special occasions, or just because we enjoyed them. When we were in Italy when I was ten, my father bought me a little switchblade and himself a big one, so we could sit on the Spanish Steps and use them to open the mail we'd picked up at American Express. During the shooting of *Deliverance*, he gave out hand-forged hunting knives to Boorman and Ronny and Ned, Jon and Burt.

Knives were piled on top of a cabinet in my father's bedroom. Old keychains and watches, cheap tie clasps, and dusty compasses were thrown among them, all part of the chaos of collections that filled the house. I was looking for one that might be useful in the garage when, deep at the bottom of the pile, I came across the dagger I'd sent my father from El Geneina, a village in Sudan, right at the center of the African continent. I'd bargained for it under a lean-to made of acacia twigs as turbaned men strolled through the desert marketplace carrying swords over their shoulders and daggers hidden by the loose sleeves of their long white robes. El Geneina was as beautifully, cleanly primitive as any place I ever hoped to be, and the knife I bought for my father was as handsome as any I could find, the contours of its blade etched with wavering lines like tribal scars, its handle made of tiny leather strands tightly woven one over another to make the grip solid in your hand, its scabbard fitted with a large handmade set of tweezers for extracting thorns, and a needle for sewing cloth or flesh.

The scabbard was gone now. The handle had been chewed by a dog and raveled away. The Sudanese dagger was buried here among all the little knives bought at truck stops or ordered through the mail.

The gifts I gave my father in those years when we were far apart, like the letters I wrote, the phone calls I made, were lost offerings, sacrifices that brought no favor. Each time we tried to pull together— and I think there were times when we both were trying—we wound up pushing further apart.

A week after Carol and I were married by a judge in Philadelphia's City Hall, in March 1980, I was at the funeral of Archbishop Oscar Romero in San Salvador, on the steps of the city's huge unfinished cathedral.

During the months I'd been in Central America, I ached with fear. I was spending most of my time in El Salvador, and no place there felt safe. I'd seen lawyers with their heads shot to bits as they drove home from the office for lunch. I'd seen human bodies left like road kill along the highway from the airport. The slaughter was relentless and savage, but it was not indiscriminate. The right-wing death squads were wiping out the entire infrastructure of the left. To do that, they threw a wide net. Archbishop Romero was such a powerful voice for peace and humanity, and so firmly opposed to the exterminating machine, that everyone knew he would be killed by it, and now he had been. He was shot with a sniper's single bullet to the heart while he was saying mass at a hospice for the poor. He was killed just as he raised the chalice toward heaven. The last good man was gone. There was nothing left for El Salvador but war, and now I was in the middle of it.

I supposed that I was a target, too, and not without cause. In a country where many of the rich and the military believed fascism's bad name was undeserved, and some proudly described themselves as National Socialists—yes, Nazis—the *Washington Post* was looked on as a communist rag, and its reporters were seen as agents of revolution. I started to tell myself each time the plane touched down at the San Salvador airport that I was dead, and if I felt those wheels come up under me again in a few days, well, that was just a bonus. The fear was terrible and real, intense and unrelenting. It was—incandescent. And it began to burn away other fears I'd carried with me since childhood. I didn't imagine death any more. It was right at hand. I still took as few risks as I possibly could. But I began to understand that being this close to the edge gave me a kind of license to do whatever—to be whatever—I would. "Intensity, where have you been all my life?" Now I knew. And this intensity was mine.

On the steps of San Salvador's cathedral, as a cardinal from Mexico read the eulogy, *los muchachos*—the boys—from the guerrilla movements raised their fists in a salute and started chanting.

An explosion. Another. A quick burst of shots.

I was between the crowd and the high fence at the bottom of the cathedral steps. With a huge burst of adrenaline pumping through me, I half climbed, half vaulted the steel barrier. I shouldered my way up the stairs through the crowd of priests and chanting demonstrators to get a better view of the square below.

Now automobiles exploded at each corner of the plaza, sending waves of liquid flame spreading across the pavement. Now hundreds, now thousands of people were pressing against the locked fence at the bottom of the cathedral stairs. Some were making it over, but many were not. Old women were crushed to death in front of me. The screams, the shooting, the bombs were deafening, and the priests—their cries for calm now altogether lost—fell back into the cathedral, stumbling, some of them trying to drag the coffin with them.

The gates broke open at last, and people poured into the building. Desperately they sought out friends, relatives, some touch of safety. The cathedral was filled with the groan of prayers, the rattle of machine guns. Everyone's fear was that the military would come up the steps and start firing directly into the building. But, slowly, the shooting began to wane. Then, very slowly, people began to trickle outside. Smoke from burning cars still hung heavy in the air. Shoes were piled near the fence—hundreds of shoes—where their panicked, scrambling, climbing, screaming owners had lost them. Rescue teams were starting to appear. They were loading unconscious mothers and grandmothers, old men and boys—the possibly alive—into trucks and ambulances to be taken away.

I made my way back to the hotel and placed a call to Washington. When it got through, I asked the editor on the desk to call Carol —"Before anything else, call Carol and tell her I'm okay." I knew she'd see what had happened on television, and she wouldn't be able to say, "Tell me when it's over." She was going to hear that thirty-five people died right where I was. She had to be told before that happened that I was all right. "And call my father," I told the desk, "and give him the number of the hotel here." Later that night, Carol called. I do not remember if my father got through, or if he tried. I do not remember talking to him at all.

This was my war.

* * *

In October 1980, six months after our courthouse marriage, Carol and I solemnized our vows in a church outside of Philadelphia. Her parents treated that as our "real" wedding, complete with a tent, an orchestra, a sit-down dinner, and engraved invitations. I had not really wanted my father and Debbie to come and after they were invited hoped they wouldn't, but they did. My father was trying to keep his drinking under control, which made him nervous and talkative. In the limousine from the church he told my new in-laws what a fine wife and mother my *first* wife had been. He made Italian-American jokes. During the picture-taking session he cut a fart that was straight from hell. Then, during the toasts to the bride and groom, Deborah made a toast to herself. She announced to the assembled guests that she was pregnant. I had not known that. I'm not sure how long my father had.

The baby, named Bronwen, was born seven months later. She was the little daughter that my father had always wanted, and for the next two years my father and I lost contact almost completely.

In the bedroom at the house in Columbia in the summer of 1996, I would come across the photo albums Debbie kept from those days. There is a picture of Bronwen in her father's arms when she's about six months old: her chubby baby face and my father's jowly, aging one look almost identical. Another picture shows her posing in her first ballerina tights beside the bust of Dante in the front hall. She was adorable. But I didn't know her at all. Jim Dickey and his wife, Deborah, and their new baby were a new family, self-contained, inured to the outside world, and uninterested. And I was now far, far outside.

Then, in January 1983, Deborah actually called me at the Camino Real in San Salvador. I picked up the phone in the lobby, and for a second, when I heard her voice, I thought my father had died. But no. Deborah had tracked me down because Jim's sixtieth birthday was approaching, and she was giving a big party for him and wanted me to come. I thought about it. I thought maybe it had been too long since we saw each other at all. I said yes.

But I could not go. Central America was the biggest news story in the world in those days. The Reagan administration was putting together a not-so-secret war against the Marxist Sandinistas of Nicaragua. Groups of CIA-trained guerrillas called "contras" were starting to operate in the mountains near the Honduran border. The Pope was coming to Central America to make his own stand against godless socialism. The *Post* wanted to know everything it could about everything that was going on. I had to work seven days a week. There was no time, and *this* was no time, my boss said, for me to go to a party in South Carolina.

I called my father on his birthday. He thanked me. But I don't think he understood why his invitation was turned down.

A few weeks later, I was on the run in the mountains of Nicaragua.

James LeMoyne of *Newsweek* and I had linked up with a former Somoza sergeant turned contra commander who called himself "Suicida," and his woman, "La Negra," and his second in command, a wiry, half-stoned killer who called himself "Krill." In their forest camps in the mountains of Nueva Segovia province, they'd told us about their lives and about their wars: how they escaped by sea after Somoza's defeat, how they linked up with Argentine and American intelligence agents, how they were going to retake the country. But on the second day with them we'd been ambushed by the Sandinistas, and for two days after that, often under fire, we were working our way back toward the safety of the Honduran border. Exhausted and dehydrated, I'd been delirious the last night. Someone had found a broken-down horse for me to ride. Now I looked down the mountainside at the Poteca River and knew if I could make it across I would be safe.

I slipped off the horse and slogged toward the water, wading into it in my shirt, pants, boots—to my knees, to my groin in the cold. My body had betrayed me badly, and I knew by now it could do worse. I'd warned Krill and the rest, warned myself, that if we came under fire the adrenaline might not suffice. But here we were at the river, gathered at the river, at the border. Safety. I looked up at the mountains on each side of the narrow valley. Ah, God, it was good to have made it here. The men were splashing and laughing. There were women contras, too, and they had stripped to their bras, washing in the cold water and giggling and flirting with the men. Krill was buck naked, and he was playing and splashing like some crazy Huck Finn in the river. And I was in the middle of the stream now, and lying down, and letting the water rush over me—my chest, my shoulders, my head deep in the water—and holding on to the bottom against the current. My pores were drinking. Every inch of my skin was alive to the sensation. Was . . . alive.

And the shooting started. The Sandinistas had followed us. I remember Krill with his rifle, standing naked, spraying bullets across the hillside, as I tried to make it up the mountain into Honduras. I couldn't do it. Halfway up, everything quit. I lay down totally exposed, unable to go farther. I listened to the sound of my own breathing. I waited for the shot that would kill me.

No shot came. The Sandinistas fell back into Nicaragua. The contras got me safe to Danlí, the nearest town, late that night. We ate a meal of scrawny chicken and Coca-Cola, and the Coke was better than champagne. I was utterly exhausted, intensely conscious. Risk made everything delicious, for as long as you survived.

I told myself then, and have told myself ever since, that I did not wish for death. But that is not entirely true. What I was looking for was resurrection. And now I sensed that I had it.

By the summer of 1984, when my brother, Kevin, got married, I'd lived for a year in New York City as a fellow at the Council on Foreign Relations, but returned to Central America often. I was just starting my first book, about Suicida and Krill and the combat we had seen, and what happened afterward, when they became murderous renegades, hunted down and killed by the agency that made them.

I saw my father once or twice during that time in New York. He would come to town for some function at the American Academy and Institute of Arts and Letters. (He eventually took John Steinbeck's chair in its pantheon.) We would meet for a drink, or we would go to the oyster bar at the Plaza. He ate, I remember, very little. He drank a lot. The evenings ended early. I do not believe he ever visited my apartment.

There was also one time when Carol and I flew down to Columbia, although I don't remember what the occasion was. Debbie came to the airport with Bronnie, who was about three by then, and who was listening to everything anyone said. Debbie was talking nervously as we drove through town, trying to explain, although I hadn't asked, why she'd lost an amber necklace I'd sent her from Florence in 1979, when I was still trying to do the right thing, still trying to make peace. "I don't know what could have happened to it," she was saying. "It must have just disappeared or something down a mouse hole."

Bronnie perked up. "Asshole," she said in her tiny Southern drawl.

"Mouse hole. Mouse hole!" said Debbie.

Everyone laughed. Bronnie was talking like a Dickey already. But Debbie seemed very nervous.

Carol and I hadn't been back to that house in Columbia in four years, and for us they'd been very long years. It had not changed much. The clutter of books and bows and guitars was a little denser. There were still photographs of my mother on the wall, where they had always been. If Miss Havisham had lived in a suburban ranch house it would have been like this, frozen in dust. But Bronnie gave it life. She and my father had a whole act they put on for visitors.

"Bronnie? Who am I?" my father would ask her. "You're an old geezer," she'd say, drawing out the word as if she thought it were onomatopoeic. "Geeeeezer." Or my father, so tall, would look down at Bronnie and say, "Fly up to the nest," and she would flap her arms like wings and he would pick her up and lift her high, then settle her into the cradle of his arms. The scene was sweet, but the whole feeling of the house was strange. Why was everyone so nervous having us around?

In the living room I could hear the maid calling my baby sister. "Bronnie? Now, where'd you go hiding those knives, Bronnie?"

You could imagine easily enough what was going on. The madness suppressed for our visit could not be hidden completely. Debbie and my father did not want me to know how much they drank, how much they fought. They didn't want me to see the hole in the bedroom door where a foot went through it, or the blood—menstrual blood, I think—that had dripped all over the back rooms of the house.

But I did not care.

I was going through the motions as a way *not* to deal with the family, with the history, with the pain. I was just playing defense. I wanted to get through these encounters without any huge scenes and go back to my own life. It was hard to play that game, though, with people who didn't seem to know any rules.

When Kevin got married in Savannah, Debbie decided not to come. She stayed with Bronnie in Columbia. There were no explanations. But there was, I remember, a general sense of relief.

Kevin had done great things with his life. He was a doctor now, and so was his wife. But when my father gave a toast at the rehearsal dinner it was dedicated to his son Chris. Kevin, the groom, was mentioned in passing. Sally Haskell, the bride, was barely spoken of at all. It was so awkward, so odd—half performance, half private rumination on his firstborn son—that no one knew what to say. So we all said he was just drunk. He was just Dad. We tried to think about other things.

Late on a warm Sunday morning in New York, I was walking down the wide, empty sidewalk of Park Avenue when I saw, a block or two away, a tiny round man staggering as if he were drunk or hurt. We were still far apart, and I couldn't really see his face. "He looks sort of like Truman Capote, but even worse," I thought. I had never met Capote, but knew him from his magazine and television appearances. The photographs taken of him when he was young, when he was so boyish and beautiful, and those taken of him more recently, looking so bloated and sick, had left a strong and disturbing impression. When we drew still closer together, there was no mistaking him. He was completely, utterly, out-in-the-noonday-sun gone. He was staggering from one doorman to another, wandering back and forth across the empty avenue each time he saw a uniform framed by brass. Now we drew even on the sidewalk, and I thought I should introduce myself and offer to help. I imagined my father in this situation, and hoped a Samaritan might help him. But I couldn't do it. Capote walked by me and I said nothing. He looked around as if he were lost in a desert and wondering what lay behind the next dune, and staggered across Park Avenue to another doorman.

Toward the end of 1985, I heard that Jim Dickey had completed his long-awaited novel *Alnilam*, which I'd begun to think he intended to finish just enough to hold for posthumous publication, and I sent him a note of congratulations. I was living in Cairo by then, farther away than ever before. My own book, *With the Contras*, was just about to be published and I hoped that somehow it would bring us together. Looking at the galleys I realized I'd written a scene on the sea off the Nicaraguan coast with undertones of *The Rime of the Ancient Mariner*. The fleeing members of Somoza's army drifted for days on a barge with no fresh water, their voices lost to thirst, like the many men, so beautiful. Unconsciously I gave the life-and-death chase near the end some of the flavor of *Deliverance*. I pointed all this out to my father. "Anyway, Dad, spotty though it is, I hope you like it. More than I knew, I wrote it for you."

When the contra book came out in early 1986, I went back to the United States, and back to Columbia as part of a publicity tour, and I realized more than ever before how much my father and I had lost the habit of being together. We talked a little about our books. He read me a little of his and praised mine with such enthusiasm that I believed not a word of what he said. And at night I just—lost him.

He was trying not to drink too much in front of me, so he would just go to his room to drink out of sight. Debbie would already be there. She had gained a tremendous amount of weight and seemed to be sleeping all the time. I would let them be and I would go to what used to be my room, now filled with books people had sent to my father that he never got around to reading but couldn't quite throw out. This had never been my house. I would not sleep here again, I thought.

I was approaching thirty-five, far too old to be thinking seriously about vows I'd made when I was fifteen. But when bullets were cracking against walls where I hid, or I drove down lonely roads wondering if they were mined, I would think about the promise I'd made one day on the porch in Leesburg to live as if I would die in twenty years, and as if nothing could kill me in all that time. It was just a mind-trick, a mental rabbit's foot. But now that I had survived this long I was a little bit amazed, and unexpectedly depressed. I was a father—Tucky, whom we now called James, was sixteen years old. I was respected as a reporter. I was the author of a book. That first year in the Middle East I had this extraordinary life, so filled with event and risk that I was walking in a fog of adrenaline. I went to Beirut to interview Americans taken hostage on a TWA flight, and narrowly escaped being kidnapped myself. I was on the ground in Tripoli, Libya, when American jets rained bombs around the city. I witnessed coups, famines, hijackings, bombings.

But suddenly, after Libya, almost overnight, I decided I was intensely tired of being Christopher Dickey the *Washington Post*. And I thought that, if I changed jobs, maybe that would change enough about my life to fill in a little of the hollowness I was trying not to think about. I stayed in Cairo, but left the *Post* for *Newsweek*.

In the summer of '86, I visited New York to meet my new editors, and while I was there got word my father was in the hospital. He'd had a hemorrhage on the surface of his brain. Doctors had to take a piece out of his skull to relieve the pressure. It was the kind of problem that often occurs after a blow to the head.

"Dad," I said, "Dad," putting my cheek next to his on the hospital bed. The top of his head was completely bandaged. His smile was weak, his tongue thick and sluggish from the sedatives. "Son," was all he said. I held his hand. "You tough old son of a bitch," I said. He looked puzzled, as if he wasn't sure what I meant. I stepped back to let others greet him. Carol was there, and Kevin and Sally. Students were coming by to bring flowers, and when one of them, a plump little country girl, appeared in the door, he brightened and invited her in. We waited until she'd finished saying how much she hoped Dr. Dickey—my father, who never earned a Ph.D. but was given innumerable honorary degrees and titles, including colonel in the Alabama militia, loved to be called Dr. Dickey—how much she hoped Dr. Dickey would be better soon. I waited for the parade through the room to end, but it didn't.

"I'll come back later," I said, and leaned close to my father. "Dad," I said in a low voice, "did Debbie do this?" He looked at me and hesitated for a second. "No," he said. "No. I don't know how it happened."

His tone was a little like Lewis's in that scene near the end of the movie *Deliverance*, when he's in the hospital barely conscious, and Ed comes to him, and the two of them fix their stories about where the canoes crashed and how Drew died. But I was not part of the conspiracy.

THE SEA
AND
OLD MEN

In the summer of 1987 Carol and I were vacationing off the coast of Naples, on the island of Ischia. We were not far from Positano, and the dark clear sea, the pebble beaches and pedal-boats, the smell of olive oil and tomato, even the stocky little body of the maid who cleaned the house brought Positano back to me. But I would not go back to Positano. Not then. My family had been too happy there.

I was trying to read my father's novel *Alnilam*. The story was simple: Frank Cahill's son Joel, whom he barely knew, was killed in flight training early in World War II. Although Frank had recently lost his sight to diabetes, he went to the base where his boy was killed to try to discover what happened to him and, more essentially, what kind of a boy he was. What the other cadets told him was that Joel was a kind of messiah. At the climax of the book, Joel's disciples created an inferno of crashed planes on the runway as Frank wandered sightless through the raging wind of the propellers.

James Dickey's voice was huge, the kind of a voice you don't find in American prose but about once in a generation. But Big Jim, drunk or half-drunk about half the time he was dictating the novel and just about every time anyone tried to edit him, had decided that when he felt like it he would split the text in two columns, with one reflecting what happened in the sighted world, and the other recording the perceptions of Frank in his world of blindness. It might have worked had there been any discipline, any coherence to the technique. But as it was, the twin columns of type seemed perverse and capricious. Jim Dickey wouldn't hear of changing them. And when the book was published to mixed reviews and scant sales, he only insisted with greater vehemence that the technique was the right one, and this was the best of his novels by far. Just as the flatulent *Zodiac* was the best of his poems.

He also said, often and to any interviewer who asked him, that Joel Cahill was based on his son Chris, although Chris was not so charismatic.

I searched for myself that summer on every one of *Alnilam*'s 682 pages. I didn't find any version of me that I knew.

What could he have been thinking? How could his vision of me have anything to do with this dead messiah? I had not yet read his poem and letters from 1951 describing me when I was still in the womb. It was only on the mountainside in Ischia, as a man almost thirty-six years old with this massive, muscular novel on my lap, that I even began to think, half smiling, half horrified, what it meant to be the imagined son of an aspiring god.

I reduced the whole thing to an "Ain't Dad weird" anecdote I'd tell friends, and when I wrote my father a note after reading the book it was very short and simple. I didn't want to engage him, just congratulate him, and pass on an interesting coincidence. Each of the big ferries that brought tourists to Ischia was named after a star used for navigation. One of them was called *Alnilam*. I sent him a picture. I thought he would enjoy that. But I never heard back from him.

Every contact we had was becoming more formal, and his voice, on those rare times when we talked by phone, was sounding more distant, even suspicious.

When Kevin's first daughter was christened in Savannah, an easy drive from Columbia, my father didn't make it. Debbie came instead. She had lost weight again, and was starting to take care of herself again, and she talked to me, as we drove together to the church, about how frustrating it was to be a young woman married to such an old man. I didn't want to hear what she was telling me.

In late 1988, I was reassigned from Cairo to Paris, and Debbie called me that fall—the only time I could remember anyone from Columbia calling me anywhere in five years. She and my father and Bronwen wanted to come visit the following August, if that was okay.

I had visions of her wallowing in bed in the house all day, of my father drunk and breaking furniture. But also of us walking the streets of Paris, maybe going to the Jardin des Plantes with Bronnie. August was ten months away. I had ten months to plan, ten months to steel myself. "Sure," I said. "Sure, Debbie. We'd love to have you."

Carol began to plan our summer around my father's visit. It would

be the first time he'd ever come to any place we lived. Carol wanted
to show him our home, try to make him feel at home.

As the date approached, I had a story to write near Antibes. I
went back for the first time in twenty-seven years to the hill below
the lighthouse.

The narrow driveway to the Villa Lou Galidou still wound
through a yard so dense with cactus and undergrowth that it might
hide slithering masses of imagined serpents. Here were the bushes
where chocolate money had been hidden. There was the door to the
furnace room where my father had shoveled coal to keep us warm and
I, the precocious three-year-old, had helpfully tossed in a pine cone
or two. Almost nothing about the place had changed, except that
through a window in the kitchen I could see a refrigerator where the
icebox had been.

My voice must have sounded like a child's when I got my father
on the phone. "Dad, listen, I'm in Antibes. I found Lou Galidou."

"Oh," he said distantly. "That's nice."

"Let's come down here when you come in August."

"Well, we'll see," he said.

A few weeks later I called him again to check on his plans. The
visit was canceled. He was just too busy, he said.

I was now traveling constantly, writing stories from the Middle East,
Panama, even Illinois. Carol had made me a beautiful home, but I was
never there. My roots seemed to be in hotel rooms with late check-
outs, in waiting lounges with self-serve bars.

Then in 1990 I traveled through the Valley of Assassins, in north-
ern Iran, with a group of rescue workers from France and Britain, to
reach villages where every house was so thoroughly destroyed by the
shaking of the earth that no one was left even to pick through the
rubble. I had never seen such utter devastation. In each settlement, as
I tried to help those digging for survivors—or for some hint of survivors—I would ask people how many members of their families were
lost, and they would say "seventy-eight" or "one hundred and thirty-
two," and I would question them again, because I didn't understand.
"You mean from your clan," I'd say, "or from your tribe." But they did
not understand me.

I realized there, near the town of Rudbar, on the edge of a lake
high in the mountains above the Caspian, something about Americans
—about us—that I'd never stopped to think about before. When I
talked about family, I'd talk about it and the people in it as something
I "had," almost like I'd have a car or a house or, perhaps, a diploma: "I

have a father, I have a son, I have a wife, I have a brother." But for these people, and most people in the Old World, families were not something they had. Families were something they belonged to. And that, in the most general and the most existential way, was what I missed.

I began to see that difference between having and belonging as a great divide in the world's societies. You could try to define yourself to yourself the way we did in America, by what you had, or maybe by what you'd done. But if you didn't know where you belonged, then you didn't know who you were. In America, it seemed to me from my vantage among the crushed homes and lonely mourners of Iran, we had a great surplus of having, and a great deficit of belonging. And I had always tried to have so much to do that I wouldn't have to stop and think about that.

A group of rescue workers from Scotland were digging where their specially trained dogs had found signs of an air pocket in a crumbled house. A little girl, who had lost her mother and father and every other sibling, shouted that her baby sister had been in that place. She watched the Scots gently pulling away the rocks, sawing the beams, peering down into the cavity with spotlights. I'd been with them for a day and a night and knew from their faces they knew that if the baby was there it was dead, but they kept digging until they pulled it from the shattered cradle. They gently wrapped it in the blanket that had covered it while it slept, and gave it to a local worker for burial.

Ah, shit. We were all so goddamned busy. My father was so busy. I was so busy. My own son's childhood had passed me by. He was in college now, training to be an officer in the army. People who had been good to me, who had meant a lot to me, had died while I was far away, in places like this. I last heard the voice of my uncle Tom over the phone as he lay in the hospital bed in Atlanta suffering from cancer and I looked out on the floodlit waters of the Persian Gulf from an apartment in Dubai. There had been no way to go home. To be with him. To be with my father when he lost his only brother.

My mother's mother still lived in Columbia, but she was very old, and alone. In the autumn of 1989, I had gone to see her. I stayed in a hotel. I didn't let my father know I was there until the second day, when I called him to tell him I was about to leave. I didn't go to the house. We had lunch at the University of South Carolina Faculty Club, and struggled to find things to say to each other. All was well at home, he told me, and showed me pictures of Bronwen taken for a child model's portfolio.

A year later, my mother's mother died. My wife, Carol, and my brother, Kevin, and his friends in Columbia had helped care for her in the last months of her life. But I was back in the Gulf then. The war with Iraq was coming. I couldn't get away.

I began to write about old men, and about fathers and sons. This was not by design. I thought that I was doing research into the background of the Middle East, or of espionage, or the environment—all subjects that I wrote about often. But to learn more about Arabia I sought out Wilfred Thesiger, the last of the great explorers of the Empty Quarter. And when I had met him and talked to him, what I wrote about was the way he had tried all his life to recover something of the excitement and the sense of home that he'd had as a little boy in Abyssinia, where his father was the British consul. He had gone away to school, and his father had died, and there was never any real home for him again.

I read everything I could find about St. John Philby, another great British explorer of Arabia, and his son Kim Philby, the infamous British spy. There was something in their story, the way they lived apart for so long: St. John was given a slave-girl bride by the king of Saudi Arabia and spent most of his later life in a rambling, wind-cooled mansion in Jeddah. The anecdotes about the last night St. John and Kim spent together seemed to me to be important. St. John was old and ailing and Kim was about to defect for good. They went drinking and whoring all one evening in Beirut, and then St. John collapsed. He went into a coma, and Kim sat there by his bed in the hospital. St. John was supposed to have recovered consciousness only once, and briefly, and said, "God, I'm bored."

I was assigned a long piece by *Rolling Stone* about killing men to save elephants in East Africa, and built it around Bill Woodley, a hard-drinking old white hunter who had tracked and shot both men and beasts since the days of the Mau Mau. He had lived the most dangerous game. He had seen and done in Africa all the things I was taught to dream about when I was a child. This was the world of *Trader Horn*, I thought as I drove through Tsavo. When I camped at the bottom of the Ngorongoro Crater, a world of gigantic animals in the bottom of an enormous caldera, I looked around at noon from the edge of a lake filled with flamingos, near the skeleton of a zebra picked clean by hyenas, and saw that the horizons curved upward. I had seen Pellucidar at last.

All through 1993, I was trying to finish a long article about Jacques-Yves Cousteau that I'd been reporting for four years. Here was a man who made it possible to explore the blue planet. He had changed the way we see the world. But he was a memory from childhood for most people in my generation, and even though the man himself remained intensely active, the idea of the man had about it a musty air of anachronism.

Cousteau had an apartment and offices just around the corner from me in Paris. I saw him often. I traveled with him to Washington; visited him at his other apartment, in Monaco; had long, lazy lunches with him. But I never could make the piece work. Partly that was because editors just felt they knew as much as they wanted to know about the captain of the *Calypso*. But mainly it was because the more I knew about Cousteau the more what I wrote was really about my father.

One summer Sunday afternoon in 1991, at the Brasserie Lorraine on the Place des Ternes, Cousteau had talked about the death of his wife, Simone, a few months before. He was eighty-one. His face was flushed, and the lower lids of his eyes were red. Flakes of dandruff speckled the eyeglasses he used to read the menu. "For me it was terrible," said Cousteau. "For her the good thing was, I spent the last three days with her.

"The night she died, we had a very joyful dinner," he said. Simone was a tiny woman, tough and reserved, who had spent most of the last forty years at sea on the *Calypso*. She was known to the crew as "La Bergère," the shepherdess. But when I met her she had looked as if beneath her leather skin there were bones of excruciating fragility. For most of the four months a year she was not on the boat, she was in Cousteau's little apartment in Monaco. She did not like Paris. Often alone, she left the radio and television turned on all the time to keep her company.

That night, however, Simone was "gay, alert, joking," Jacques Cousteau remembered. They stayed up late drinking and talking before finally going to bed. "At five o'clock in the morning she asked me to help her to the toilet. And I did. And"—as he hesitated, I wondered uncomfortably why he was telling me this—"she died in my arms."

Cousteau called an ambulance and the doctor in Marseilles, but there was nothing to be done. "I knew she was not well, but I had no idea what was wrong with her," said Cousteau. He told the doctor he thought "she was drinking too much red wine." But the doctor said, "Jacques, it was either wine or morphine."

The old explorer did not understand.

For the last five years, the doctor explained, Simone had had "a generalized cancer."

"She made the doctor promise not to tell me," Cousteau said, "so as not to disturb my work."

The story made me cringe. The whole Cousteau family history

troubled me. Cousteau had played favorites with his sons, taking an intense and angry interest in Philippe, his anointed heir, until Philippe crashed in his plane. Then Cousteau turned by default to his other son, Jean-Michel. He worked with him for years, then rejected him, too. Cousteau had built a second family even before his first was gone. Simone did not like Paris not least because Cousteau's mistress was there, along with the little boy and girl she bore him when he was more than sixty years old.

Cousteau's writing and philosophizing—what he called his "crazy ideas"—conjured memories and sensations I couldn't keep under control. In his first book, *The Silent World*, his descriptions of his first dives in the clear waters off the Côte d'Azur made me think of my father flying in the water above the rocks at the Plage de la Garoupe. I found myself crying as I read them. Cousteau wrote an essay of which he was very proud called "The Exploration of Happiness." It ought to be possible, he said, to teach "the science of joy." Cousteau wanted it all. I admired him for that, but couldn't forgive him for it, because I knew everyone around him had paid the price. The dispassionate, slightly puzzled way Cousteau told me about Simone's death "made him seem a man filled with oblivious self-fascination," I wrote in one version of the failed article. And then I wondered about Simone's real motives for keeping her sickness a secret. "Like suicide," I wrote, "such long, mute agony carries with it a suggestion of revenge." I was thinking of my mother in that line, of course. I realized that as I read it over. But I was thinking, too, of myself.

It was time to end the passive agony, time to go home—if that time was not past.

FATHER
AND SON

I am thinking of how I may be
The savior of one

Who has already died in my care.

—"The Lifeguard"

VECTORING

I was forty-two years old. I had fair reason to think I'd discovered the world as it is, and that I could take that home, and that somehow it would protect me.

"Dear Dad," I wrote in May of 1994, "I'm looking out on the Bosporus. It's a brilliant morning with the sun coming up from Asia a few hundred yards away."

I was straining to be upbeat, trying to convince myself.

"On mornings like this," I went on, "when there's a moment to relax and the thrill of strange and beautiful places is high, this life is irresistible and I wish that we all could, as you say, share the adventures. Why not gather the clan at Ngorongoro, where the lions walk beside your car and elephants visit your camp for breakfast? Or here on the Hellespont where Byron used to swim? There are so many places, Dad, that you made part of us when you raised us just by dreaming about them; so many other places that you actually took us to. I can't walk up the Spanish Steps without seeing us sitting over there, just to the right beneath Keats's house, opening mail from American Express. I never pass the Jardin des Plantes without looking for that special entrance through the wall."

I was dreading the trip home. I hoped there was going to be too much going on in the world to allow me to make it. But Carol, who had worked so hard to keep our marriage together and me together with my son and with my brother while I was running away after other people's lives in distant corners of the world, would not let me out of my own life. Not this time.

We flew to Raleigh-Durham and rented a Lincoln Town Car to

float along the interstates. If I was going to go back to South Carolina to meet my father on his home turf in the heartland, I wanted to have some fun, and the Lincoln was so absurdly deluxe. I set the cruise control, revved up the stereo, and let it roll. As we got nearer to Columbia, I was getting excited. I'd rented a phone and was calling to check in every hour or so, giving my father my ETA. It was working. I could hear from his voice that he was excited, too. Happiness was rising through me like a drug, warming my blood, making my skin tingle, making everything feel all right. I didn't trust it, but I felt the comforting embrace of family just the same.

To be coming home like this was suddenly such a relief after all the false starts and disappointed expectations. Only a few months before, my father had come to Europe with Debbie and Bronwen. He told me he'd be in Rome, and that seemed perfect. It was neutral territory; full of memories, and just the right memories. At the very least I could see him, and, well, whatever happened, that would be something, and there was a chance that we could really begin to talk. "Just tell me when you'll be there," I said. "Debba will call you," he said. But no one called. Then, a few days later, his secretary told me he was already in Rome. I left a message at his hotel. Finally Deborah called back to say they were just about to leave Italy, and they'd had a wonderful time, and she was so sorry we hadn't been able to get together. I felt as if I'd reached out to take hold of my father's hand and seen it ball into a fist. But I told myself he hadn't meant this. He was just careless. She was a little worse than careless. That was all.

But they couldn't not be in Columbia. And Dad—and I—we were counting the miles. He was the control tower. I was vectoring in toward Lake Katherine.

The day was sparkling. The sweaty summer humidity, the weight of Carolina heat, hadn't set in yet. The neighborhood smelled like newly mowed lawns. I pulled the Lincoln next to my father's Dodge van in front of the garage. I detached my seat belt, ejected the cassette from the stereo, looked to see if there was anything I wanted to take into the house with me. . . . I was using up as much time as possible. I wanted my father to be standing in the doorway of the house when I came to it. I looked around the inside of the Town Car again, glanced up at the house. There he was, framed against the blue door, and coming now to greet me as I got out of the car. He was thinner than I remembered, and maybe not so tall as he used to be, but Jim Dickey looked pretty good. We hugged and I could feel the memory of his strength. "Ah, son," he said. "Ah, son."

There was a blur of first impressions. Deborah's long hair was ragged and showing threads of gray, but she was not the total wreck I'd remembered. And Bronnie was not a little girl any more. At thirteen, she was tall and graceful, poised and intelligent and full of enthusiasm. She wanted to show us all around the house. She took me to her room, which used to be mine, and for a second I remembered the long afternoons locked away in there, brooding to the sound of The Doors, dreaming of any escape from this place. Now there was nothing left of me here—and suddenly I was glad of that. On the bookshelves in one corner Bronnie had crammed dozens of her worn-out toe shoes, their ribbons hanging down, trophies of all the years she'd been dancing with the Columbia Ballet. This was her life here. This was her place. Good.

My father's bedroom had a new, enormous television in it next to the unused Soloflex, but the bed was in the same place it had been for as long as I'd known this house. The bed was once my mother's, but I did not see, as I looked at it, any shadow of her here. Those last years she was alive, she had been loath to sleep in it; had sought out almost any other place in the house, drinking until she could pass out on one of the sofas or, if Kevin was gone, in his bed.

"Same old view of the lake," I said, talking to the emptiness of the room. "Such a pretty view from here."

A scene erupted in my memory. It was that afternoon a few days after my mother died when I lay beside my father here, holding his head against my chest and running my fingers through his thin, damp hair, and tried to find some strength in my own arms to steady him as he shook with the bone-rattling cold of alcohol withdrawal; that time when I was so much younger, and hoped that with a little love I could save his life. I had been naïve. I had thought I could do more than I could, then (thinking in absolutes, as young men do) convinced myself I could not do anything. To save him I would have to sacrifice myself, I thought. I would have to move to Columbia and take care of him when he would let me, take his abuse when he would not, fight with him, then flee him—drive aimlessly for hours, seek some other place in the house to sleep—as my mother had done endlessly, until her end. So I had said to Debbie, "You do that," and gone on. . . .

"Chris?" Bronnie was calling me across the hall, to the room I always thought of as Kevin's. "This is sort of Mom's room," she told me. Patterns repeating, I thought.

But I was not here to be horrified, I was here to be happy. "Let's go find the rest of the folks," I said.

My son, James, drove in that afternoon from Fort Benning, where he was now a lieutenant, and the next day we headed out for Litchfield. With all the arrivals, the plans, the getting acquainted, there was not much time to be with my father, but I thought that was okay. We'd take it in stages. We'd get used to being around each other again. Then we could talk. Debbie had hesitated about going down to the beach. She said she didn't think she should, didn't think she could. I had to beg her to come, and finally she consented. She sat in the front seat, next to me, a Bible poised on her lap. Carol and Bronnie got in the back. My son and my father followed in my father's van, with James behind the wheel. Things would get better when we got down to Litchfield, I thought. There, I'd be able to talk with my father.

On the three-hour drive, Debbie talked about herself and, every so often, clutched her Bible. Sometimes she talked about her problems with drugs, and her problems with treatments, and how sorry she was for all the time she'd wasted in her life. "We all make mistakes," I'd say. "I just love you all so much," she'd say, and feel the rough texture of the cover on the book she held. "We love you, too," I'd say, hoping I could find some way to mean it.

Long before Deborah met Jim, she suffered from terrible insecurities. When she married him, she must have had some idea that the problems would go away, or at least get better. She was going to be the prized wife of a famous man. He was a kind of god, at least in her eyes. She'd have money, prestige, and a chance to be as smart and beautiful as she really was.

But everything he did played on the weakest parts of her character. Who was she? What good was she? As his wife she suddenly had to be the country girl *and* the prostitute. He made it clear in a thousand ways that he expected her to be one and all of the women he loved who had died: not only his wife, Maxine, and his mistress, Robin, but also his mother—and also the daughter he'd never had. She was there to help him forget his guilt, then expiate it, and when she couldn't do that, she came to represent it.

Debbie was in love. Debbie wanted a happy marriage, a happy family. But she would come back to the house in the afternoons those first couple of years thinking she would tell Jim something funny that had happened to her, just tell him about her day, and she would find him sitting in the living room looking at the lake silently weeping, and nothing that she could say or do seemed to make a difference. The more she failed to be all that she was expected to be, the more she became the child that is all she really knew how to be—the bad, beloved child who demands that her trespasses be forgiven so she can go out and trespass again. She became, without ever wanting or meaning to, my father's penance.

Deborah needed professional help, and she started looking for it soon after she got married. But Jim didn't approve. Discipline and intelligence ought to get you through anything, he thought. It took more than three years of screaming and a little violence before he decided Deborah could start seeing a psychiatrist. The man they chose was well known: a respected professor at the university and something of a local celebrity, who was often called to testify whether criminals were sane enough to stand trial. She hadn't much liked him, she said later. But in hindsight, after he was arrested, almost nobody admitted to liking him. The good doctor, it turned out, was leading a double life. At night he was the most infamous cat burglar in the state. It was a terrible irony, and terribly funny, except that Deborah needed someone so badly.

Debbie's experience with the night-crawling shrink gave my father more reasons to be skeptical of psychiatrists, and made it harder for her to get help. But I don't think that Jim Dickey objected to therapy because he thought the lunatics were the ones taking notes. He didn't fear that therapies would fail. What bothered him was that they might work, and take away the magic. My father liked to surround himself with a certain degree of what he thought was madness —what Rimbaud called, in a phrase he liked to cite, *"dérèglement de tous les sens,"* the dissolution of the senses. But Jim Dickey was a dilettante of madness. It was something he imagined, an idea he played with, like his diabetes, or killing a deer. Before Deborah, my father didn't have much experience of the real thing. None of us did.

Bronwen's birth changed the dynamic again. Now Deborah could be the mother of my father's daughter. But as Bronwen grew up, grew into her own mind, made more of her own decisions, and then became more of a woman, Deborah couldn't play that game any more, and Debbie was left once again with no clear idea who she was, or even what my father wanted her to be. She called herself a mother and tried, transparently, to be Bronnie's sister. She became, again, my father's troubled child, and moved deeper into the world of drugs.

And all of that might have been darkly amusing or at least *interesting* for Jim Dickey. But he never reckoned on how profoundly, excruciatingly disturbed Deborah was—beyond the power of his intelligence, discipline, or love to touch—and how explosive she could be when his cruelty ignited her pain. He made the heads of his other children, me and Kevin and Bronwen, but he had not made Deborah's, and her mind was a mystery to him. Nor had he reckoned on what it would mean that she was so much tougher than my mother, and ultimately so much stronger—physically stronger—than he. "Rougher than a night in jail," was the way he described her to me before I ever met her, but that was just something he said. He had no idea it was a prophecy.

Halfway from Columbia to the coast, we stopped at the Central Coffee Shop in Manning, South Carolina. The place looked like it had been there since the 1930s, with all the chrome and vinyl and linoleum worked in and worn out long ago, and big murals on the walls where every detail was lost to the film of grease and smoke. The owners, George and Penelope, always remembered Jim Dickey and his wife and daughter. The hot roast-beef sandwiches on white bread tasted just like America. We drank sweet tea. Nothing but that. We were all trying hard, I thought, as I sopped up the last drop of gravy. Real hard.

A few hundred yards before the entrance to Litchfield Plantation, we passed my mother's grave. "We've tried to take care of it," Debbie said. "I appreciate that," I said. "I'll come back here later. Let's go on now to the house." We turned through the gates and down the allée of live oaks in front of the old plantation house, then left to our place. And there it was, all three stories: a house of windows and stairwells. "Root-Light." I remembered when we'd bought it and it had seemed so *modern.* . . .

Now it was a wreck, but the excitement was holding. We were circling around each other like restless planets—veering off to run errands, or walk around the plantation grounds, or go to the pool or the beach. But the gravity was pulling us back together, and closer.

We planned a big dinner that night at the plantation's restaurant. It was still light, I remember, when I went to the house to pick up Dad and Debbie. He came downstairs first, dressed in a polo shirt with a tie, and a loose suit with his Phi Beta Kappa key on a chain that hung outside his pocket. I hadn't seen him in a suit in a long, long time. He'd dressed up for me.

We sat by the window, where the dead wasps littered the rug, not paying any attention, and I can't tell you what we talked about, just that we *were* talking and listening, and I felt like I was settling into home, when Deborah came downstairs.

Something had gone wrong. Somehow she had, as they say in the South, worked herself into a state. Maybe my father had said something upstairs I never heard. Maybe Debbie just looked in the mirror and didn't like what she saw. But, standing there in the living room, she started to talk about the way she was dressed, and apologize for the way she looked, and say how much prettier Carol was, and how bad she felt. . . .

"C'mon, Debbie, you look great," I said.

"You look just fine," said my father.

But she wouldn't believe us, and wouldn't quit apologizing. And now she was launched on a whole flood of apologies, each of them more sensational. She was talking about her drinking and her drugs, and the men she'd been with. She was starting to call herself names, and each new confession, each new apology, was a little more humiliating for my father to hear, and for him to see that I was hearing.

"C'mon, Deb. Let's not do this," I said. But she wanted forgiveness, and she wanted it now. Right now. So she went on attacking with her confessions, until my father erupted. "You have brought murderers into our lives," he said. "You have endangered my life, and Bronwen's life, and your own—"

"Dad," I said. "Wait. Debbie, I want you to tell me all about all of this." I looked at her eyes, trying to steady her a little bit. "But not here. Not now."

"That's right," said my father.

"That's right," I said. "Now, come on. Let's go eat."

It was four-thirty in the morning, and the glowing screen of my laptop looked like headlights in a tunnel. I was trying to finish a story I'd left undone before I came to Litchfield, sitting alone in the dining room in the dark, trying to be as quiet as possible. The same sentences kept reshaping. I couldn't get the piece in focus. I rubbed my eyes, and a rush of anger surged through me like bile in my throat. Why the hell had I come back here?

The second day at Litchfield, Carol and I and James and Bronnie thought we'd drive to Charleston for lunch. But Debbie and Dad decided they wouldn't go, and when we got back, they were drunk. Dad staggered down the stairs, literally staggered, to eat some of the soup that Carol and Bronnie had made him. But Debbie couldn't make it down at all. "I'll go get her. I'll talk her down," I said.

"Don't go up there," my father said. "Don't," he said again, shaking his head loosely. "You don't want to see." He sat down heavily on the sofa. He was wearing shorts and I could see his ankles were red and swollen with fluid. They looked like my mother's had looked in the last year or so of her life. After a few spoonfuls of soup and a little more slurred talk ("Your, um, office called; I don't remember the name"), he staggered back upstairs. I hadn't seen him since.

I rubbed my eyes again, and took a break to check for e-mail. Then I decided to look at the online newspaper archives. I punched in "Deborah Dickey." A handful of headlines appeared, among them "DEBORAH DICKEY GETS TWO YEARS' PROBATION."

"Jesus," I said under my breath. I hadn't heard anything about this. The date was May 1991, a little after the end of the Gulf War. I must have been in fucking Kurdistan when all this was going on in Columbia. But probably no matter where I was, I wasn't going to be told. "Jesus."

A reporter for the *Columbia State*, John Allard, had written a story that was very clean, and very much to the point:

> Tears flowed down the face of the wife of writer James Dickey on Tuesday when her private battle with cocaine became public in a Richland County courtroom.
>
> Deborah Dickey, 39, admitted being caught injecting cocaine with a stranger in an abandoned house at 2314 Pendleton St. Ronald Middleton, 29, of 1311 Maple St., injected the cocaine for Dickey because she did not like doing it herself, said 5th Circuit Assistant Solicitor Duffie Stone.
>
> Circuit Judge Carol Connor sentenced Dickey to two years in prison, suspended on serving two years' probation, after she pleaded guilty to possessing cocaine. While on probation, she must submit to drug testing and continue drug treatment, which she started after her arrest in March.
>
> Dickey cried while telling Connor that her drug addiction had humiliated herself and her family.
>
> James Dickey stood at his wife's side during a short hearing and told Connor that he wanted to help her overcome her drug problem.
>
> "I will stand beside her until death and mourning," James Dickey said.

I knew, after Deborah's compulsive confessions, that there was more to the story than that. But I didn't want to know any more details, I didn't want to have to forgive any more than I had. I just wanted to be able sometimes to be at home here, in peace, with my people.

I was going to have to be patient. But patience was something I thought I had acquired. Partly it came with the inevitable mellowing that any man feels when he reaches his early forties. Partly it was something I learned in the Middle East, where all obstacles seem immovable and all progress is the result of patience and a search for alternate paths. Here in South Carolina, I had to remind myself, patience, forbearance, and forgiveness were the price of love within a family, and that price was not too high. I took a deep breath. The air at Litchfield was—in the broadest, best sense of the word—familiar, and it filled me with hope. We were going to have difficult times, but the worst was over. Now at last we had made a new beginning.

The gray light of morning was just beginning to sift through the Spanish moss outside the sliding glass door. I would lay flowers on my mother's grave later in the day.

At the end of the summer, I was back working in Cairo and Carol and I took another brief vacation, far from South Carolina, on the Egyptian coast of the Red Sea. It was my birthday, I was forty-three, and Carol presented me with diving lessons. Twice a day, in a state of barely subdued terror, I dropped below the surface of the water with lungs and fins, until finally the fear started seeping away. Then I swam free-style far out into the sea, stroking, breathing, moving across the water in that motion I had never before been able to master. Stroking, turning my head, breathing. I reached the anchor rope of a small boat near the reef and looked back at the shore, hundreds of yards away, and I could not stop smiling. By the fourth day I was diving out in the deep where the coral walls faded down to blue, and the depths dropped away forever, and the quicksilver surface lost its shimmer—floating weightless, like a man in space or the dream of a womb.

On the long drive back through the Sinai I wrote in my head a children's poem about the ocean, and a little boy swimming free. A lot of it sounded like "Kevin the Diver." I sent a copy to my father.

THE
NIGHTMARE LIFE
IN DEATH

Late October 1994. Yet another message from Debbie on the answering machine. "Chris, you better do something," she said in a weird croon with a rising pitch. "Your father is in the *hospital,* and he's yellow, yellow, yellow—yellow as the Yangtze River." I thought she was playing another of her fantasy games. She had left so many obscene, incoherent messages for me. "Leave us *alone!*" she'd scream. Why was I persecuting her? Why wouldn't I just leave her and her family in peace in South Carolina? Through the maid and the secretary in Columbia, I heard that Debbie was bragging she would take out a contract on me.

The proximate cause of this murderous fury was my invitation to Bronwen to come visit us in Paris during part of her Christmas vacation. When I'd proposed the idea over the summer, everyone seemed enthusiastic. Even Deborah approved. But it was easy to say yes to things like that in Columbia. Plans were made all the time and nothing ever got done; nobody there really believed it would happen. So I booked the tickets. The advance-purchase reservations lapsed. I booked them again and worked with my father's secretary to make sure they got bought. I was determined to break the fatal torpor on the edge of Lake Katherine. When promises were made, I wanted to make sure they were kept.

Then, when it looked as if this trip might happen for Bronwen, the abuse began. Deborah would call in the middle of the night and we would hear her electronically filtered rage smoldering on the speaker of our answering machine in the next room; or she would send faxes scrawled as if the pen were held in a clenched fist, words written and scratched out, and scrawled again. Then—she would change her mind. Bronnie could come, Bronnie should come. Then she would change it again. I was trying to steal Bronwen from her. Then my father would call—or Debbie would, and put him on the phone—and he would say, with the voice of a dead man, "Bronwen cannot come," and I would listen, knowing Deborah was still on the line, and agree with him, then call him back a day or two later, when she was not around, and keep moving forward.

All this for a one-week visit.

So, when I got the message about my father turning yellow, I filtered that out, too. Then Bronwen faxed me a short handwritten note that said, simply, "Dad is in bad shape," and I knew it was real.

Jim Dickey's condition was serious this time. His liver had started to shut down on him, and he'd had an attack of hepatitis the likes of which many people do not survive, and neither Kevin nor I had known what was happening, or believed what we were hearing, until the immediate crisis was over. From our separate edges of the map we had talked to Debbie, again and again, but all she talked about was what she had done, how she had taken care of him, how no one could be trusted in the hospital, how she had been with him when he fell down and banged his head there, and how he'd bled all over the place and no one helped. Only her. Now we were talking to Dad, and he sounded weak, but he'd made it.

I should have gone to South Carolina, should have gotten on a plane that day and gone back, but I did not. I believed, because it had always been that way in my family, that dramas were played out in inverse proportion to the seriousness of the problem. There had been so much hysteria this time, the situation couldn't be as serious as all that. Or maybe it was.

Ambivalence is easy to understand but hard to forgive when it touches on issues of life and death. After keeping Columbia at a distance for all these years, now I felt it reaching out to grab me at every turn, and my instinct was to resist. I was in the middle of their lives, they were in the middle of mine. They didn't seem to like it. Neither did I. Was reconciliation with my father worth this price when, one way or another, I'd done without it for so long? Did I need to be roused from hard-earned sleep by Debbie's malevolent, maudlin hysteria? And if I did go back, what could I do? My brother was the doctor. He could talk to his colleagues. All I could do was hold my father's hand. Would that be enough for him? For me? I thought a lot had been resolved, and a reconciliation begun, but maybe it was just a last goodbye. And maybe, just maybe, that was all I needed.

I waited. Thousands of miles away from my father's hospital bed, I waited. In the half-dreaming hours before dawn, remembering my mother's voice screaming, dying on the phone, I waited. Eighteen years before, she had died without me. She had gotten better every day that I was with her—every day that I had kept my father away from her. Then I had gone, and he'd come back to her bedside, and she had died. That was what had happened. That was fact. And I knew, whether it was true or not, that if I'd stayed with her, I could have saved her, at least for a while, at least for a few more days, or months, or years. I might have had her with me still.

All these years I had blamed my father because he was easy to blame; because he asked for it; and because it was the only way I knew not to blame myself.

Could I save him now as I had not saved her?

Still, I waited. A week passed. Then two. The doctors said my father's condition was stabilizing, but if he started drinking again, he'd be dead.

We talked often on the phone. I learned to call when Deborah would be out of the house. The maid, Mayrie, and the secretary, Phyllis, kept me informed. Both were ferociously loyal to my father.

Jim Dickey was frustrated with his condition. He was weak. Excruciatingly weak. But his voice sounded better to me than it had in a long, long time. He was sober.

"When you get better," I said, "let's go to Africa." He had given me the idea, long ago. I wanted to give him the real thing.

"I'd like that."

"I told you about the Ngorongoro Crater. The horizons curve up. Like—Pellucidar."

"David Innis! Those are my favorites of the Burroughs books."

"I know," I said. "When you go to the Ngorongoro, it's like you're there."

"That's in Tanzania."

"Yeah."

"What about the Selous?"

"I—don't know about the Selous." He could always surprise me, my father.

"Have you read Peter Matthiessen's book *Sand Rivers*?"

"No."

"It's pretty good. That's about the Selous. That's where I'd like to go if I'm up to it."

"You'll be up to it."

"Sure I will."

He was already planning his comeback. We were starting to plan it together.

I asked him if he still wanted Bronnie to come to Paris. "She's going," he said, no question about that. "But Debbie—" I said. "You just let me take care of that," he said. He sounded as if he would. As if he really would. Since he wasn't drinking, he'd discovered—we'd all discovered—that he could make a promise and keep it, too.

My young sister's contagious intelligent interest in everything she beheld made her dazzling in the City of Light, whether she was dressing up for a formal evening at the Opéra de la Bastille (and counting off the *fouettés* in a production of *Swan Lake*), or charming a hair stylist who was used to working with top models, or searching out the grave of a favorite author, Oscar Wilde, in Père Lachaise Cemetery. More than pretty, she was charismatic.

I had met Bronwen three times in my life that I could recall: Once when she was the little girl who flapped her arms and flew up to the nest of her father's arms. Once, when she was five, and my father was in the hospital, and the maid had asked her where she'd gone hiding those knives. And once that summer of 1994, a few months earlier, when we'd all gone down to Litchfield. And yet I knew her, I felt, in my soul. Bronwen was thirty years younger than I, but she had snuggled beside Dad on the same armchair and been read the same poems. She'd been taken out to the suburban night to look at the same stars, and been summoned to sit on the old ottoman and strum the same chords on the guitar. She had seen our father raging drunk and incoherent, and felt his effulgent excitement. She had seen his bitter fights with her mother, and rushed to defend him. He had adored her and spoiled her, frightened her and inspired her. He had made her head.

Who else but Kevin and I had ever shared those experiences? How could we not love her?

And she was so bright, and had had to work so hard. In the bad times, she had had to make her own life in Columbia. She'd found refuge in dance and the hours of relentless, focused practice it required. She'd found protection and love in the homes of Deborah's sister, Elaine, and the maid, Mayrie Maclamore, who would rescue her when life at the house became too crazy to ignore.

Beneath the oversweetened manners of a Southern schoolgirl, she was very damn tough. Kevin and I did not have to start thinking about self-preservation until we were in our teens. Bronnie was born a survivor, and she knew the only way to keep surviving was to have a sharp, clear vision of what went on around her. When she came to Paris, we talked a lot about home, of course, and Carol and I made the usual excuses that adults make for each other—even for Debbie. Bronwen would hear none of it. She knew what her mother's problems were, and her father's. She knew that, with my father sick, her own future was at stake. And she forced us to admit that we knew that, too.

Still, I did not go back to Columbia. Bronnie went home just before Christmas and Carol and I went to visit Carol's relatives and my son in Florida. Then, at last, just after the holiday, we drove up to South Carolina.

As I had that summer, I called my father from the car. But he sounded weak, too weak to talk. I would have to vector in without him in the tower.

We rolled down the driveway of the lake house a little after dark, about an hour later than I'd planned. The drive was a lot longer, a lot more wearing than I'd expected. I was apprehensive about my father's condition—anxious to see him, but afraid of what I'd find.

Before I could get out of the car, Deborah appeared at the door of the house screaming obscenities: "You almost killed your father, you son of a bitch, and that bitch wife of yours," she shouted. "You're not coming in this house." I sat back in the seat of the car, watching. Debbie's eyes were wild, her hair was flying: she was the woman who liked to grab for knives. Carol froze and said, very quietly, "You go in. I'm not." I started to get out of the car. Debbie was still screaming. "Your father wanted to be sitting in a chair when you came, and he waited up and waited up, and then he fell down when I was trying to get him back to bed. You almost killed him," she screamed. "You are not coming in this house." But she was wrong about that.

When I opened the door of the bedroom, I tried not to show how horrified I was by the way my father looked, but I could feel the pressure of tears behind my eyes and a chill that ran through my shoulders. The flesh on his face was tight around his skull. On his forehead, where eight years before the bone was removed and blood drained away from the brain, there was now a hollow pit. He had a bristle of white beard, and his gums were as red as blood oranges. Beneath the sheet, his body seemed to be a soft, bloated mound. He smelled like sweat and sickness, and when I looked up I could see that a spray of vomit had gotten on the bookshelf behind him and been wiped away but not cleaned.

"Ah, Dad," I said.

"Son. I'm so glad you're here. What was all that—"

"Nothing, Dad. Nothing. I'm here. You get some sleep. We'll talk tomorrow."

I never expected, never wanted, to stay that night with him. But it was hard to leave. His condition was horrifying, and mesmerizing: hidden in this quiet house by a suburban lake, in this bedroom hell with this Cerberus wife at the door.

"We'll talk tomorrow," I said. We had a lot we would have to talk about.

Carol and I went home to the hotel where we'd reserved a room, and Bronwen came with us to show us the way. We unpacked the car. We sat for a while and talked. Bronwen was bright and cheerful—I could not imagine how. Finally I took her back to the only home she knew and let her out at the door. She would be okay, she said. She was used to it.

At the hotel, the telephone began to ring. Mayrie Maclamore wanted to come by and tell me what really had been happening in the house. One of my father's friends from the English department called to find out how long I would be staying. There were some things I should know, he said. Each told me horror stories. But there was nothing by now that I could not guess. The question was what I planned to do about it.

I did not know. I felt as helpless, at the age of forty-three, as I had felt at the age of thirteen. Then, it had been my mother who raged in desperation and drunkenness. She had not been as wild as Deborah, or as dangerous, but there was a sameness nonetheless—the way she and my father had played on each other's weaknesses, goading each other to anger, sliding between hysteria and stupor, staying together for their children, they said—staying together to see who would be the first to die.

Jim Dickey was never going to stay sober and get well, Debbie was never going to get better, and Bronwen was never going to get the education and opportunities she deserved unless we could break the circle of destruction in that house.

I held the tape recorder close to my father's mouth. Bronnie sat on the other side of him, on the arm of the old corduroy-covered chair. Debbie had left the house for a few minutes, and while she was away I wanted him to say clearly, and on the record, that he approved of Bronwen's going away to school.

That would be a beginning, I thought. I knew that he had wanted me to go to Exeter or Andover. I knew that he wanted the best for his daughter, just as he'd wanted the best for me. But when we'd talked about this before, on the phone, he'd always said that prep school was out of the question. Bronwen did not want to leave Columbia, he said. Now, I knew she did, and I knew that once she was out of the house, Deborah's hold on my father would weaken.

I started the tape recorder rolling. Did Bronwen really want to go away to school? "No ifs, ands, buts, or anything else," she told him.

"All right," said my father. "It shall be. It shall be."

Ess muss sein.

I suggested that he not bring this up with Debbie—at least not right away. This was a first step, and I didn't want him to plunge everything into chaos just to see how that looked. If he was going to get better, I told him, he was going to have to live in a healthier, quieter environment. He shouldn't have to face the ranting and intimidation.

"I think that's quite a good decision," he said. "Because it's hard to get well being ripped and torn to pieces emotionally all the time. And to have to fight off your wife because your son is coming to visit you, who you haven't seen in thirteen years or thereabouts. It's not right to try to throw all kind of monkey wrenches into that situation when there's not anybody in the world that I wanted to see more. She seems to think that there's some—something wrong with that. That I have done it as an insult to her. But it's not true at all. I just wanted to see my boy."

"Yes."

"But as soon as you come on the scene, then things start to get bad."

I said I understood.

"For God's sake," he said, and there was a note of real fear in his voice, "for God's sake, keep hold of that tape. Don't let Deborah get hold of it. It would be worth my life. And she would actually kill me. She's not above it. She has wounded me. It was her who caused all this to happen." He touched the old pit in his forehead where the doctors had drained his blood. "Repeated blows to the head. And she stabbed me. Almost cost me the use of my left arm. I didn't proffer charges, although the lawyers and legal people were urging me to do so, because I figured that she just lost her temper and she would straighten out. She never did."

I was not sure what to believe at that moment. Deborah has since told me that she did stab my father with a broadhead arrow, years ago. But the hemorrhage on the surface of his brain was something else, she said. It could have been caused by a fall he took on the stairs at Litchfield, or by a smack on the skull from the boom of the little sailboat he used to take out for drunken sails on Lake Katherine. She never hit him with a blunt instrument, she said. Nothing like that. And maybe, that morning as Bronnie and I sat with him in Columbia, Jim Dickey was using a lie to dramatize reality. But whatever had happened in the past, he seemed to be frightened in a way I had never seen him frightened before. And I was frightened for him.

Now we could hear Deborah pulling into the driveway. She was coming in the door. She saw me and Bronwen with our father, and a rage rose up in her that you could see cross her features like a cloud. She demanded to know what was going on. I said we were just talking. She ordered me out of the house. When I said I wasn't going to go, she started screaming. I moved as close to her face as I could and told her that no one was going to listen to her, no one was going to obey her, no one was going to do a goddamn thing she said. I didn't threaten her, and I didn't raise my hand, but if she thought, looking at my face, my eyes, my anger, that I had murderous intent, well, that was fine with me.

And then she cracked. She broke down in tears. "I thought you were going to hit me," she said. "No," I said, and took her in my arms, and I walked her to the sofa, and I let her cry on my shoulder and held her hand and told her we were only trying to do what was good for everybody.

Kevin was in Connecticut with his wife and children, but he had arranged an appointment for my father with a liver specialist in Charleston. It seemed likely that the only way to save Jim Dickey's life would be with a transplant, and this was the best man to do it.

Carol and Bronwen and I drove down the day before and stayed in an elegant little bed-and-breakfast on the Battery. It was supposed to be a quiet change of scene. Debbie had agreed to it. But as soon as we'd left she'd started working the phones, trying to find ways to drive me out of the grim little world ruled by her fury. Out of the blue, my ex-wife called me in the hotel. It was the first time I'd heard from her in years. Debbie had talked to her, Susan said, and she just wanted to say that she thought Debbie was right, that the best place for a child was with her mother. I told Susan I really didn't think she understood the situation, or needed to be involved.

That afternoon, when Bronwen, exhausted, went to her room for a nap, I transcribed the tape of our conversation with my father and e-mailed it to my brother. Kevin had a lot of friends in Columbia, and one of his best friends was a lawyer. I wondered if we could have Deborah institutionalized. It seemed that might be the only way to protect our father. But by the evening we had our answer. The law wouldn't help us, and probably would hurt us. The state might even step in and take custody of Bronwen. That wasn't an option.

We could only hope that our father would stay sober long enough to take control of his own life. We could only keep working to get Bronwen into school, and keep hoping that Deborah could be persuaded that the best way for her to show her love, and the best

way for her to survive, was to get out of the house and get straight.
Nothing was going to be easy.

I helped my father urinate in the lavatory of the doctor's office, and
helped him undress in the examination room. When he lay back on
the table, his whole chest, from his collarbone down to his groin, was
full of liquid. The doctor tapped on my father's belly, and ripples
spread across his body like the undulations of a water bed.

"My God," I thought, "my father is going to die. He really is
going to die."

Deborah and I sat together listening to the doctor lecture Jim
Dickey about the need to quit drinking. His liver disease could have
led to many complications, including dementia. And death, of course.
It still could. Jim had to join Alcoholics Anonymous. Unless he did
that, there was no way he could even begin to be eligible for a
transplant, which would be the last chance to save his life. "Yes," my
father said. He would do that. Debbie would help him. She knew all
about Alcoholics Anonymous, she said.

My father was lying. He absolutely despised the confessional
organizations where Deborah had spent so much time to so little
effect. As far as he was concerned, Alcoholics Anonymous was a place
for people with nowhere else to go who had nothing else to talk about
but drinking, and Narcotics Anonymous was a place, as he put it, for
"assignations." (He liked to draw out the word and make it hiss a
little.) I knew he had no intention of going to any meetings, or earning
any chips for abstinence.

When I left Columbia that first week in January 1995, I could not
be sure I would see my father again. All I could do was try to keep up
the little momentum we had for change. I contacted half a dozen prep
schools, all the ones I'd ever heard him talk about. I began arranging
for Bronnie to take her boards, to get her letters of recommendation. A
Bronwen team took shape in Columbia, headed by her godfather, Matt
Bruccoli, and my father's friend Ward Briggs, to see that she got her ap-
plications filled out, her essays written, the checks sent in on time. She
proved herself as brilliant as we knew she was. Within three months,
she'd been accepted at every major school to which she applied.

I had promised to fly back to Columbia in March for my father's
next appointment with the specialist in Charleston. Again, Jim Dickey
and Deborah and I sat in the doctor's office. But my father was stronger
now, that was clear. The doctor said, frankly, he hadn't thought Jim
would make it this far, and he was well satisfied with the improvement.
"You've been going to Alcoholics Anonymous," he said. "I have," said

my father, holding up a little red plastic key fob—a chip—embossed with the legend "90 Days Clean and Serene." "That was the finest thing you ever did," said the doctor. "It certainly is," said my father.

Later on, knowing how Jim Dickey felt about AA, I asked him what it was like to stand up and confess to alcoholism.

"I never did," he said. He'd just gone to a few meetings with Debbie.

"Right. But—didn't you get your little chip?"

"Nope." He shook his head and smiled like he had me on that one. "She gave me hers."

"That was the finest thing you ever did," my father said, mimicking the doctor's accent and starting to chuckle. "It certainly is," he said, repeating his own line and erupting in laughs broken by a breathless cough. "It certainly is—to put one over on you, you asshole. I never did like that fella. My liver is the best thing I have got to show right now. It's a hundred percent. And I won't do a Mickey Mantle on him. Or a J.R. or whatever that guy's name is. No, we ain't gonna need that."

Jim Dickey's liver did seem, throughout the spring, to be on the mend, and that seemed a major miracle. We were settling into a kind of rhythm. Bronnie was getting ready to go to school, and Debbie was gradually being edged out of the house. Her money was cut back, and she couldn't beg or threaten any more out of him. He was talking to divorce lawyers. My father was sober. There was no going back on that one. His will was holding—and it was pure will. All his. "What God does, we will," Joel Cahill told his disciples in *Alnilam*. Amen. As long as Jim Dickey was sober, he was in control.

Medications helped drain the bloat from his abdomen, and he started talking now about really getting back in shape, and what we'd do then. "The Selous," he'd say. "The Sand Rivers." But he was still frighteningly gaunt, like a sculptor's armature stripped of clay, and each time we talked he was more frustrated. Nothing seemed to help him start coming back, and his breathing was so damned difficult.

Bronnie came over to Paris for several weeks in the summer, then went away to school in Connecticut, not far from Kevin. Still my father's liver was improving. Still his will was holding. The divorce proceedings were starting to take shape. There were scenes, sometimes frightening scenes, but nothing my father couldn't handle. And then Deborah was gone. She moved out of the house to start a new series of treatments at a clinic in southern Georgia.

My father was free at last, but terribly lonely. Mayrie Maclamore, who'd taken care of Bronnie for so long, was there now to take care of him. Carol Fairman, his new secretary, doted on him. His students and best friends from the university, Matt Bruccoli and Ward Briggs and Don Greiner, spent a lot of time at the house. I was coming from Paris every chance I could get, and on the least pretext, whether researching the novel I'd begun, or seeing friends at CNN in Atlanta. My son, James, who adored his Fun Man, was visiting, too, from Fort Benning. At Christmas 1995, we all gathered with Kevin and Sally and their two little girls at Litchfield.

The first night in the house on the coast, my father managed to climb all the way to the bedroom with only brief pauses, but it cost him. He was exhausted. The next day, when he climbed up he did a little better, and then each time after that there was improvement, until the ascent of the landings was almost easy. We were going to beat this weakness. We were going to do great things.

But the breathing—the breathing was so damned hard. He kept going back to the doctor to find out what was wrong, and the answer kept coming back the same: a fibrosis was slowly petrifying his lungs, but they didn't know why, and they didn't really know how to stop it. It had been there even before his liver started to fail, but then, when his whole body shut down on him, it got much worse.

Kevin had looked at the X-rays. "The fibrosis will be what kills him," he told me. But it seemed to be moving slowly. When Kevin and I and our families left South Carolina a little after New Year's 1996, we thought that, with therapy and medication, and the love of his family and friends, Jim Dickey would hold on for a long time.

There had been so many friends in the old days. So many had been driven away. Now a few, when they heard that Deborah was gone and my father was sober, began to come back. Michael, who had been estranged for almost as long as I had, began to call his beloved Jim Dickey from New York several times a week. Carolee Guilds, a beautiful divorcée who lived across the lake and had loved my father from afar, from just that far, for more than twenty years, now began to visit almost every day. We all wanted to surround him with attention, with love, and it was pure pleasure to see how he thrived on it. My father would read, and talk, and hold court—and he was starting now to write with a renewed clarity and intensity that hadn't been there on his page for a long time.

We talked on the phone several times a week. My father got his first computer so he could get e-mail. My son set it up for him. Dad started to imagine the way *Crux* would take shape. We talked about the movie that was going to be made from *To the White Sea*. Who would star in it. What was happening with the script. Who the director might be. We even began to talk about what I was writing—the novel that I was trying to finish, this book about us that I was trying to start.

My father told me about the oxygen generator sometime in the spring. It was a big help, he said. A big help. So we had come back to Litchfield in July of 1996 accompanied by the sighing of the machine, but it did not seem to me then to be whispering of death.

I thought, at the end of that summer, as I left the landings and the dank garage behind me, that I had saved my father's life. I had descended into Jim Dickey's hidden hell on the quiet shores of Lake Katherine. We had ascended the landings of Litchfield. I had preached reason—and truth. And I had brought him back. Now all we had to do, together, was keep him alive.

My father, always so fascinated by coincidence and vastly grounded in literary reference, must have been a little bemused by the Orphic plot that had taken his family apart, and put it back together, and returned him to the light. It was the kind of thing he'd imagine himself doing.

One afternoon at Litchfield he had wanted to talk about all the poets of his generation and the generation just before his—so many that he knew—who killed themselves, or might as well have. Jarrell and Berryman, Roethke and Lowell. "Too much sensibility," he said. Which seemed an odd judgment. He was always puzzled by their kind of madness.

Just then he was reading John Haffenden's 1982 biography of John Berryman, which he'd brought down from Columbia. He motioned me over and handed me the book. "Page 408," he said. "I never knew that before."

I turned to the place he'd marked, in the chapter called "Last Months, 1971–72":

> For the summer his AA group contained and supported him; he proudly earned sobriety pins. At an AA picnic, to everyone's surprise, he entered a foot race with Kate on his back. He had found reasons for committing himself to group sobriety as early as the winter, when he read James Dickey's novel *Deliverance* and identified himself with the following quotations:
>
> > Survival depends—well, it depends on *having* to survive. The kind of life I'm talking about depends on its being the last chance. The very last of all.
>
> > I bound myself with my brain and heart to the others; with them was the only way I would ever get out.

WALLS OF BOOKS

It was Christmas and I was going home to South Carolina, and for just about the first time in my adult life, it felt like home. The work of the summer was finished. We weren't going to be cleaning the garage any more. We weren't going to be plotting anyone's rescue. That job was done. It was two years since my father's hospitalization, and all our lives were different, and all of them certifiably better. The divorce decree had been approved by the court, and Debbie was still straight. Bronnie was on the dean's list. Kevin and I were beginning to feel, at last, like we belonged to a family.

My father and I had found so much to talk about. Wherever I'd be, I'd call him about almost anything. We'd talk about my son and my wife, my sister, Bronnie, and her school; about our books in progress. My first novel was finished. It had started as an experiment with the thriller genre, intended to make several political points, but had turned ineluctably toward the character and identity of the narrator. It was supposed to be about terrorism, and it wound up being about family. The narrator, holed up behind enemy lines in the Gulf War, waiting to try to escape through a storm of fire in a ferocious allied bombardment, wonders how much you can ever really learn about your father: "The man I knew as a child was a man no one else had known, and the man known to everyone else was a stranger to me."

Now my father and I had the chance to know each other as men, grown father and grown son. I started to read him more passages from the novel. He read me scenes, or described them, from *Crux*. We tried to come up with the right title for my book. "Muj" and "Mission Unspoken" and "A Portion of Wrath" were all used at one point or another, before I finally settled with my editor, Alice Mayhew, on *Innocent Blood*. But I was constantly trying out different ideas. Jim Dickey loved to play with titles.

One late-autumn day, I'd gone with Carol and her mother to a video installation by Bill Viola in the eighteenth-century chapel of the sprawling Hôpital Pitié-Salpêtrière, not far from the Jardin des Plantes in southeastern Paris. Inside, there were recurring projections of a man drenched in a shower of water that began as a trickle and ended as a deluge; and another man consumed by fire; and another who sank deep below the surface of water until he was a blurred impression, then surfaced again, his breath exploding on the screen, then sank away again, until his form dissolved into a memory distorted by the ripples on the surface. At the entrance to the show, as an epigraph, was some poetry of Walt Whitman: "By the sea under the yellow and sagging moon, / The messenger there arous'd, the fire, the sweet hell within, / The unknown want, the destiny of me."

It seemed to me "The Hell Within" might be the title I was looking for, and I wondered if Jim Dickey would know just where it came from in Whitman. I called him from the street in front of the hospital to ask him what he thought of the line. He thought for a minute, wondering aloud if it might not be from "Starting at Paumanok," then thought better of that. "Sea-Drift," he said. "Look up 'Sea-Drift' and see if that isn't where it is." And I didn't know why, but I started to cry, there on the street in front of the working part of the Hôpital Pitié-Salpêtrière, where ambulances came and went. It was just so good, so sweet to hear my father's voice—like this. Ah, God, it was great to have him back. Tears flowed down my cheeks in the October chill. After I hung up, I was weeping until I lost my breath, and Carol tried to comfort me. Never before in our lives together had she seen me weep from joy.

So it was good—it was great—to be back with him now in Columbia. I knew he couldn't get up to come to the door when I pulled in the driveway. I didn't wait. I walked right in. This was my place now, too.

He was in the corduroy chair, surrounded by stacks of books in every direction that could be reached by his hands. The wall they formed around him had grown, in the months since I'd actually seen him, into an elaborate, teetering structure of well-thumbed volumes of poetry and art and architecture, fiction and criticism and film, with a bowl of cereal balanced precariously on top of one column, a big glass of Ensure on another, a phone list and a letter opener on still another; and just beyond that first line of defense, other, lower walls, and books piled on the big coffee table, and among them, strangely, various castings of the aluminum life-masks made twenty years before, when his face had been full and strong. I kissed the hollowed cheek of the living man and hugged him to me, trying not to tangle my feet in the clear plastic hose that ran to his breathing machine, feeling his ribs beneath my fingers.

There were a lot of little things to take care of those first couple of days. There always were. Jim Dickey was about to start teaching again, and he was worried. "You don't realize really what a close thing this physical thing is. It's real close, Chris. I am just on a knife edge. I can function—barely." The trip to the university, the wheelchair ride to the elevator, the struggle with oxygen bottles, was a calvary he dreaded. But he wanted to teach. He said it was for the money. But it was really so he could be around people, so he could interact with students, so a couple of times a week he could get that dose of admiration and inspiration that was better than any medicine. The solution was simple, of course: he would give his seminars in the house. Columbia is a small city. Jim Dickey's home was only ten minutes from the humanities building. There was plenty of room. Meg Richards, who replaced Carol Fairman as my father's assistant, was full of energy and enthusiasm and anxious to make the classes work at home. It was absurd that no one had thought of doing this before.

The university was always looking for a way to exploit the old poet, but was always a little embarrassed by him. USC (this "other" USC) was as insignificant on the national education-and-arts scene as it had ever been. It was still answering to a state legislature steeped in the cracker traditions of politicians like Strom Thurmond. Despite a string of ambitious presidents, at least one of whom had notions of largesse in public and private life that got him in trouble with the law, the university was a stagnant backwater. When it decided to start a publicity campaign to raise its profile a little, where else would it turn, where else could it turn, but to James Dickey? So there'd been a new television spot made about him. My father showed it to me proudly. In it, he had taken off his oxygen tube, and stood near his desk just long enough to get an image for the lens with focus soft enough and light warm enough not to shock the viewers. I told him it was good, that he looked great, but it was sad, and painful to watch for anyone who had ever known him before.

I wondered why the university didn't have a whole archive of video- and audiotapes recording the twenty-eight years of classes he'd taught there. They could have had scenes with any number of his students who went on, like Pat Conroy, to be nationally known writers. They would have had a line on the Jim Dickey method of teaching, which was all about discovery and excitement and personal transcendence through the discipline of craft. They'd have had a record of those classes that he always worked on so hard, filling the house with notebooks and syllabi outlining his courses, and sorting books onto special shelves, or special columns near his chair, because they were the ones he needed to pass on the magnificence of what a poet could do. But no one at South Carolina had ever gotten around to recording those classes. Not in twenty-eight years. It seemed it was about time to start. I called Don and Ward and Matt. We got that arranged.

And then we just talked.

"Well, how is *Summer of Deliverance* coming?" my father asked, shuffling some papers that Meg had brought him, and making sure she didn't step on his oxygen tube—or "the mortal coil," as we'd taken to calling it. "I'll be finished panting in a minute," he said, then got down to business. "We start at Springer Mountain," he said.

Jim Dickey and his son had a project together at last, this story of a movie and how it was made, and what happened before it and after. He was sketching it out in his head. It would start with us hunting together.

"I think I was about eight," I said. "We wound up sleeping together in the same sleeping bag in a little tent. I don't even think we really did any hunting. There was a lake in the mountains, up in the fog."

My father smiled. He was floating through the forest, weightless as an owl. The woods burned in his head. "Yeah, that's right," he said. "Rock Creek Lake."

"I was a real little boy then."

"Yes."

"And we wound up—and we had—I don't even . . ." The words were rushing out of me, but not fast enough to keep up with the rush of memories, the surge of emotion they brought on.

"Those, too, were great days," said my father.

"Yeah. Oh, yeah," was all I could choke out in my utterly inarticulate need to seize some part of that irretrievable past. "And we wound up sleeping—"

"Son—"

"We had a . . . we had a . . ."

"Son."

"Yes?"

"I do love you so much."

And for me at that moment it was as if he had never said it before. "I love you, too," I said, and wanted to tell him, to show him, to know for sure that he knew how much. But that was all I could say. "I love you, too."

"I love you so much," he said again. "Now go on."

I tried. I wanted it all back. "I think that was the first time you ever said I had more guts than a burglar. I think."

"You do."

"That is the first time I ever remember you saying that. And I don't know why I had so many guts. . . ."

"That has certainly proved out."

"It started raining like hell and the tent leaked."

"Oh yeah."

"It wouldn't, it wouldn't stay dry."

"Oh no," he said, and laughed. "No."

"It was cold. We didn't have an air mattress or anything. We were —the sleeping bag was on the cold, cold ground."

"Just had the ground sheet."

"Oh yeah. Fuck, it was cold. And we wound up in the same sleeping bag. I was so little."

"I shouldn't have taken you up there at that age."

"Oh no, but it was great."

"Except that you just wanted to go so bad."

"It was a great adventure. I built campfires, I remember that." And there was a remembered twinge in my fingertips to remind me of the matches I'd rubbed together in my coat pocket.

"Sure."

"Then there was another time. I must have been older. I must have been closer to ten. And that was when I was in the hole and you were in the tree."

"That was a wonderful adventure, that was a beautiful little field there, with a creek running through it."

I remember the sun was going down and we had been on the edge of the field for hours. I had my little bow and my father had put me in a low hole camouflaged by a few branches. He was in a tree-stand twenty or thirty yards away. I was shaking with the cold, more cold than I could remember or could endure. But I was afraid to move, because I knew the little car-coat I was wearing was the color of a deer, and there were other hunters staking out the field, waiting for the deer to come down at just this hour, ready to loose their arrows at a color or shape glimpsed moving in the twilight.

I tried to signal my father. I wanted to call out, but I couldn't make a little-boy fool of myself in this world of men. My hands and feet were deathly numb with cold. Tears were hot against my cheeks. Why wouldn't he look in my direction? His eyes were fixed on the broken stalks of corn, the wooded edges of the field, the thin stream of water that ran through it. I looked around to see where the other hunters were, there among the trees and bushes. If I stood up a little higher could they see me clearly enough not to shoot? I could not know. I could not see any of them.

My arrows rattled in the quiver on my back as I inched myself out of the hole. "C'mon, Dad, look at me. Help me." I walked slowly toward the tree where he sat on a board, bracing his feet at odd angles against the branches. "Come on, Dad," I said, clinching my teeth to try to keep them from chattering. And now he saw me. He saw the panic on my face, and a look of panic crossed his. "Chrissy!" "Please, Dad, come down," I said soundlessly with the movement of my lips. He looked out quickly over the field to see what the other hunters were doing. "I'm coming," he said. But for a terrible moment—it couldn't have been more than a few seconds—he could not twist himself free of the branches, and in that moment I had felt what it would be like to have him beyond my reach, and for me to be beyond his. For just that second I had seen my father, my savior, helpless.

Didn't my father remember that? I wondered as we sat talking in Columbia.

"I look back in horror now," I said. "Because you—you left me, you were up in a tree. You were like stuck up in a tree. I mean not . . . You couldn't get down, Dad."

"But you had your own full equipment to hunt."

If my father would just keep writing and creating and thinking about all that was possible in the future, I thought he could hold on. And better than hold on. But his loneliness was becoming dangerous. He missed Deborah, and called her all the time, although he liked having her at a distance more than having her in the house. He missed Bronwen, who was away all year at school, then away in the summers, too, and dating now, and driving, and not there at the house much even on vacations she spent in Columbia. And there were times when he was scared, too, by the loneliness. Mayrie was there for him all day every day and often late into the night. If he was really worried, he'd call a good friend like Ward Briggs, who would come over and sleep in the house with him. But he couldn't do that every night. Jim Dickey was frightened by his own frailty, and beside him now in the chair, not just because he liked the way it looked but because he hoped it could help him, he kept one of the enormous Rambo knives with a serrated edge that someone had given him years before.

I was not here enough for him. I knew that. I hadn't seen him since the summer. My father had given me that moment when we remembered the tent, and the cornfield, and the stream. It was the pure moment of understanding, of reconciliation, that I'd been looking for all along. But now I found that I was in the tree and he was scared and he had come looking for me from the hole in the cold ground, and I could not come down.

So I made more plans. Always more plans. I would be coming back in a few weeks—maybe for his birthday on February 2. He was going to have a physical therapist to help him get back into better shape without putting the kind of strain on him that going to classes at the university had done. And we were going to work on his projects together every day. I'd use e-mail to send notes back and forth with Meg.

I was thinking that we'd work on *Crux*. But then he pulled two other manuscripts from among the piles of books and folders closest to his right hand.

One was a slim binder of completed poems that he called *Death, and the Day's Light*. He turned to one of them, "Drift-Spell," about going with my brother to visit my mother's grave beneath the Spanish moss in the old cemetery on the coast, and preparing to join her there.

> . . . *Without words, we shall know*
> *That we have her forever: are learning to the full*
> *What we have: death, and the day's light,*
>
> *The three of us in love. Moss,*
> *Your mother's eyes, and an owl in stone.*
>
> Love and the day's light?
>
> *No, she is honest with us*
> *Anywhere, son. Death and the day's light*
>
> *With us here, full of the drift-spell.*

The other manuscript was in a thick folder; each page was covered with notes, and the notes themselves were annotated. "I have been working on this for almost twenty years," he said. "I don't know if I'm going to be able to finish it."

"You'll finish it," I said.

"*You* will finish it," he said.

"No," I said, but he started to walk me through the folder anyway. There were two poems, in fact: "Two Poems on the Survival of the Male Body." The first was called "Show Us the Sea," a long expansion of a poem published several years before about an aging father watching, through binoculars, his lifeguard son on the beach with other young men, bodysurfing and striking poses like weightlifters.

> . . . *Real God,*
> *Through both hands and my head, in depth-bright distance, roll*
> *In raw caught sharpness*
>
> *Of sight, and let my son come,*
> *Exploding with proximity, and with him bring voices*
> *Faintly around him, the sounds not matching*
> *The size of their magnified bodies. No harm; I am invisible*
>
> *With sand.*

The second of the poems was "For Jules Bacon," who was Mr. America when my father was young. It is about a flier in the Pacific in World War II who puts together barbells from the junk and spare parts that accumulate around his base, thinking that, if he could just perfect his body, make it like Bacon's, he would become invulnerable somehow, that even high in the air, living with invisible fear, the mystique of perfection would keep him alive.

> . . . *I rose. War, Jules, and nothing else*
> *Jules, not death*
>
> *But body. War. I rose. War, war, Jules,*
>
> *War. War roared with life, and you saved me.*

We would work on those, I told my father. Yes, we would. I couldn't write them, but I would type them according to his directions, and maybe take a couple of guesses at the choices he hadn't quite been able to make, and e-mail them to Meg, and he would look at them and figure out what I had done wrong, and in correcting it take his own work further toward completion, and we would go back and forth like that and talk on the phone every day. There was so much to do. So much that was so good. And I would be back in a month, just a month, for his birthday.

"Son, I do love you so much."

"I love you, too."

"I love you so much. Now go on."

CLOSINGS

My father died late the night of January 19, 1997. I was not there. One last time I had not wanted to believe, had waited too long, and I will always wonder and never know if I could have saved his life, even if only for a few more days. I would have wanted that time with him. I want it still.

When he went into the hospital, no one thought it would be for the last time. He was more concerned about an infection in his foot caused by his gnarled toes and bad circulation. It was the childhood fear that he would lose his leg. When I talked to him on the phone, he gave me the good news that his foot, at any rate, would be okay.

The breathing was coming hard now. The tissue in his lungs was turning to fibrous stone. But the disease still seemed to be moving slowly. He would rest in the calm of the hospital, with good care; he would begin the physical therapy that he had been avoiding. He would begin to mend as much as could be mended. All of us were optimistic, or, at least, as optimistic as we could be.

Once again Jim Dickey was visited in the hospital by a long procession of friends and students. The whole team of people who had come together for him in the previous months and years was on the scene now. Mayrie and Meg kept the house and his correspondence going. The beautiful Carolee Guilds went to see him often, raising his spirits just by being there. Matt Bruccoli was there, and Don Greiner. And Ward Briggs, who had spent so much time at the house.

When he saw my father's weakness, Ward remembered something that my father had told him a few weeks before, one morning after Ward had slept over. Jim said he'd had a dream. He'd been back at North Fulton High School and scored three touchdowns, including the one that won the game, then gotten a date with the most beautiful girl in Georgia, and been with her in a car with the top down bathed in the light of the moon. Everything was right with the world. But Jim couldn't be happy, he told the girl, because this was just a dream. And the beautiful girl had said, "It's all real within the dream, Jim. It's all real in the dream." Now Ward, who knew my father so well, leaned over him and held his hand. "It's all real within the dream," he said. And my father smiled. "I know it is," he said.

Debbie did not come to the hospital. She stayed at her apartment in Georgia and talked to my father on the phone, and I'm sure he was glad to hear her voice now, so loving and so reasonable. She had been completely sober for almost a year, and would remain so. She was a different person, redeemed and confident. But he asked her not to visit him. He needed love. But he also needed quiet.

When James Dickey went into the hospital, that was news in Columbia, South Carolina, and it went out on the wires. People who had known him well, and people who had wanted to, started to send messages of encouragement. And people who had seen in the idea of the poet some reflection of their own insanity, or relief for it, started to lurk around the hospital, stalkers looking to share in the ecstasy of his genius or the excitement of his death.

Among these was a former student, a well-to-do middle-aged woman from North Carolina, an obsessive admirer who decided she loved him and hated him—just another incidental lunatic sycophant who wanted to embrace him and kill him. She was the kind of person whose attentions the old dilettante of madness had enjoyed or endured when he was drunk and numb and could write it all off as inspiration. But now he had no desire and was in no condition to deal with her. He couldn't withstand the blood fear of all the madness and guilt, trivial and monstrous, all of it coming back to him in the form of one tawdry little woman with an empty life who thought the great poet could fill it.

She came to the hospital at a moment when no one was there to protect him. Not Mayrie or Meg, or Matt or Ward, and not one of his children. It was the moment, precisely, when I should have been there and was not.

Later she told me her own story over the phone, in a long conversation that began with her using an assumed name and was interrupted many times by her tears and accusations, pleas and apologies. It was a kind of discourse that had grown familiar to me, and I listened without apparent emotion, and even took notes to give to the police, just in case they needed to make a case against her in the future.

This is her account of what happened that night in the hospital:

> I walked in and he said, "How did you know I was here?" And I thought, "Well, he can't be too bad off. He is as mean as a snake." I said, "I will never tell." . . . Then he said something about, "You get out of my room! You get out of the hospital!" Then he goes, "This relationship is over!" I thought, "My God, the nurse is going to think we were lovers." I said, "Jim, *a student-teacher relationship is never over!*" And, ah, and I am not sure if anything else went on. Then I said, "You are cruel, Jim. You are cruel." I went out and I said, "Get me a taxi. Get me out of here." And I curled up in a wheelchair and I cried my heart out, Chris. [She started to weep over the phone.] I cried. God, I cried. Then I went downstairs and the taxi took too long. I was completely out of my mind and I said, "I ought to go back up there and shoot the old bastard. He was so cruel."

Nurses at the hospital, including Debbie's sister Elaine, heard of the threat and decided it was time to move my father to a different, safer room. But that, too, panicked the old man. When I reached him on the phone, he was upset and scared. And I began, too late, to make plans to go home.

The day after the former student's visit, my father's condition was dramatically worse. I was talking to him and to Carolee, to Meg and to Mayrie. Kevin was talking to them and to the doctors, too, and keeping Bronwen informed at school. Jim Dickey was in bad shape. We all decided it was time for us to go home, and I booked my flight, but to get from Paris, France, to Columbia, South Carolina, was going to take me twenty-four hours. It suddenly seemed as remote as El Salvador or the Sudan.

Kevin and Bronnie got to the hospital early on the evening of the 19th, and our father was just barely holding on. Each breath was a work of ferocious, exhausting concentration. Kevin and I had talked about whether he should be put on a ventilator, which would have meant he was heavily drugged and completely incapacitated for as long as the machine kept him, technically, alive. That was not a choice. "Let me die my own death, and not the death of doctors," he had always said, quoting Rilke. My father was afraid of being alone, but he was as unafraid of dying, I think, as any man could be. He would know the great secret. It would all be real within the dream. So our concern was that the doctors in Columbia not take his death out of his hands when he lost consciousness. But they handled it right. When Kevin checked the chart, he found the simple notation "DNR." Do not resuscitate.

Kevin and Bronnie stayed with our father that night as long as they could bear it, and went back to the house, planning to see him in the morning. Carolee Guilds paid a visit, too, and left. Mayrie stayed. "Don't leave me, Mayrie," he said. "Don't leave me."

In Paris, I gathered up papers. I tried to work on "Show Us the Sea," so I could show him some more of it. I tried, finally, to get a little sleep before going to the airport. The call from Kevin came a little after five in the morning. It was already January 20 in Paris. "Chris, he's dead," said my brother.

Jim Dickey had given one class in his home by the lake, and it was recorded by the university, just as we'd planned. Meg got me a copy of it, but I did not listen to it right away. Preparations for a funeral are marvelously distracting, with so many people appearing who have been unseen for so long, and gifts of food and flowers to be dealt with, and, too, lawyers and accountants. All of it so distracting, some of it so reassuring. So good to be close. Michael met me at Newark Airport when I made the connection to Columbia and he flew down with me. James, who was serving in Korea at the time, flew back around the world to make it to Fun Man's funeral. It was so good to be together. We only missed the one person we all wanted most to be there.

I finally put the tape in the player of the rent-a-car as Michael and Kevin and I drove back to the house from some errand. "This is a class for poets," it began. Technology makes strange ghosts for us, I thought. At the push of a button, our father's voice had filled the car.

"Poetry is a matter of luck," he said. "You can't teach it. You can point it out when it occurs, but you can't teach it. Verse, however, you can teach." Our father's voice was cadenced by his short breath. "This is a class in verse hoping to become poetry, with luck."

We were driving past the shopping malls and filling stations, the automatic teller machines and the fast-food restaurants of Columbia, coming to the tree-lined streets of a suburbia that looked, I thought, like Atlanta looked when I was a child, full of tidy houses for people who wanted tidy lives. What strange places these were for us.

On the tape, Jim Dickey paused to take a drink of chocolate milk. "I teach this semester what I call 'creature poetry.' Poetry written with the whole, the whole, the *whole* of the sentient organism: mind, body, guts, blood flow, breath. In everything that enables you to be a living being we have a resource. So we start with dreams. And with automatic writing. Anything to break through the barrier that leads from the conscious mind to the unconscious and to the dream life."

I wondered if he would talk about the happy swimming pool or that moonlit night with Miss Georgia. But no.

"I have the most terrible dream of pursuit," my father said. "I am always moving against a terrific wind. Which doesn't bother my pursuer at all, but I have to grab the grass and try to inch forward, you know? And something is just gaining on me in leaps and bounds. It is some sort of guilt, I guess. If I were a post-Freudian I am sure I would have to admit to it. But in the dream it is only the terrible pursuit."

God, our father's voice sounded weak—so much weaker, even, than it had been two weeks before, when I was with him. But now he was changing the subject again. He was getting stronger as he started to talk about exactly what it means to be a poet.

"Invent," he admonished. "Invent is the guts of it. 'To invent.' You can say as much as you like with stuff you know. But don't be confined to it. Don't think about—honestly—don't think about telling the truth. Because poets are not trying to tell the truth, are they?"

No, I thought, poets are not trying to tell the truth. We pulled into the driveway of the house by the lake.

"They are trying," Jim Dickey told his students, "to show God a few things he maybe didn't think of. It takes us to supply that. We are not trying to tell the truth. We are trying to make it so that when we sit down to write we are absolute lords over our material. We can say anything we want to, any way we want to. The question is to find the right way, the best way to do it. This is what we are going to be looking for."

Still we sat in the car. When I closed my eyes, I could imagine my father beside me on the long highway through West Texas. My mother, ahead of us, sees the desert open before her and throws her arms wide to embrace the horizon.

"This is going to take us through some very strange fields, across a lot of rivers, oceans, mountains, forests. God knows where it will take us," my father said. "That is part of the excitement of it, and the sense of deep adventure. Which is what we want more than anything. Discovery. Everything is in that. Everything is that."

Yes. Everything.

"We have to fight for it. We have to fight through to it. We have to cut the angel out of the marble, out of the rock, the form of the angel. Michelangelo used to say the angel is already in the stone, all I got to do is chip the rock from around it and set it free. Well, the shape is already in there. It takes a lot of chipping to get that angel to stand up, much less to fly. Sort of heavy for that." Jim Dickey chuckled at his own little joke. "So, as I say, this is a strange and long journey that we are undertaking."

Then his tone changed again. "With my current physical shape this will almost undoubtedly be my last class forever," he said.

I listened, breathless with loss.

"But what we start here I would like you to continue on your own," he said. "When we get started, I want you to fight this thing through, with your own unconscious, with your own dreams, and see where it comes out. That is the excitement and the fun of it—deep discovery, deep adventure. It is the most dangerous game, and the best.

"Flaubert says somewhere that the life of a poet is a hell of a life, it is a dog's life, but it is the only one worth living. You suffer more. You are frustrated more by things that don't bother other people. But you also live so much more. You live so much more intensely and so much more vitally. And with so much more of a sense of meaning, of consequentiality, instead of nothing mattering. This is what is driving our whole civilization into suicide. The feeling that we are living existences in which nothing matters very much, or at all. That is what is behind all the drugs and the alcoholism and suicide—insanity, wars, everything—a sense of nonconsequence. A sense that nothing, nothing matters. No matter which way we turn it is the same thing. But the poet is free of that. He is free of that.

"For the poet, everything matters, and it matters a lot. That is the realm where we work. Once you are there, you are hooked. If you are a real poet, you are hooked more deeply than any narcotics addict could possibly be on heroin. You are hooked on something that is life-giving instead of destructive. Something that is a process that cannot be too far from the process that created everything. God's process. You can say what you can of God. I don't know what your religion might be. You can say what you want as to whether this is a chemist's universe or a physicist's universe or an Old Testament, New Testament God's universe—whatever kind of universe you might want to attribute the cosmos to. You can attribute it any way you want. To an engineer, as I say, to a physicist or an astronomer. Or whatever you might want the deity to be.

"Those are things that he *might* be. What this universe indubitably *is* is a poet's universe. Nothing but a poetic kind of consciousness could have conceived of anything like this. That is where the truth of the matter lies. You are in some way in line with the creative genesis of the universe. In some way—in a much lesser way, of course. We can't create those trees or that water or anything that is out there. We can't do it. But we can re-create it. We are secondary creators. We take God's universe and make it over our way. And it is different from his. It is similar in some ways, but it is different in some ways. And the difference lies in the slant, in the slant that we individually put on it and that only we can put on it. That is the difference. That is where our value lies. Not only for ourselves, but for the other people who read us. There is some increment there that we make possible that would not otherwise be there.

"I don't mean to sell the poet so long or at such great length, but I do this principally because the world doesn't esteem the poet very much. They don't understand where we are coming from. They don't understand the use for us. They don't understand if there is any use. They don't really value us very much. We are the masters of the superior secret, not they. Not they. Remember that when you write. You are at the top level, and they are down there with Elvis and Marilyn Monroe and the general idols of the schlock culture we live in. We are the elitists. I don't mind saying that at all. Quality is what we strive for, best standards. My grandmother was born in Germany, and she used to quote from Goethe, a lot. One of her favorite sayings was, 'He who ever strives upward, him can we save.' That is what we are going to do."

A blankness settled over my memories of my father in the months after his death, like a blanket of ash that obscures everything beneath it, and I would have lost him almost entirely if I had not had this book to finish, if we had not both written so much already, and talked so often onto tape, and worked so hard those last years of his life to know each other.

In March, six weeks after his death, I went back to the house in Columbia with Bronnie, and slept there for the first time in ten years. I slept in my father's bed, in the room that looked out on the lake. The sheets had been washed, but it still smelled of him, the light smell of an old man's frail body, a scent not of sweat but of dust. Here, too, walls of books were piled around, and by reaching out with my right hand I could touch the last ones he had touched on the top of those unstable pillars. There was a magazine there, closest at hand, a *National Geographic* explaining, complete with maps and photographs, the history of the Palestinians. He had been trying to know what I did. He had been trying.

In June I went back again, with Bronnie and with Kevin, and in July I took Bronwen to Antibes to see the hill below the lighthouse, to swim off the Plage de la Garoupe. Carol was transcribing the many tapes that I could not yet bear to listen to, and falling in love with the voice of my father as she had never believed she could do, but whenever I read the transcripts they showed me how much I had remembered when my father and I were talking a few months before, and how little I remembered about those same things now. If the memories were starting to come back at all, it was slowly. Beneath the ash, where he had been, there was only a hollow semblance.

I was trying to learn from my father now that he was dead all that I never allowed him to teach me while he lived. In Antibes I read back through every one of the poems and the notebooks, and found what seemed to me to be clues planted long ago to a dialogue we never had, or that I had never heard. I read again and again the letters to my mother before I was born, the early poems about fathers and sons. I read "Dover: Believing in Kings," and "Breath"—"This is done with your father again / In memory"—and I read once more "The Owl King," written in the 1950s.

> The breath falls out of my voice,
> And yet the singing keeps on.
> The owls are dancing, fastened by their toes
> Upon the pines. Come, son, and find me here,
> In love with the sound of my voice.

We make of coincidences what we need them to be, I suppose. And there were all sorts of coincidences as I tried to write. Before dawn on my birthday, August 31, I found myself back at the Hôpital Pitié-Salpêtrière, talking on the phone from the street, just as I'd done ten months before, when my father and I had been searching through Whitman for the sweet hell within. Now I was just covering a story, the death of Princess Diana, and talking live to CNN, which was relaying my reports around the world. When I told them word was official that Diana had been killed, my voice broke, and I guess it was a memorable television moment, but the choked tears were not for her.

In early October, I went back to Positano for the first time in thirty-five years, and at last the memories began to rush to the surface. I sat in the Buca di Bacco and looked up at the window where John Steinbeck had stood. I sifted through the pebbles for the bits of colored tile my father had taught me to spin across the surface of the Mediterranean. I walked along the cliff path and, looking down, remembered him swimming around the point, alone and powerful. I climbed the stairs and saw that the secret place he took Kevin, high above the sea, was still there.

It was all still there, and it was all to be found now in my head. The head that he had made.

At the end of the month, the house in Columbia was sold and I went alone to pack it up and close it down. It was, it occurred to me, exactly twenty-one years ago that week that my mother had died.

I was supposed to meet the estate manager from the bank, but she was not there, and I did not have a key to the house by the lake and could not get in. Around back, the curtains were open to my father's bedroom, and a couple of lights were on. I could see that all the bookshelves had been emptied by Matt and his graduate students, thousands of volumes taken to the university for safekeeping.

It was just dusk. I was punchy from the long flight, eight hours to Atlanta, and the layover, and then here to Columbia, and not sure how close I was to breaking down. I kept wanting to see my father at the front door, moving slow but—so glad to see me. Not sure how to act. Neither of us sure how to act. But—there. I didn't think of him then as the old man with the oxygen machine, but as a man just my age loading up the back of the Toyota Land Cruiser with his guitars and his bows, heading off to the mountains of North Georgia to watch them make his movie.

Ah, Dad.

One of the neighbors was standing in the driveway looking at the rent-a-car I'd come in, just keeping an eye on things. We talked about the house being sold. He told me the new owners were going to tear it down.

Two days later, the bows and the guitars and a few pieces of furniture from the house safely packed away, I went down to Litchfield. I was alone by my parents' graves, alone in Root-Light, and alone on the November beach. My intention was to write. I had gotten to the chapter in this book where my father and I went camping on Rock Creek Lake when I was eight, but now I had lost my concentration. The family pictures that I arrayed on the old desk on the top floor of the Litchfield house, the uncollected poems I'd found in the one un-cleaned corner of the garage, all of them should have inspired me. But the loss of the house in Columbia left a hole in me that I could not get around.

I'd also found, in the clutter I cleared in the last days moving out of the house, a pair of Tasco binoculars I'd had when I was about ten.

They were with me at Litchfield, and I thought, in the late afternoon, that there might be deer running along the edge of the marsh, or maybe an alligator in the shallows. So I put the glasses around my neck and went for a walk.

Near a tall stand of pines I heard an owl. I hadn't been thinking about owls. But the low, rhythmic hoot was impossible to miss. It was somewhere up in the trees, beyond my 7x35 power to see. I moved farther along the edge of the woods, looking deep into the branches, hoping to discover the owl somewhere up there in the slender tops of the pines as they swayed in the early-evening breeze, but all I could find of him was his call.

I took a blade of grass and held it between my thumbs and blew through the reed. No sound came, and that did not surprise me. This was something else that my father had tried to teach me that I never was able to do. I tried again, trimming the blade of grass a little, testing different ones, adjusting the tension between my hands. And then the reed vibrated. It squealed to life like a thing dying; like a wounded animal made of breath and grass, it screamed at the treetops. But the owl was not fooled. Or not for long. There was a pause in the rhythm of its call. Just a very brief pause. And then it started again. The owl did not swoop out of the trees to find this creature calling in pain. The owl did not give itself away.

It was a strange coincidence to hear the owl at Litchfield that I had never heard before, but it was not a dream, and the moment was beyond my power to invent. It was only the truth as it is. As it must be.

BIBLIOGRAPHY

James Dickey's name appears on scores of books, but the core of his work —the best of the poems, the criticism, the fiction, the notebooks—can be found in seven volumes.

POETRY

The Whole Motion: Collected Poems 1945–1992, published by Wesleyan University Press (now University Press of New England), Hanover and London, 1992. This volume, which is still in print, includes most of the best-known poems from *Into the Stone* (Scribners); *Drowning with Others* (Wesleyan); *Helmets* (Wesleyan); *Buckdancer's Choice* (Wesleyan); and *Poems 1957–1967* (Wesleyan)—which is the single best and most consistent volume of his work—as well as later poetry, verse and translations.

FICTION

Deliverance, published by Houghton Mifflin, 1970, and reprinted in paperback many times, most recently by Houghton Mifflin in 1994.
Alnilam, published by Doubleday, 1987.
To the White Sea, published by Houghton Mifflin, 1993.

CRITICISM, ESSAYS

Babel to Byzantium: Poets and Poetry Now, published by Farrar, Straus and Giroux, New York, 1968, includes the essay "Barnstorming for Poetry."

JOURNALS, INTERVIEWS

Self-Interviews, James Dickey recorded and edited by Barbara and James
    Reiss, published by Doubleday, New York, 1970.
Sorties, journals and new essays, published by Doubleday, New York, 1971.

Also of some interest are *Night Hurdling: Poems, Essays, Conversations,
Commencements, and Afterwords,* published by Bruccoli Clark, Columbia, S.C.,
1983; and *Striking In: The Early Notebooks of James Dickey,* edited with Introductions by Gordon Van Ness, published by University of Missouri Press,
1996. This became an important book for my father in the last couple of
years of his life, and several previously uncollected early poems are published here, including "The Father's Body."

Jericho: The South Beheld and other coffee-table books were published
by Oxmoor House in Birmingham, Alabama, in the 1970s and 1980s.

Recordings of James Dickey reading *Deliverance* (audio cassette from
Durkin Hayes, 1986) and *To the White Sea* (audio cassette from Brilliance
Corporation, 1993) can still be found, but the best recordings of all are
the LPs of him reading his poetry: *The Poems of James Dickey (1957–1967),*
directed by Arthur Luce Klein (Spoken Arts, 1967); and *James Dickey
Reading His Poetry* (Caedmon, 1971). These are very hard to come by, but
include him reading all of his best and best-known poems.

There are also two beautifully produced children's books: *Tucky the
Hunter,* illustrated by Marie Angel (Crown, 1978), which my father wrote
for my son, and *Bronwen, the Traw and the Shape-Shifter: A Poem in Four Parts
by James Dickey* (Harcourt Brace Jovanovich, 1986), which he wrote for
my sister.

ACKNOWLEDGMENTS

When my father died I was deep into the writing of this book—too deep to turn back—and suddenly I was in very lonely territory. I felt by myself inside myself. I was often lost, and I could not have found my way through without the enormous support of my friends, colleagues, and family.

My wife, Carol, and my oldest friend, Michael Allin, were my constant companions as I explored the past. Carol, with extraordinary devotion to both my father and to me, spent weeks transcribing the many taped conversations I made in Columbia. Michael has been, since the day I met him more than thirty years ago, the most able recorder and raconteur of our family's life. My brother Kevin and my sister Bronwen brought their own perspectives to the story of Jim Dickey, and someday I'm sure that both of them will tell it in their own ways. Deborah, too, was supportive, and in several talks about our long and difficult history together we found how much we shared in the experience of my father's love.

At Simon & Schuster, my editor, Alice Mayhew, was always a source of good judgment and quiet inspiration. She had her own personal losses to deal with, and her strength was a powerful example to me. Roger Labrie, with creativity and patience, greatly facilitated the process of trans-Atlantic editing, and it lifted my spirits just to hear the voices of Liz Stein and Lisa Weisman on the phone. Kathy Robbins, my agent, was a fount of energy and encouragement. Henry Hart shared some of his exemplary research.

The editors of *Newsweek* were extraordinarily understanding and supportive during the years when I was working on one side of the globe and trying to care for my father on the other. The thoughtfulness of Maynard Parker, Ann McDaniel, Michael Elliott, and Michael Glennon at the time of my father's death was a source of great comfort to me and, in every sense, made me proud to work in their company. I would also like to thank Sharon Sullivan, whose kind voice and willingness to listen saw me through some difficult moments.

Newsweek has a terrific team of people in Europe at all levels of the operation, and many of them are longtime friends. Stryker McGuire in London and Rod Nordland in Rome both pinch-hit for me when I had to go back to the States or take time off to work on the book. Lars Malmqvist and Chantal Mamboury in Geneva have a wonderful, contagious sense of enthusiasm, which is just what I needed on many occasions. Judith Warner in Paris helped talk me through my book while she was working on her own. Ginny Power Jestin, a great friend as well as a colleague, always helped me keep my life and work on track.

In Columbia, nothing and no one could have been saved were it not for the loyalty and love of a handful of people around my father: Matt Bruccoli and Ward Briggs, who were his best friends and his only peers at the university; Mayrie Maclamore who watched over him and protected him at the house; Jim Kitchens, who saved him more than once from financial ruin; Carol Sanders and Rita Cullum, who started as the family's lawyers and became our good friends; Carol Fairman and Meg Richards, who were my father's efficient and devoted literary assistants, and have remained cherished members of the clan. They are all, as Jim Dickey would say, our people.

INDEX

PHOTO CREDITS

Printed in the United States
By Bookmasters